This diary is the only eye-witness account of the English Civil War by a participant on the King's side who was not an officer. The diarist, Richard Symonds, was a royal Lifeguardsman for the crucial two years of 1644–5, which included the battle of Naseby and the Royalist defeat. Symonds was also a scholar and antiquarian and his diary includes much topographical detail of the time. The value of his diaries to our understanding of the Civil War is considerable. It provides a distinctive picture of the face of battle in the Civil War, of the feelings of a sensitive and passionate follower of the King, and of the variety of military experience the war afforded.

This reissue enhances Symonds's diary by placing it in a rich historical context for the first time, and adding a great deal of new material supplied by recent historical scholarship. This book will be invaluable to scholars and students of the English Civil War, as well as to local historians, war-gamers and Civil War re-enactors.

RICHARD SYMONDS'S
DIARY OF THE MARCHES OF
THE ROYAL ARMY

Camden Classic Reprints is a select series of classic editions which are reissued on behalf of the Royal Historical Society by Cambridge University Press. The series serves to bring to light editions of private papers or diaries of particular historical significance which have been unavailable for some time. Each volume contains a new introduction by a recognised expert in the field which contains fresh insights informed by recent historical scholarship, and which places each text in an appropriate historical context.

The first titles in the series are:

RICHARD SYMONDS'S
DIARY OF
THE
MARCHES OF THE
ROYAL ARMY

Edited by

C. E. LONG

With a supplementary introduction by

IAN ROY

CAMDEN CLASSIC REPRINTS 3

FOR THE ROYAL HISTORICAL SOCIETY

University College London, Gower Street, London WC1E 6BT

CAMBRIDGE
UNIVERSITY PRESS

PUBLISHED BY THE PRESS SYNDICATE OF THE UNIVERSITY OF CAMBRIDGE
The Pitt Building,Trumpington Street,Cambridge CB2 1RP,United Kingdom

CAMBRIDGE UNIVERSITY PRESS
The Edinburgh Building,Cambridge CB2 2RU,United Kingdom
40 West 20th Street,New York,NY 10011–4211,USA
10 Stamford Road,Oakleigh,Melbourne 3166, Australia

First published by the Camden Society,Old Series,74,in 1859

Reprinted with supplementary introduction by
Cambridge University Press 1997

Printed in the United Kingdom at the University Press,Cambridge

Typeset in Monotype Modern 12/15 pt

*A catalogue record for this book is available from
the British Library*

Library of Congress cataloguing in publication data

Symonds,Richard, 1617–1692?
[Diary of the marches kept by the Royal Army during the great Civil War]
Richard Symonds's diary of the marches of the Royal Army/edited by Ian Roy.
p.   cm.–(Royal Historical Society Camden classic reprints;3)
"For the Royal Historical Society."
Originally published as: Diary of the marches kept by the Royal Army
during the great Civil War. London:Camden Society,1859.With new introd.
ISBN 0 521 62308 1.– ISBN 0 521 62656 0 (pbk.)
1. Great Britain–History–Civil War,1642–1649–Personal narratives.
2. Symonds,Richard,1617–1692?–Diaries.   I. Roy,Ian.   II. Royal
Historical Society (Great Britain)   III. Title.   IV. Series.
DA400.S96   1997
942.06'2–dc21   97-27995 CIP

ISBN 0 521 62308 1 hardback
ISBN 0 521 62656 0 paperback

TAG

CONTENTS

INTRODUCTION TO THE 1997 EDITION

Richard Symonds's family, originally from Shropshire, was by the early seventeenth century settled at Black Notley, a rural parish near Braintree, Essex. The senior branch of the family owned a small estate at Great Yeldham, and he claimed cousinage with Edward Symons, the rector of Rayne, all neighbouring parishes. Both branches produced a high proportion of men who attended the inns of court, and – more unusually – entered the law as a profession. As well as being minor landlords Richard's wider family supplied, over the generations, cursitors in Chancery. At any one time in the reign of Charles I the cursitors' office (twenty-two strong) contained three or more members. Daughters of the family married other cursitors, and the office descended from father to son. This department of Chancery was as closely associated in the period with the Symonds family as was the Treasury (and a florid complexion) with the Fanshawes. Richard, the eldest son of the Black Notley branch, entered Emmanuel College, Cambridge, in 1632, and became a cursitor in due course. There is no record of his having attended an inn of court.

In the great division of the nation in summer 1642 the county of Essex was more inclined to Parliament than most. Many of its MPs and leading clergymen were sympathetic to the cause, and protected by the patronage of one of the great peers of the popular party, the Earl of Warwick. The minority of local gentry which could be identified with Royalism or recusancy was unpopular, and victimised: the houses of the Countess Rivers and the Lucas family were attacked. The extended Symonds family was divided. As gentry in a predominantly Parliamentarian area, and with strong legal and officeholding connections in the capital, it might be expected that they would side with the majority. To do otherwise would be to invite unwelcome reprisals. The senior branch of the family declared for Parliament, and Richard's first cousin, of the same name, fought in the New Model Army and died at Naseby (see 'Pedigree of Symonds', below, before p. 1).

But Richard Symonds, who had inherited the estate on the death of his father in 1636, took a different line. It is no doubt significant that he was a devout member of the church, and the rector of Black Notley was a man who welcomed the Laudian innovations of the 1630s. In doing so he quarrelled with the churchwardens and this may be why Symonds himself, the local squire, seems to have taken over the keeping of the parish register just before the outbreak of the Civil War. Several entries are in his hand; one of them records his mother's burial in 1641. Head of the family in that revolutionary year, at age twenty-four, responsible for younger siblings, and out of sympathy with current trends, he faced many dangers in a local environment increasingly hostile.

It is clear from his writings that he found reassuring, in a time of troubles, his own religious faith and strongly held political beliefs. His commonplace book, now in private possession, reveals a solitary, introverted man, who – with the onset of the revolution and the loss of his patrimony and office – became increasingly embittered. An impression of his seal, in red wax, exists among his surviving papers. If the head depicted is a true likeness of the owner, Symonds, aged about thirty, bore some resemblance to the conventional image of the Cavalier, with long, flowing locks and Van Dyckian cast of face. But he was not a laughing Cavalier; his long pointed nose and bulging eyes make him look decidedly testy. Had he survived the Restoration and met John Aubrey, another keen and eccentric antiquarian, he might have merited the latter's well-known observation: 'great goggli eies'.

Symonds's study of the past, even his musical and artistic tastes, may also have aided his withdrawal from society. Did they also provide private consolation in an alien world? He never married. He admired the antiquity and othodoxy of the church, perhaps especially as recently reformed to express the 'beauty of holiness', and the nation's equally ancient and honourable temporal institutions, the crown, nobility and landowning gentry (England's 'nobiles major and nobiles minor'). Hereditary rank and ancient lineage, like the church by law established, embodied those timeless verities which the conservatively inclined found reassuring in the turbulent 1640s.

For whatever reason Symonds became a fiercely partisan defender of the Church of England and the monarchy of Charles I. In his particular locality he would suffer for his cause, and he must have lost his office in Chancery. He later claimed that he was imprisoned by the Essex Parliamentarian Miles Corbett in March 1643, but that he escaped from prison in October of the same year ('Pedigree', below, before p. 1). As a delinquent his estates were sequestrated. If he wished to help the royal cause he had little alternative but to uproot himself, take what he could (he probably travelled with a couple of servants) and join the King at Oxford, where Charles I had set up his headquarters after the battle of Edgehill (October 1642). Several prominent Royalist officers were from Essex. His younger brother Edward died at Oxford in October 1644.

On the way he may have passed through London. With his connections in the governmental and legal world he was no doubt familiar with the politics of the capital. As a Royalist sympathiser he shared the view that London had been the major instigator of rebellion and was now its principal supporter. He took a close interest in the leading figures involved in City and Parliamentary politics, and although (if the dates he supplies in the 'Pedigree' are correct) he could not have seen the return of the regiments of the London militia from the Newbury campaign, at the end of September 1643, he had speedy and privileged access to an eye-witness account of that occasion. He not only copied the full notes taken by another Royalist, a courtier acting as a spy, but was able to correct and supplement it from his own knowledge, and decorate the cover with a drawing which symbolised the malice of the City of London. A satyr or devil, with cloven hoof and forked tail, and bearing the City's arms, holds two cornucopias full of snakes. This valuable list names the units mustered on that occasion, estimates their numbers and sketches their banners. It was, like other notes made by Symonds in his Civil War journals, a piece of private intelligence gathering (p. xxxiv: BL, Harl. MS 986).

By December 1643, when the war was already more than a year old, he was at Oxford, and it must have been about this time that he joined the Royalist army, as a trooper in the mounted Lifeguards. He was not, as is sometimes claimed, an officer in this elite corps. The Lifeguards had been raised in summer 1642, at the beginning of the war, and comprised two troops: the first, entirely manned by gentlemen, was commanded by Lord Bernard Stuart, the King's cousin and younger brother of the Duke of Richmond; the second, consisting of their servants, by the courtier and playwright Sir William Killigrew. To be one of the eighty men who rode in the first troop was easily the equivalent of being an officer in a line regiment. One of their number, Sir Philip Warwick, claimed that altogether the troop was worth £100,000 p.a. If so, Symonds was one of its least wealthy members; his yearly income was less than £100. It was gilded, aristocratic and glamorous: its

special function of guarding the royal person gave it inde-
pendence from the army command – a point of contention
later – and usually preserved it from the ordinary hurly-
burly of battle. This had not been the case at Edgehill and
First Newbury, but nevertheless, as it seemed to the casual
observer to be more for decoration than for fighting, it had
gained the nickname 'the Troop of Shew' or 'the Shew
Troop'. As such, it was an early example of what was to be
a source of merriment in the British army later: 'What is
the role of cavalry in modern battle? To lend distinction to
what would otherwise be a vulgar brawl.'

While the troop was in winter quarters, and as we
might expect from a man of his character, Symonds would
use his leisure to observe and record the antiquities of the
ancient city and university, which served as the royal
headquarters, and which were new to him. He began to
visit sites of historical interest and to jot his observations
and sketch pictures in the first of the series of notebooks
he was to employ. As a scholarly, Chancery-trained civil
servant, who reverenced the past, he was well equipped to
record accurately what he saw or heard. He was methodi-
cal and orderly, and wrote a neat if small hand, only occasionally indecipherable. His drawing is serviceable but
lacking in flair; in an often fast-moving campaign he had
little time to do more than put down a simplified version
of what he saw as he stood before it. Passionately interested in ancient buildings and the monuments they contained, and in heraldry, the record of ancient lineage, he

must also have been moved by his emotional partisan-
ship: his political and religious commitment to the institutions, now subject in the Civil War to sacrilegious abuse
and destruction, he lovingly recorded.

He included in his jottings at this time one or two of the
colleges – including the books in Balliol library, which
remained in place though the college community itself
had dispersed – and the remains of Osney Abbey, just the
kind of medieval ruin which would have a special appeal
to the author. He was also an eye-witness of the pompous
funerals of two leading Royalist officers, one killed by a
fellow officer in the garrison, but whether as one of the
horse guards on parade on that solemn occasion, or as an
interested bystander, is unknown.

The portrait of the writer and artist which has emerged
so far has been drawn in the main from his own notes
scattered through several of the small octavo leather-
bound volumes he used, containing all sorts of material
and composed at different dates. He considered the series
of four books which he began to use in April, on the eve of
his departure with his troop from Oxford, however, as a
discrete collection. Like the others the four contained dif-
fering kinds of information, but all relating to the move-
ment of the Royalist forces in which he served, from April
1644 to February 1646. They comprise the text now
reprinted. He entitled the first volume 'A Diary of the
Marches and Moovings of his Maties Royall Army,
Himselfe [the King] being personally present', and, at the

close of the campaign, when its hundred ink-numbered
pages were mostly used up, he noted with satisfaction on
the same first page that the story ended 'with the Ruine
of two great Armyes', those of Essex and Waller. The fact
that he indexed the volume also indicates that although it
has all the appearance of a diary, with entries made, at the
time or shortly after, on a day-to-day basis, but with some
gaps, the author felt free to add to his work or amend it
later.

On 10 April 1644 the garrison of Oxford, including the
horse guards, marched out to meet the rest of the army
already in the field, which had been worsted at Cheriton by
Sir William Waller two weeks before. This was Symonds's
first experience of active service, and it was almost bloodless.
The army rendezvoused on the Wiltshire Downs and in the
notebook in which he had copied the musters of the London
militia Symonds listed the colours, chief officers, and
strengths of the regiments assembled, adding to these notes
later to record changes in personnel (p. xxxiv). The troop
guarded the Queen on her way to Bristol and the West, and
then returned to Oxford with the King. In complicated
manoeuvring around the city in the following weeks the
royal army, the more mobile cavalry separated from the
slower infantry and artillery, proceeded to avoid as best it
could the attempt of two powerful Roundhead forces to
surround and destroy it. The Royalists were forced to
abandon their main infantry base at Reading and 'slight'
the defences; at the same time they deliberately gave up

Abingdon, a decision they would later regret. But in his celebrated 'night march' (2 June 1644), the King, accompanied only by his cavalry, eluded his pursuers, rejoined his Foot, and moved without loss to Worcester.

On all this, in which the troop protecting the King was much involved, Symonds preserved, for a man on his first campaign, an air of scholarly detachment; his account is spare and laconic, and he found time to visit some of the local churches and great houses his troop passed by, and note their contents. At Reading he recorded the regiments in the garrison, and their numbers, in the 'musters' volume. His first lengthy description, in the text printed below (pp. 10–13), is of the city and cathedral of Worcester, and the Royalist forces raised locally. Here as elsewhere he usefully lists the garrisons held by both sides, with their commanders. He marked Parliamentarian garrisons 'R'. For Symonds, as for his royal master, the opponents of the King were always identified as 'Rebells'.

The first battle he witnessed was the encounter at Cropredy Bridge, on the 29 June 1644, between the King and Waller's forces. Historians of that battle consider his account, not much more than a page in length (pp. 22–4), 'short and confused'. Probably the great distance between the different actions fought that day, cavalry being mainly involved, and the apparent inactivity of the King's troop, would have made it difficult for any member of it to see the whole battle. It was drawn up 'near the enemy', but was not called upon to take part.

The pace quickens with the march of the army westward, following this success, in pursuit of the Earl of Essex's main army. The Parliamentarians had embarked on what looked at first like a triumphal progress, to raise the siege of Lyme Regis and exchange supplies with their last remaining stronghold and port in the south-west, Plymouth. Persuaded by leading Cornish sympathisers – who must have hoped that a successful expedition would lead to the recovery of their estates – that his army would be well received, Essex found his forces, the further west he penetrated, in contrast badly treated and environed by not only the pursuing Oxford forces but those which had been occupied before the besieged towns: by the middle of August he was surrounded by four armies, those of the King, Prince Maurice, Lord Hopton and Sir Richard Grenville. Hemmed in at Lostwithiel, in Cornwall, while his cavalry escaped back to Plymouth, and he left by boat, the main body of his infantry, some 10,000 men, was forced to surrender.

This great victory for the Royalists was well described by Symonds, whose account is one of the most immediate and valuable to have survived. The events of 31 August to 2 September are recounted in some detail (pp. 62–8), the longest connected narrative of any in the four volumes. He set the scene: the atrocious weather, the lack of shelter in the field and the shortage of provisions, the strange country, of thick-set hedges and narrow lanes, which made cavalry fighting difficult. He described the desperate plight of the

Roundhead Foot, trapped between the sea on three sides and the Royalist armies on the other. His account of the fighting tallies with others, and possesses many individual touches. Although the troop was once more paraded, with the several units of mounted Lifeguards belonging to the other commanders-in-chief, behind its colours, and endured salvoes of musket fire which emptied a few saddles, it was again not brought to the charge. This did not prevent Symonds seeing a good deal of the scattered actions which gained valuable ground for the encircling Cavaliers, and providing an intelligent appreciation of the situation. As an observant topographer he noted the dispersal of the soldiery in search of provisions and the consequent difficulty of concentrating their forces which incapacitated both sides in those conditions. He learned right away of the flight of the enemy cavalry, and unlike the contemporary official Royalist history (and Clarendon, who followed its error) he saw that no forces of the King could have prevented it escaping.

The nature of the conflict is brought home by his description of the captured gunner, so drunk that he had not fired his piece more than once, and of the '8 or 9 of the enemyes men dead under the hedges'. His picture of the sodden and dejected state of the infantry after their surrender is memorable (pp. 66–7).'It rayned extremely as the varlets marched away', and the captives were as downcast as the weather. 'The rout of soldjers', he observed, were 'strucken with such a dismal feare' that, passing through the ranks of their captors, they 'presst all of a heape like sheep, though not so innocent'. Their colours were furled (a mark of disgrace), and they were without arms (except officers their swords) to protect themselves against some undisciplined and vengeful Cavalier soldiery and an even more hostile population.

As well as compiling the diary narrative Symonds continued in his, presumably self-appointed, role of intelligence gatherer, noting, when he had the opportunity, the size, disposition and leading personnel of the forces in the field, and other key bits of information. It is to him that we owe the best listing of the King's tertias of Foot taken on the Western campaign, and the names of the officers of one of the regiments of Horse. He was later at Oxford to ask the colonel of one of the Foot regiments for a complete list of the companies and their captains, and the history of the unit (pp. 102, 159–61). He supplies a great deal of information about another Lifeguard troop, that of Prince Maurice, perhaps to compare it with his own: but, if that is the case, it is an even more curious omission that, in the four volumes he filled, he said so little about the composition and leadership of the King's troop (pp. 181, 223, 245, 258).

He seems to have had access to what would now be termed classified information. In Cornwall he copied two papers taken from captured Roundheads – a list of the regiments of the Parliamentarian cavalry quartered at Tiverton (Devon) in July, and the route of march of

Essex's army to the West (pp. 73, 97–8). Later he had more important documents to transcribe. No doubt copies were circulating, some already in print, in the army's quarters, especially those guarding the royal headquarters. These were the sensational disclosures which accompanied, and justified, the sudden sacking of the King's cavalry commander, Lord Wilmot, and his replacement by Lord Goring, in early August. Forty-four of Wilmot's subordinate officers signed the petition to the King, which asked for an explanation, and prompted the publication of the charges and counter-charges which Symonds saw (pp. 106–10). Although he diplomatically omits their names when he came to copy these papers, and forbears to comment on their contents, his notes are a valuable source for this episode. Even in sight of the enemy, over whom they were about to score a resounding victory, the divisions in the Royalist camp could not be contained.

The main event of the campaign which followed was the second battle of Newbury, where the 'Shew Troop' belied its name by again getting into action. It defended its position near Speen (not, as the editor has supplied in the text, p. 145, Shaw House), chased from the field the enemy cavalry which charged into it, and slaughtered the musketeers lining the hedgerows: 'wee cutt their throats', Symonds noted grimly. In spite of this success, however, in a confused, bloody and lengthy struggle for position the Royalist generals decided the King was unsafe in the field at the end of the day, and his guards rode with him

through the night and the next day the fifty miles to
Bath. One has to read between the lines of Symonds's
account to appreciate the stress and danger undergone by
those involved.

Neither side could claim the victory. There were
recriminations in the Parliamentary camp over the per-
formance of their generals; and Symonds records the
changes in command which the King made after the
battle. Rupert, not involved at Newbury, was made effective commander-in-chief; but almost immediately he
threw up his commission because the Guards, though
recently enlarged and reofficered, were to remain, as they
had been since the beginning of the war, independent. As a
guardsman Symonds no doubt awaited the outcome of
the dispute with some interest, but he recorded it in his
usual low-key style. 'It was all quiett that day' (Friday
15 November), he wrote, but eventually Rupert 'yeilded
to the King's resolucion' (p. 152).

Symonds's third notebook continued the story with the
start of the Naseby campaign on 7 May 1645. The
Parliamentarians had remodelled their forces during the
winter, and Cromwell and Fairfax make their first appearance in his pages. It is due to him that we know the
strength of the several components of the royal army
which manoeuvred in the Midlands, something of its
munitions train, and which of the local garrison forces
were drawn out to augment the marching army before the
first test of battle in the summer. He provides some basic

information about the garrisons, for and against the King, maintained in the Midland counties at this time.

Till now, as a chronicler, Symonds has been self-effacing, rarely slipping into the first person singular. But as the Royalist army prepared to assault Leicester in the last days of May he reveals more of himself and his private activity. There were few duties for Horse in a siege and he appears to have gone off with friends on scouting expeditions, on one of which they visited the mansion of the great rebel, Sir Arthur Haselrigge. These sorties were probably unauthorised, for he kept the note of them cryptic and in French (pp. 179, 185). Symonds was present, however, at the storming of Leicester, for he saw for himself the dead piled up against the inner defences of the town after it was taken.

His account of the decisive encounter at Naseby is sparse in the extreme. No doubt conditions following the battle, and his own state of mind, were scarcely conducive to an extensive or considered description. He had beforehand accurately noted the order of battle of the King's veteran infantry, and found time to draw some of their regimental colours (pp. 180–2, 194). Most of the Old Foot of the army was lost at the battle. By August 1645 he was able to list the reduced number of Horse, only 2,200 effective, following the King (p. 225). The Lifeguards had been augmented, however, and now consisted of four troops, amounting to 300 men, a sizeable and important elite force in the attenuated ranks of the royal army.

If Symonds allowed himself the occasional unofficial foray in the relatively favourable circumstances of the army's progress before Naseby, his inclination to go his own way was strengthened rather than diminished by the military catastrophe of June 1645. His bald account of the flight of the defeated army (interspersed by his anti-quarian diversions) through Wales and the Welsh borders, then eastward as far as Huntingdon and north to Chester (and another crushing defeat before the walls of that city in September) conceal a widespread demoralisation among those remaining with the King, which he must have shared to the full. A note of bitterness is occasionally apparent: the knighting of a local worthy, though non-combatant, the perfidy of the Glamorgan 'Peaceable Army' ('these rogues', p. 239), the poverty and rudeness of Wales, the misleading and over-optimistic news fed the King's men – all attracted his contempt. Though, typi-cally, he does not mention it, his regiment's colonel, Lord Bernard Stuart, was killed at Rowton Heath, where twenty of the first Lifeguard troop (a quarter of the whole) were captured (p. 243). The 'long and tedious marches' over the barren mountains of North and central Wales were dispiriting (p. 245); at every turn they were harassed by the enemy, who were able to beat up quarters and capture stragglers. Inevitably there was much deser-tion to the other side.

While he does not spell out the catalogue of disasters – he fails to record the surrender of Bristol by Rupert in

September 1645, or detail the Rowton defeat – for a Royalist irreconcilable like Symonds the situation would be increasingly hard to bear. But there was a ray of hope. He contrasted the poor state of the remnant of the field army, and the defeatism of those in the high command, like Rupert, who saw the war as already lost, with the high morale and fighting qualities of some of the local forces still operating in Wales and the Marches. These were often the professional soldiers, blooded in the Irish wars, who had been waging a fierce rearguard action against the increasingly dominant local Parliamentarians. Symonds had already seen and admired the 'gallant' troops brought by Charles Gerrard from South Wales to the King (p. 242). He praised the little army commanded by Sir William Vaughan, at the core of which was the regiment he had brought from Ireland in late 1643, and which ranged widely through Shropshire and North Wales. If the war was to be carried on, these were the men to do it, and, exhausted as he was by continual and futile marches, Symonds left the Lifeguards and carried his sword, and no doubt his servants, into these troops when they went to 'refresh' themselves in Bridgnorth garrison in October 1645 (p. 245). Disbanded officers and men ('reformadoes'), rather than formed units, now made up a large part of these forces.

The rest of the diary is a fascinating (though increasingly fragmentary) record of their last stand against all odds, fighting a ferocious guerilla war in increasingly desperate circumstances. The King had raised his first army in Shropshire; Symonds's own family came originally from there. The previous year most of the garrisons had been Royalist. Now, in the summer of 1645, eight out of eleven (including Shrewsbury) had fallen to Parliament (pp. 248–9, 256). The powerful local Roundhead general, Thomas Mytton, was able to pen the remaining King's forces into a smaller and smaller area. Vaughan had placed his Headquarters at Shrawardine Castle ('Shraydon', p. 256), six miles west of Shrewsbury, and appointed as governor his clergyman brother. But it fell in July, and the castle was rased to the ground. Today only heaps of grass-covered stones mark the spot where Vaughan acquired his evil reputation as 'the Devil of Shrawardine'.

When at Chester Charles had promised the governor, Lord Byron, that he could expect relief from the still effective loyal forces in North Wales. This did not materialise, and in November Vaughan's small army, mainly cavalry, was dispersed by Mytton in a skirmish just outside Denbigh. Symonds, as usual, passes over this last disaster almost in silence, but takes the trouble to copy (p. 280) the friendly letter from the governor of Denbigh to Vaughan, welcoming his infantry to the protection of the castle, and soothingly noting that Mytton's army had greatly outnumbered his. The guerilla forces of the area were so infamous that they were often refused entry by the remaining Royalist garrisons (Vaughan's party was shut out of Ludlow later), and so were always in danger of falling prey to the better disciplined enemy. Symonds may have judged the action of the governor of Denbigh so unusual and laudable as to be worthy of record.

The news everywhere was bad. Symonds must have got hold of a copy of the printed account of the famous quarrel at Newark between the King and Rupert and his fellow officers, which followed the sacking of the Prince on his surrender of Bristol. He entered it into his journal (pp. 268–70), but tore it out when one of the participants, Sir Richard Willys, much later told him it was 'all a feynd [feigned] form'd lye' (p. 270; BL, Harl. MS 944, f. 66). Willys no doubt preferred to be remembered for the scheme, which he had presented to the King at Newark somewhat earlier, to collect from the remaining garrisons a force large enough to face the New Model Army. Symonds dutifully recorded Willys's version of these events. He also, usefully from the historian's point of view, copied out Rupert's declaration of October with the twenty-two signatories, and the King's letter to the governor of Worcester (pp. 270–2). These additions to his MS show that he was revising it as late as 1659, the date of his conversation with Willys. Symonds was suspected as a Royalist plotter in the 1650s, as was Willys. Presumably he did not know that his informant was also a Cromwellian spy.

Otherwise there was little to record but the bad behaviour of the King's men before their final liquidation. They foraged, plundered, quarrelled and fought amongst themselves; two officers killed each other, and there was an

attempted suicide, at Bridgnorth (p. 250). They carried
fire and sword through the little towns and villages of
Shropshire, Worcestershire and Herefordshire (pp. 261,
276). Not surprisingly Symonds begins to note the resistance of the local people to these depredations, although
he does not call them Clubmen (p. 263). The new general
for the King in these parts, Lord Astley, came to Worcester
before Christmas (p. 277), and spent much of his time
thereafter attempting to compose the quarrels of the
local commanders.

It was time for Symonds to make his last move. He left
Bridgnorth in the new year, 1646, and joined one of the
garrisons, Tutbury castle in Staffordshire, of the energetic
East Midlands general, Lord Loughborough. Symonds
was already familiar with this 'flying army', for he had
noted a year previously its dispositions and officers'
names in his 'musters' journal (BL, Harl. MS 986). It was a
natural step for him to retreat from Tutbury to
Loughborough's Headquarters at Ashby de la Zouch. It
was there that he ended his war, being granted a pass from
the local Parliamentarian governor to return home with
two servants, horses and arms, in March 1646. He com-
pounded on Ashby articles later that year, with a fine of
one sixth of the value of his estate, £295.

Symonds's military career was now over. He had been a
conscientious recorder of antiquities and the end of the war
(and the victory of a hostile regime) gave him both opportunity and incentive to extend his knowledge by foreign

travel. Having settled his remaining income on his sister, borrowed money from her and the local rector, Edward Symons, he set out for the Continent. Of his travels in France and Italy, from 1649 to 1651, the year-and-a-half-long stay in Rome was the most formative experience. He learned the language, saw the sights and, discovering a taste for modern art, met and conversed with several painters, including Nicolas Poussin. Until his money ran out, he bought as many books, prints and drawings as he could. Among art historians Symonds has an honoured place. His notebooks of this period are as valuable a record of contemporary art and artists, their workshop practices, and the contents of private collections in Rome, as his earlier diaries are for the Civil War. Back in London thereafter he listened to gossip about the artists of the time and recorded some of it. Symonds is the source for many of the stories of the period in Walpole's *Anecdotes of Painting*, such as the legend of Cromwell's nocturnal visit to the coffin of King Charles (p. xxxiv).

An old mystery, the date of his death, which baffled the editor of the diary (pp. xxxvi–xxxvii), and the author of the article on Symonds in the *Dictionary of National Biography*, has been solved by a modern art historian. Dr Mary Beal, in *A Study of Richard Symonds: His Italian Notebooks and their Relevance to Seventeenth-Century Painting Techniques* (New York, 1984), has shown that Symonds died intestate in June 1660, at the age of forty-three, and was probably buried in London. The will of his one remaining brother, who died in the following year, hints that the family were having difficulty regaining their estates, and possibly their offices, at the Restoration. Richard Symonds's papers were dispersed, probably not long after. If, however, like John Evelyn, he was able to witness the 'miraculous' event of May 1660, the triumphant entry of Charles II into London, he must have died a happy man.

The value of his diaries to our understanding of the Civil War is considerable. No other narrative by a soldier who was not an officer, on the King's side, exists. Of course, as a cultivated gentleman, he was not an ordinary trooper, but his record is of someone who was obeying orders rather than giving them. While a careful reading, some of it between the lines, is needed to appreciate its merits most fully, it provides a distinctive picture of the face of battle in the Civil War, of the feelings of a sensitive and passionate follower of the King, and of the variety of military experience the war afforded, so different from pre-war existence. The Civil War changed lives. How other than in those troubled times would a pious and artistic Essex squire end his personal Odyssey fighting alongside the ruthless 'Devil of Shrawardine'? When later, in 1649, as a traveller and connoisseur, he waited for an escort to enable him to cross the brigand-infested mountain passes to Rome in safety, did it ever occur to him that he had himself acted this role in the inhospitable hill country of North Wales only four years before?

INTRODUCTION.

THE author of the following Diary, Richard Symonds, was descended, as will be seen on reference to the accompanying pedigree, from a respectable gentleman's family, sometime seated at a mansion called the Poole, in the parish of Great Yeldham, in the county of Essex. He was himself, however, a native of the parish of Black Notley, in the same county, where his father had acquired a small property in right of his wife.

At the outbreak of the great Civil War, between Charles and the Parliament, our author joined the royal standard; while his cousin, of the elder branch, and of the same name, took the opposite side, and fell in the cause of his country at the crowning fight of Naseby. The royalist was, as he tells us, in the troop of horse commanded by Lord Bernard Stuart, a younger son of the Duke of Lenox, and during the various operations in which they were engaged he seems never, in his leisure moments, to have lost sight of his ruling passion, the love of topography, with its handmaids genealogy and heraldry; and, on all occasions, to have had his note-book in his pocket to jot down, from time to time, whatever, in churches or in country mansions, might elucidate his favourite pursuit. We are indebted to him, then a very young man, for many a family record which time, neglect, and Vandalism have since swept away; and, if his narrative is not always lively, and attractive to the general reader, it is valuable as affording corroborative testimony to the truth of other publications of that period.

The manuscript labours which he has left to us are, in the first place, the three small volumes in the Harleian collection which form the contents of the present article, together with the volume preserved among the Additional MSS., completing the set, and which latter was purchased at Mr. John Bohn the bookseller's sale in 1847, by Sir Frederic Madden, for the Trustees of the Museum. It had been supposed that one or more volumes still remained in private hands; but this point is cleared up, first, by the dates of the several volumes, and, secondly, and conclusively, by the fact that Symonds, on leaving England, consigned his books and various boxes to the custody of his sister, and among the contents of one of the latter we find that he makes mention of "4 bookes of marches bound in leather."

The other manuscript volumes of Symonds are:—

Harl. MS. 964:

Notes of Monuments, &c. Oxford, Dec. 1643 to April 1644.

These, though not distinctly included in the Diary, are, nevertheless, virtually a portion of it, inasmuch as the dates show that they were made during the leisure hours of his winter quarters.

Harl. MS. 965 :

Similar Notes taken in Oxfordshire and Berkshire Churches, and in Worcester Cathedral, 1644.

The same observation applies to this volume, although, in a note at page 3 of the text, the Editor has, somewhat hastily, hazarded a different opinion.

Harl. MS. 943 :

This is a Memorandum Book, containing notes made during his journey from Calais to Paris, and whilst resident there, and then to Italy, and at Rome, from January 1648-9 to 1651. It contains, at the beginning, some family *memoranda*, a copy of his father's will, together with lists of his books and boxes at Black Notley and elsewhere, &c.

Harl. MS. 1278 :

Notes of Churches and Public Buildings at Paris, dated 1649.

Harl. MS. 924 :

Notes of Churches, &c. at Rome.

Additional MS. 17,919 :

Notes of Churches, Pictures, &c. at Rome, dated 1649 and 1650.

This was formerly in Dr. Mead's library, and purchased of Rodd, the bookseller, in 1841.

Egerton MS. 1635 :

Notes of Pictures, &c. at Rome, 1651. Purchased, with the next, at Sotheby's auction rooms in 1853.

Egerton MS. 1636 :

Secrets in painting learnt at Rome in 1650 and 1652, together with notes of "certain old paintings I have seen in London since my return from Italy."

All the above MSS. are extremely curious, and it is to be hoped will some day see the light in a legible form, under the auspices of the Camden Society, and with the assistance of some gentleman whose knowledge of art may enable him to do that justice to the subject, which the present Editor's incompetency would deter him from undertaking.

Harl. MS. 991 :

Collections of Anecdotes and Memoranda relating to different contemporaneous individuals, extending to 1660.

These were partly printed in the Gentleman's Magazine, vol. lxvi. p. 466, and vol. lxxxvi. p. 498. The latter records the story of Cromwell lifting up the lid of Charles's coffin and gazing on his body.

Harl. MS. 986 :

" The Ensignes of yᵉ regiments of yᵉ Citty of London, both of trayned bands and auxiliaries; together with the nearest number of their trayned soldiers, taken as they marched into Finsbury feilds, being their last generall muster. Tuesday, Septemb. 26, 1643. Anno pestiferæ rebellionis."

To this he has added some musters of the King's army on various occasions.

Besides the foregoing, there are three volumes of Col-

lections for the County of Essex, now in the library of
the College of Arms, to which they were presented in
1710 by Gregory King, then Rouge Dragon Pursuivant
of Arms, and who appears, by a note in one of the
volumes, to have become the possessor of them in 1685.
These now form, as we have said, three volumes, but
Symonds speaks of them in the Harl. MS. 963, as " my
two volumes, bound up, of Essex Visitations." Morant
obtained extensive materials from them for his History
of Essex. The dates of his journeyings in his native
county are given in the volumes themselves, and show
at how early an age he was imbued with archæological
ardour ; a feeling shared and indulged in by the Editor,
in his own native county, at the same age, but, unhap-
pily, without the same profitable results. As a prelude
to his own pedigree, under Great Yeldham, we have a
rather ludicrous endeavour to trace the derivation of
the name of Symonds, and to exalt its origin, by numerous fanciful and fantastic quotations, beginning with
" Simonides the poet," and ending in " one Richard
Simon, a subtil priest who lived in Oxford," and " had to
his pupil the baker's son Lambert Simnel." A reference
to Camden might have relieved him from all these ab-
struse investigations by the information that it was
merely transformed into a surname by the simple addition of a letter to the baptismal name of Simon.

Reverting to the Diary, the Editor would observe
that it has been frequently referred to by County histo-

rians, and, in some instances, partially transcribed.
Copious extracts will be found in Parry's Royal Visits
to Wales, and in Shaw's Staffordshire. It is also quoted
in Hutchins's Dorsetshire, Nichols's Leicestershire, and by
Lysons, &c.; and in Walpole's Anecdotes of Painters there
are frequent allusions to Symonds, as well as a note re-
specting the author and his manuscripts, but accompanied
by the error that he was " born at Okehampton," whereas
he tells us, in his pedigree, that he was baptised, and therefore no doubt born, at Black Notley. We may, however,
notice that he has himself committed a palpable blunder
in the same pedigree, viz. by stating that his father died
in " 1627." The Register of Black Notley tells us that
he was buried there, Dec. 9, 1636, and the date of his will,
as transcribed by Symonds, in MS. 943, is Oct. 12 of the
same year. It may be remarked that, in close proximity
to his own name in the family pedigree, we find the impression, in red wax, of an admirably engraved head in
profile. Its identity is certainly incapable of direct
proof, but there is every reason to believe that it is the
portrait of Symonds himself, and that the artist was, in
all probability, Simon, whose works of the period are
well known.

The Editor has to lament his inability to show what
became of Symonds after his return to England. We
can trace him down to 1660, when he was forty-three
years of age. The family pedigree, which he entered in
his Essex collections, has the usual mark of marriage

appended to his name, but evidently only meant to be indicative of the possibility of such an event. It can hardly be supposed that he had parted with these manuscripts during his life, and we know that they were in other hands in 1685. The calendars of the Prerogative Office have been searched without success, and the Will Office at Chelmsford has been as fruitlessly examined. A further attempt was made to find a list of the Cursitors at the Petty Bag Office, yet, as far as he was personally concerned, to no purpose. The will of his uncle, Richard Symonds, dated June 1, 1663, and proved in the Archdeaconry Court of Middlesex, January 11, 1680, is at Chelmsford; and it appears that Anne, the sister of the author, and to whose care, when he left England, he had consigned his personal effects, was then alive and married. She is thus spoken of, "Anne, the daughter of my brother Edward, and wife of Mr. Wright." The Wrights were an Essex family of some repute, and a branch was seated at White Notley; but Morant, who mentions them frequently, makes no allusion to this marriage.

The will of Samuel, the nephew of Richard, a clergyman of Colne Engaine, proved in 1667, and also that of John Symonds, of Great Yeldham, brother of Samuel, proved in 1693, both in the Prerogative Office, have been examined; but, with the exception of a cousin, William Symonds, living at Ipswich, in New England, n 1693, doubtless a son or grandson of the Samuel who emigrated there, and a Mr. Thomas Symonds of Farnham living in 1663, no collaterals of the name are mentioned.

The house in which Symonds and his father had lived at Black Notley is that now known as " the Buck." Its ancient name was Plumtrees, and it is so called by Symonds in his memoranda (Harl. MS. 943). It is now a farm-house, with but a very small portion of the old mansion still standing; yet part of the garden wall, and a very aged cypress tree, attest the existence, at one time, of a place of greater pretension. A reference to Morant's Essex, will show (vol. ii. p. 124) that this property came, subsequently, into the Carter family, and it further appears, that the Carters were related to Symonds, being descended from Elizabeth Wolmer, the sister of John Symonds, of Great Yeldham, before-mentioned. This gentleman was a man of distinguished philanthropy, and his funeral sermon was preached by the Rev. John Brooke, the then incumbent of Great Yeldham, on the 24th of February, 1692. It was after-wards printed, with a dedication to Jane, the widow, who was the testator's second wife, a daughter of Sir Robert Burgoyne, of Sutton, in Bedfordshire.

Sir Edw. Bysshe's Visitation of Essex in the College of Arms, begun in 1664 and finished in 1668, has no entry of Symonds. In C. 21, f. 113, Coll. Arm., the Visitation of 1634, there is a short pedigree entered, when Richard Symonds of Lincoln's Inn, brother of John Symonds of Great Yeldham, who attested it, seems to have adopted the whimsical signature of "Fitz Symonds," as he also did when signing his will in 1663.

The Editor must here take the opportunity of returning his sincere thanks to the Rev. T. Overton, the Rector of Black Notley, and to Mr. A. C. Veley, of Braintree, the Registrar of Wills, for the kind manner in which they have met and seconded his endeavours to trace out the latter part of his author's career. Such instances of courtesy and disinterestedness, especially towards a perfect stranger, are most gratifying to the literary inquirer, and when we find persons not only ready to waive their legitimate profits, but taking an interest in the research, some acknowledgment beyond the barren thanks in a private letter seems justly due. The Editor must also record his obligations to Mr. H. W. Holden of the Petty Bag Office, by whose exertions a box of old Cursitor deeds was discovered and examined.

As far as the incidents of the great struggle, on which the liberties of his country depended, came under his observation, our author is entitled to the credit of strict accuracy. His dates agree with those in the *Iter Carolinum*, and his narrative accords with Sir Edward Walker's printed account. If the details of some actions, especially that of Naseby, are somewhat meagre, there are others, such as that of the second battle of Newbury, where a much more minute and interesting description is afforded.

It was, at first, the wish and intention of the Editor to have given far more copious topographical and genealogical notes in the way of illustration, but the time required for such a purpose, and the reluctance to attempt such a task without, in numerous instances, a personal visit to the different localities, rendered this an impossibility, unless the publication had been postponed to an indefinite period. The diary is therefore offered in its crude form, with only, here and there, an effort at elucidation, when the Editor happened to be aware of any fact bearing upon the point at issue. It may further be observed that all the very numerous shields of arms recorded in the MS. are what is technically called "tricked" by Symonds, thus necessitating a description of the bearings, and involving much labour and delay in the transcript.

The Editor cannot conclude these few prefatory remarks without tendering his thanks to Sir Frederic Madden and his colleagues in the Manuscript department of the Museum, for their very kind assistance in deciphering the occasionally minute and perplexing penmanship of the author; as also to Sir Charles George Young (Garter), and the Members of the College of Arms, for the liberal manner in which the MS. collections in their library have on this, as on all other occasions, been placed at his disposal.

CHARLES EDWARD LONG.

8, Chapel Street, Grosvenor Square,
        April 9, 1859.

CORRECTIONS.

Page 3. " Red heath." The Editor was too precipitate in pronouncing this to be " Snelsmore Common." It was undoubtedly what is now known as Greenham Common, south-east of Newbury. See also at page 142, and refer to Walker's Historical Discourses, page 108.

Page 16. " Armour of woove worke." It may be questioned whether this should not be " of a rare worke." The word is extremely indistinct. See folio 29 of the MS.

Page 39. " [few]." The brackets should be omitted, as the word is the author's.

Page 101. Note. This is not the monument of Henry Earl of Bridgewater, but of Sir Giles Daubeney, whose will, dated March 3, 1444, was proved at Lambeth March 2, 1445. He desires " to be buried in the church of St. Peter the Apostle at South Pether-ton, before the altar of St. Mary." The crest is not a plume of feathers, but a holly tree, and the same may be seen on the garter-plate of Giles Lord Daubeney at Windsor.

Same page. *For* " ploro " *read* plora.

Page 103. *For* " [? Erpingham] " *read* [Chidioke].

Page 110. *For* " [Deneband] " *read* [Denebaud]; as also *postea.*

Page 152. *For* " Fyfield Church. Nul." *read* Fyfield Church. Nil.

Page 177. *For* " quiquid," *read* qui quid'.

Same page. *For* " familiæ," *read* familiæ.

Page 183. It has been suggested that " she. R." might mean Sheriff, Rebel; but, besides the repetition of the designation R, Sir William Herrick does not appear in the list of Sheriffs.

Page 203. " Ludlowe['s] men," a mistake of the printer; it is Ludlowe men.

Page 224. *For* " [Fretchville]," *read* [Freschville.]

Page 230. " Crosse built by Edward III. in memory of Elianor his queene." This is Symonds's own error, and should, of course, be Edward I.

FROM THE AUTHOR'S MS. COLLE

[Arms. Azure, a che
[Crest. Out of a mural

John Symonds of Croft, com. Lancast

Robt. Symonds; went into Staffordshir

John Symonds of Stratto

Thomas Symonds of Stratto

John Symonds of Newport, com. Salo

John Symonds of Newport, com. Salo

Richard Symonds of the Poole, an antient seate in this parish, came out of Shropsh
one of yᵉ Cursistars of yᵉ Chancery; buried in Yeldham Church, July 8, 1627.
[Arms. Symonds, impaling, Ermine, a bend vaire or and gules cotised vert.]

Edward Symonds, 2d son, one of yᵉ Cursistars of the Chancery, borne at Yeldham; married in St. Gregories of Paul's, London, Feb. 2, 1614; died 9 of Decemb. 1627; buried in yᵉ Church of Black Notley in Essex. He lived in Notley, and had his lands there cheifly by his wife. Benefactor with yᵉ other Cursistars to yᵉ library at Westminster. [Arms. Symonds, impaling *blank*.]	=Anne, onely daughter of Joshua Draper, of Brayntree, in yᵉ county of Essex.	Samuel S. 3d son, one of yᵉ Cursis of the Chancery, bought yᵉ place Toppesfeild in Essex called Olmers, per ann.; went into New England [Arms. Symonds, with a mulle difference, impaling, Azure, a ermine between three leopard's he erased or.]

RICHARD SYMONDS, baptised at Notley 12 of June, 1617, eldest son; one of yᵉ Cursistars of yᵉ Chancery; committed prisoner by Myles Corbet for a delinquent to yᵉ State, 25 of March, 1643; escaped thence 21 of Octob. 1643, and gott into yᵉ King's army, where he was in yᵉ King's troope under yᵉ command of yᵉ Lord Bernard Stuart, Earle of Lichfield, in yᵉ battaile of Cropredy Bridge, Listithiel, Newbury (2d and 3d), Naseby, Releife of Chester, when that hoᵇˡᵉ lord was slayne; after yᵗ with Sʳ Wm. Vaughan at Denbigh, and other places. Collector of these 3 volumes. [Arms. Symonds, impaling *blank*.]	=...... Edward Symonds, 2d son, dyed at Oxford, 1645, being in armes for yᵉ King, 1645; baptised Dec. 20, 1621.	Ann Symonds, bapt. at Notley, March 31, 1631.	3. John Symonds, bapt. at Notley, April 10, 1627.	Richard S. eldest son. Student of Greyes Inn.	Dor San Har ke Eliz be wh he rie wi hir Ne En lan

F SYMONDS.

ESSEX, VOLUME 2, FOL. 613.—COLL. ARM.

ailed between three trefoils or.]
a boar's head argent, tusked or.]

laughter of Sir Wm. Lording, Kt.

laughter and h. of ...... Congrave of Stratton.

laughter of ...... Gravener of Bellaport, com. Salop, Esqre.

laughter of Tho. Worthington, Gent. — Robt. S 2d son, married and had issue.

ret, daughter of Thomas Maynard.

dau. of Thomas Bendbow.

eth, ye 2d daughter of Robt. Plume, of Yeldham Gent.; buried in Yeldham Church, Jan. 27,

William S. married and had issue.
Roger S.

. daughter of Tho. laken- of Colne.

John S. eldest son, one of ye Cursistars of ye Chancery. [Arms. Symonds, impaling, Azure, a fess or.] = Ann, dau. of Thomas Elyott, of Godalmyng, in ye county of Surrey, Esqr.

Thomas S. 2d son, dyed June 5, without yssue, 1625.

Richard S. 5th son, Barrister of Lincolne's Inn; bought ye manor of Panfeild in Essex, of James Heron, Esq. [Arms. Symonds, impaling *blank.*]

Margaret, onely daughter, married to Edmund Eyre of Windsor, Gent., one of ye Cursistars of ye Chancery. [Arms. Azure, a chevron between three wheat straws argent, impaling, Symonds.]

ichard S. eldest n, born Octob. 3, 1616; Student in Lincoln's n; in divers attailes with ye arle of Essex gst ye King; as slayne at aseby, 1645, nder ye command of Sr Tho. airfax, agst ye ing.

John S. 2d son, one of the Cursistars of the Chancery by ye resignation of his father, 1641; borne at Y. Sept. 4, 1618. [Arms. Symonds, impaling, a fess ermine between three birds.] = maried ye daughter of Sr Ralf Quarles of Rochford, com. Essex.

Sam. S. 3d son. Fitz Symonds, 4th son.

Ann Symonds, eldest daughter, married Mr. Thomas Bacon of ye Citty of London, merchant. [Arms. On a chief two mullets, imp. Symonds.]

.. ... Bacon, onely daughter.

Elizabeth, 2d daughter, married to Anthony Wolmer of Lincolne's Inn, barrister. [Arms. Gules, a chevron between three escallops argent, impaling, Symonds.]

Thomasine, 3d daughter.

Thomasine, maried ...... Pepys; Dorothy. Twins, borne Aug. 16, 1627.

Dorothy and Penelope, both dead about 1621.

SYMONDS'S DIARY.

[Add. MSS. Brit. Mus. 17062.]

A Diary of the Marches and Moovings of his Maties Royall Army, Himselfe being personally present.

Beginning April 10, 1644, ymediately after the Battayle at Alresford, which was 29 of March, 1644.

Ending with the Ruine of two great Armyes commanded by Robert Devereux late Earle of Essex, and Sir William Waller.

[The Author here gives " A Table of the Shires and parish Churches in this Booke : wherein any thing worth observacion was found concerning Armory,' but which it is conceived will be better arranged in a general Index.]

KNIGHTS BATCHELORS made by the KING in this march, A.D. 1644.

At Worcester :—

     Sir Martin Sandys,[a] Col. June 12.

     Sir   ,[b] mayor of Worcester.

At Evesholme [Evesham] :—

     Sir [John] Knotsworth, Colonel, and governor of Evesholme.

Neare Banbury in the feild :—

     Sir Robert Howard,[c] fourth son to the Earl of Berks, June 29.

     Sir Thomas Hooper,[d] Leift.-Col. of Dragoons, eod.

At Exeter :—

     Sir Hugh Crocker, then Mayor, July 26 or 27.

At Crediton in co. Devon :—

     Sir Thomas Basset,[e] 27 July.

     Sir Joseph Wagstaffe,[f] eod.

     Sir Henry Carye, eod.

At Boconnock in Cornwall, Lord Mohun's howse :—

     Sir James Cobb, Aug.

     Sir John Arundel of Lanreath,[g] under age, being a ward, which frees his wardship, Aug.

     Sir Charles Trevanion,[h] of Carhese, Cornwall, Aug.

     Sir Francis Basset,[i] high Sheriff of Cornwall, Aug.

List of Knights in MS. M. 5, Coll. Arm. :—

[a] Colonel of a regiment of Foot in the city of Worcester.

[b] Sir Daniel Tyas.

[c] Knighted at Cropredy Bridge.

[d] Knighted for taking Wemes the Scot (General of Sir William Waller's Artillery) prisoner at Cropredy Bridge.

[e] Brother to Sir Francis, General of the Ordinance to Prince Maurice.

[f] Major-General to the army under the conduct of Prince Maurice in the West.

[g] At Liskeard, 3rd of August.

[h] Knighted at Crediton, July 30th.

     Knighted at Crediton ; a Cornishman, Governor of St. Michael's Mount.

Neare Listithiel [Lostwithiel], in the feild:—
  Sir Edward Brett,[a] Aug. 31.
Upon Redheath neare Newbery [? *hodie* Snelsmore Common]:—
  Sir John Boys, Governor of Denington Castle, Octob. 2.

The unfortunate BATTAILE of ALRESFORDE in the Countie of Southt. was fought on Friday, 29th of March, 1644.

The King marched out of Oxford Aprill the tenth 1644, being
Tuesday. That night he lay at Childerley [Childrey,] an ancient howse, now the Lady Fetyplas[b] lives in it, com. Berks. Divers
ancient matches of that family in the hall windowes and the chappel. His troope quartered at Wantage, two myles nearer Oxford,
and twelve myles from Oxford. Lord Bernard[c] lay at Sir George
Wilmott's[d] howse neare Wantage. Vide Wantage Church, *alibi*.[e]

Wednesday, the King's army appeared at the rendesvouz neare
Awborne, five myles short of Marlborowe. The King lay that
night at Marlborough, the howse of the Lord Seymor's.

The troope quartered at Ogborne, a myle from thence. Lord
Bernard lay at Mr. Goddard's, a man of four or 500[li] per ann. A
small village. Thursday the King dyned at an inne in Wantage,
and came that night to Oxford.

Aprill 17, 1644. Being Wednesday in the afternoone, the Queene
marched to Abingdon from Oxford, lay there that night, and the
next morning went on to Lamborne, so for Bristoll.

The King's troope attending of her that night, and carryed her

---

[a] In the field at the pursuit of the Earl of Essex's army, Captain of the Queen's troop.

[b] This was Anne, relict of Sir Edmund Fettiplace, and daughter of Sir Roger Alford·
She died in 1651.

[c] Lord Bernard Stuart was Captain of the King's troop, to which the writer belonged.

[d] He married Margaret, daughter of Richard Aldworth, Citizen of London, and resided
at Charlton.

[e] He alludes, no doubt, to a volume of Church Notes, but which form no part of the
Diary

out of towne; then came to Oxford with the King. As we marched in Abi[ngdon] I saw a tall stout fellow, whose haire was all matted in elfe locks, very long, and his beard so too, though not so large. His nose cutt or eate off.

This coate at Abingdon, in the howse where Mr. Parme lives, which Dr. Tucker[a] owes (owns).

> Vert, on a bend engrailed argent three hearts gules; impaling, Or, a che-vron between three apples or. *Crest*, on a wreath of the colours, out of a ducal coronet or, a heart gules. [TOOKER impaling SOUTHBY.]

Thursday 16 May, 1644. The King marched from Oxon to Reading, his whole army being there, and the workes there then slightinge.

The King lay that night at Cowley howse, belonging to Hampden in right of his wife. Vachell.

Cowley howse. In the dyning-roome windowes [b]—

> Bendy of six ermine and azure, VACHELL. Impaling, Per pale azure and gules, three saltires counter-changed, LANE.[c]
>
> Quarterly, 1 and 4, VACHELL; 2 and 3, Argent, a chevron sable between three [cocks gules, COCKWORTHY or COCKWORTH, co. Devon.]
>
> VACHELL,[d] impaling, quarterly, 1 and 4, Azure, semée of cross-crosslets or, a cross cercelé voided: 2 and 3, Argent, on a chevron three roses gules, KNOLLYS.
>
> VACHELL,[e] impaling, Gules, on a chevron argent a lion rampant sable, crowned or, BROOKE. *Crest*, for VACHELL, a neat's foot couped ar-gent, hoofed or.

---

[a] Charles Tucker or Tooker, D.C.L. He married Christian, daughter of Richard Southby of Carswell, co. Berks. He was of the family of the Tookers of Maddington, co. Wilts., and was of Oriel coll. Oxford. He died 1659. C. 8, f. 119, Coll. Arm.

[b] All this glass has disappeared. The old house was pulled down; but there are on some portions of the remaining walls the dates 1553 and 1567.

[c] Sir Thomas Vachell married 2dly, Sarah, daughter of Sir William Lane, of Horton, co. Northampton.

[d] This was Letitia, 3d wife of Sir Thomas Vachell, and daughter of Sir Francis Knollys of Reading, brother to William Earl of Banbury. She subsequently became the second wife of Hampden, as mentioned in the Diary, and died in 1666.

[e] Sir Thomas Vachell married, 1st, Alice, daughter of Hugh Brooke.

In the Hall windowes are these :

VACHELL, with this motto : " It is better to suffer then revenge."

Crest, on a mound vert, between two wings erect azure, charged with four bezants, a cow passant argent, collared sable, to the collar a bell pendent, udder gules.

Vachell, in allusion to Vacca.

Adjoyning to this new built howse is the ancient habitation, but very small, which now is used as the outhowses.

In the kitchen windowes are these two shields, older than all the former :—

Argent, three pales wavy sable, on a chief gules a saltire or.
VACHELL.

On Friday the 17th the King marched with his whole army from the Leager neare Reading, through Inglefield, where in the church are these old shields :—

Barry of six gules and argent, on a chief or a lion passant azure, ENGLEFIELD. " South window, Church."

ENGLEFIELD.   " This old in the North W. Church."

" This coate in this forme South side of . . . " Here is sketched a quaintly-shaped shield or tabard bearing, Sable, six martlets 3, 2, and 1, or. [? ROSSELL.]

" This in the same North window aforesaid." ENGLEFIELD.

This quartering is in the East window of the North yle of the chancel."
A shield, bearing, Quarterly, 1 and 4, ENGLEFIELD ; 2 and 3, Sable, a fess between six martlets, three and three, or, [ROSSELL.] *Crest.* On a wreath, a double-headed eagle displayed per pale gules and azure.
Orate[a] pro aīa . . . . Inglefeld, &c. 1514 or thereabouts, as I remember."

Divers other coates of armes, but time would not suffer me to take them.

Under the south wall of the south yle of the church, under an arch, lyes the portrait of a man in compleate armor, crosse-leggd,

---

[a] This inscription was in English ; the following one in Latin, but not beginning " Orate."   Vide C. 12. Coll. Arm.

his shield on his arme. The coate of Inglefeild had beene fairely painted on his breast.

Upon a flatt stone neare the south dore of the church, the effigies of a man in brasse, and an inscription; thus as I can remember: —

> Orate . . . Englefeild, armigeri, qui obiit . . . M.V^c.

Betweene the chappel and the north yle aforesaid, stands a faire tombe of blew marble, arched at the east end, inlayed in brasse; the statues of a knight kneeling. Upon his surcoate, his armes and match. On hers, her armes, and the coat of Inglefeild, and his match between them in brasse too.[a] The inscription was faire, and was for a knight of the name. 1500, &c.

In the aforesaid east window, north yle, and written under.

> Quarterly, ENGLEFIELD and ROSSELL, impaling, Gules, on a chevron argent three bars gemels sable, THROCKMORTON.

Three or four flat stones of the same family. One new faire erected monument against the north wall of the said yle;

> A shield noted as "with several quarterings," but none given, impaling, on a bend cotised, three lions passant, BROWNE.

This family lived ever in man's remembrance till Queen Elizabeth's dayes. He was accused and dyed for treason.[b]

The manor howse is neare the church, a lofty and faire seate; and a faire parke well wooded neare it, belonging to it.

Now the howse of the Lord Marquesse of Winchester.

From Inglefeild the King and the army marched by Bradley, in the same county.

Where, neare the church, and by the roade, is a faire large and antique manor howse, now the seate of Captaine Stafford, a young

---

[a] All these brasses were gone when I visited this church about 1827. They are all noticed by Ashmole as existing; and, as he commenced his Visitation in 1664 and concluded it in 1666, the Cromwellians, who are always accused of having perpetrated such spoliations, are, in this case, most clearly exonerated.

Sir Francis Englefield was indicted for treason, fled the kingdom, was outlawed, and attainted 28 Eliz., when his estates were seized by the Crown. He died at Valladolid about the year 1592.

gent.[a] The hall, parlor, &c. were adorned with severall matches of that family.

> Or, a chevron gules, charged with a crescent for difference, a canton ermine. [STAFFORD].
>
> Same coat, impaling, Paly of six argent [or] and gules, on a chief azure a lion passant gardant or. [LANGFORD [b].]
>
> STAFFORD, with an impalement, but the charges obliterated.

From thence to Compton, which is the beginning of the Downes in the way from Reading to Wantage. Here, on the top of the playne hills, was the rendesvouz of the whole army that Satterday. The King returned home to Oxford that night.

Round about the King's chessboard this verse:—

> Subditus et Princeps istis sine sanguine certent. 1643.

Munday, the 27 of May, the rebels possessed themselves of Abbingdon.

Tuesday they faced at Cumner and Ilsley (Iffley), a myle from Oxford.

Wednesday the 29. We scouted beyond Cumner, and mett with some of them; none hurt of either side. Thursday, a great body of foote of them appeared upon Ballington greene; some bodyes of theire horse and many of their scoutes appeared on the hill, neare neare the citty of Oxford on the east side. Divers of us went out and mett them, singly. One Captayne Bennet of ours slayne.

Friday 31. The King went out of Oxford at the north gate to Wolvercote. The Lord B[ernard] and the King's troope went neare the Mill at Islep, where our army kept them from coming over. That day, Sir Jacob Ashley kept them off. And the next, and on Sunday, with losse of six or little more men too.

Sunday 2 June. At one of the clocke in the afternoone, the King, accompanied with his troope, &c. went to Woodstock and killed two bucks, and supt there.

---

[a] This was probably Edward Stafford, son of Sir Edward Stafford, knt. by Mary, daughter of Sir William Forster, of Aldermaston, co. Berks, knight.

[b] This is the coat of Langford of Bradfield, from which family, and who had previously inherited it from the De la Beches, the Staffords derived it.

Newes came at ten of the clock at night, that Waller was at New bridge, with all his force, consisting of 10,000, and that 150 horse were on Oxfordshire side, come over.

Wee marched towards O.; lay in the feild by the way. Our soldjers hung lighted matches at the mill and bridge neare Islip to cheate Essex, and so fairely left the place, the enemy shooting many times that night at the matches in vayne. Wee came safe to O. that Munday morning, brought all the King's army safe to Oxford; and that day, many of our foot and horse went towards Abingdon, with our cannon and cariages, which made Waller hast from Newbridge to Abingdon. At nine of the clock that night, the King with all his army lay in the feild at Wolvercote, marched without a cannon between New bridge and Woodstock, and left Witney on the left hand; so to Burford, a long stree and one church, where the King's troope refreshed themselves at Mr. William Lenthall's howse in that towne,[a] and that night marched to Morton-super-aquas.

Wednesday 5 of June. The King and all his army marched over Cotswold downes and Brodway hills, and came to Evesham, his owne garrison, where young Colonel Knotsforth was governour; which was the first night's rest of our army.

Thursday morning the bridge was pulled up, and Knotsford commanded to stay till he saw the enemy, of whom wee heard (by one of their captaynes who was taken scowting that morning neare Brodway) that Waller was at Brodway with all his army. Evesham being slighted.

The King marched with all his army to Worcester that night, being twelve myles the worst way. A woody and durty country.

Pershore bridge was pulld downe by our forces, because Waller should not follow, and forty of our men lost. The bridge fell from under them into the river.

This Knotsworth was knighted at Buckingham.

---

[a] This was the house, now partly pulled down, which belonged to Lord Falkland, and was purchased by Speaker Lenthall.

EVESHOLME, co. Gloucester.

Two parish churches within this mayor towne both in one church-yard, Al-Saints and St. Lawrence.

Alhallowes [*i. e.* All Saints] Church in Evesholme, more eastward placed in the churchyard.

These are in very old glasse in the north yle window of this church:

> Argent, two bars gules, a canton of the last.
>
> Barry of six, or and azure, an inescocheon argent, on a chief of the first two pallets between two esquires of the second, [MORTIMER].
>
> Argent [or], two bends gules, [SUDELEY].
>
> Gules, a fess argent, on a chief gules two mullets pierced of the field or.

East window of the church:

> Gules, six martlets argent, 3, 2, and 1.

A deepe stone cutt for a coffyn, with a place for the head, lyes in the chancel.

North window north yle:

> Gules, three human legs armed conjoined argent, [ISLE OF MAN].

In this church stands an old organ case.

Upon a flat stone the picture of a man and woman in brasse:

> Orate pro aīa Rob'ti Willys et Agnetis
> ux'is ejus ; quor' a. p. d. a.

Another—

> Hic jacet Johēs Okley, quondam mercator ville de
> Eveshᵃm, qui obiit viij. die Junii 1596 ; (*sic.*) cujus a. p. d. a.

Carved on an old stone in the south yle of the church:

> Azure, three bishop's mitres or ; in chief, chevron-wise, a chain of 24 square links, at the dexter end thereof a ring, at the sinister a padlock of the second, [ABBEY OF EVESHAM, but incorrectly drawn].

South yle, west window, this coate, old:

Gules, two keys in saltire or.

In an old roome adjoyning to the north side of the church these two in old glasse:

Azure, a chain chevron-wise, at the dexter end thereof a ring, at the sinister a padlock or, between three bishop's mitres of the second, [ABBEY OF EVESHAM].
Gules, two keys in saltire or.

WORCESTER, June 6, 1644.

Wherein is the cathedral, and a colledge adjoyning for a deane and ten prebends, worth 80*l.* a peice per annum; ten petty cannons; ten singing men; ten singing boyes; forty king's schollars.

The bishop's pallace is neare the cathedral.

Parish churches tenn.

1. St. Peter's.	6. St. Andrewes.
2. St. Michael's.	7. Alsaints'.
3. St. Alban's.	8. St. Clement's.
4. St. Ellen's.	9. St. Nicholas.
5. St. Swithin's.	10. St. Martin's.

All within the walls.

Four gates. Sidbury gate, towards Evesham, which is the east gate. 2. The Bridge gate, which is the west gate, and goes towards Hereford. 3. North gate, called the Fore gate, which leades to Yorke. 4. St. Martin's gate, towards Warwick, north-east.

The citty is governed by—a maior, recorder, six aldermen in scarlet gownes. All that are aldermen and have beene maiors do weare scarlet.

Twenty-four of the grand councel, in purple gownes faced with sathan. Forty-eight of the common councel, all in purple gownes faced with sathan.

Two coroners; one sheriffe; one towne clerk.

All the officers chosen once a yeare.

This coppy I had of Mr. William Symonds, now living in Worcester, ætat. 70.

De Crohlea, now written Crowle;[a] four myles from Worcester.

Tempore illo quo Dani hujus patrie possessores fuerunt, villa que dicitur Crohlea à dominico victu monachorum hoc modo ablata est, licet servitio ecclesie adhuc (Deo largiente) mancipata sit. Nam Simund quidam, genere Danus, miles Leofrici comitis Merciorum, possessor existens alterius Crohlea, predicte jam vicine, ut illius generis homines erant soliti, nostre tunc proprie ville dominatum avare cupiebat. Quam cum adipisci nullo modo posset, vi et potentia sua et domini sui eam tot damnis et placitis pejoravit, ut fere eam colonis destitueret. Hinc facto placito, precibus domini sui predicti comitis Egelwinus, prior istius monasterii, ei terram ipsam concessit possidendam vite sue spatio, ea tamen conventione, ut pro ea ipse ad expeditionem terra marique, que tunc crebro agebatur, monasterio serviret, pecuniaque placabili sive gabello ipsum priorem unoquoque anno recognosceret.

This in the register of Worcester was written by Hemingus, a monk in the priory in the time of St. Welston [Wulstan] Bishop of Worcester, in the reigne of William the Conqueror, at which time no armes were borne in England. It is in the booke of Sir Richard St. George, King of Heralds, and the armes there appeare.

Symond. Sable, three cupps argent, covered or. So far this coppy of Mr. William Symonds his writing, and in his hands.

A rude sketch of a male figure, above which is written, "DEVEREVX DE BELLO-CAMPO miles dedit Lodestan."

WORCESTERSHIRE.

Since the civil warr in this kingdome these regiments have beene raysed out of this county, *pro Rege*: which consists onely of 150 od parish churches.

[a] This was the residence of a family of Symonds in no way related to our author. The extract from Hemingus has been corrected from Hearne's edition, 8vo. 1723, p. 264, with the exception of the word "gabello," which appears preferable to "caballo," as Hearne printed it.

Sir James Hamilton, about May 1643, raysed three regiments. One of horse of 400 or thereabout, one of ffoote neare 1,000, one of dragoons, all at the charges of the county. These captaynes were under him of this county:

Of Horse.

Captain John Blunt, of Soddington, son to Sir Walter Blunt.

Captain William Welch.

Captaine Colt.

All these and his regiment were cutt off and taken prisoners about or neare the Devizes. These captaynes aforesaid are now in towne.

His regiment of foot lost there, so was his dragoons. Henderson, a Scot, was his leiftenant.

Colonel Samuel Sandys, of Ombersley, four myles from Worcester, about the same time raysed three regiments; one of horse, one of foot, one of dragoons, all at his owne charge. He hath 3000*l*. per annum.

The horse consisted of between 6 or 700.

John Sandys, his unckle, captain-leift.

Mr. Windsor Hickman, leift-colonel.

Capt. Savage, of this county.

Captain Langston.

One regiment of foot of about 1000.

Captain William Sandys, his unckle.

Captain Frederick Windsor.

Captain Fr. Moore, of this county.

Captain Heling.

Regiment of dragoons not perfected. Captain Thomas Symonds, of Claynes, in this county, nephew to Mr. William S. of Worcester.

Colonel Sandys gave up his regiment of ffoot to Knotsworth, who was now Governor of Evesham, of the county of Warwick, about Aprill 1644, when Prince Rupert was here.

Sir William Russel, of Strensham in this county, raysed, not long after, one regiment of horse consisting of about 300, now in being about this citty.

One regiment of ffoot consisting of about 700, about 300 still, ther rest gone for want of pay.

Colonel Sandys, younger brother to Sandys which was killed here on the rebells side, raysed a regiment of horse in this county.

The citty of WIGORN. at this present, 3 June, 1644, is thus governed and defended:—

The governour, Sir Gilbert Gerard, hath a regiment of foot. Leiftenant-Colonel (*blank*), Major Bishop, Captain Gerard, and one regiment of horse.

Colonel Martin Sandys, unckle to Mr. Samuel Sandys, hath a regiment of foot of the townesmen, consisting of about 800.

He was knighted at the palace in Worcester June 12, 1644.

The mayor of Worcester was knighted 12 of June, 1644.

Munday the 10 of June, the Lord Wilmott with his horse went from Worcester on that side of Severne next Hereford, so to Bewdley, and relieved the Castle of Dudley, which was beseiged by the Earle of Denbighe: tooke some prisoners.

Wednesday the 12 of June, 1644, his Majestie marched out of Worcester on that side of the Severne next Hereford, by the parish of (*blank*) where is a park where Sir Walter Devereux lives, two myle on the right hand the way from Worcester. Then by Shrawley, a parish. At last to Bewdley, ten myles from Worcester, where the King lay that night at the manor of Tickney, on the top of the hill nere the towne, a howse belonging to the Prince of Wales, now farmed out to Sir Ralph Clare. A fine hilly parke about the howse.

The church is a myle from the towne. In the towne is onely a chappel of ease. Two myles from Kidermister.

This is an inclosed county, small pastures and corne feilds, a narrow way, most part of it stony; the quarrie of stone of a brickish colour.

In the chappel of ease at BEWDLEY, called St. Ann's Chappel.

In the east window of the chancel:

Gyronny of twelve argent and gules.

These armes, of the towne of Bewdley, are depicted on the wall, east end:

Argent, a barrel or, enfiled by an anchor erect azure, on the dexter side a sword, erect, of the last, on the sinister side a rose slipped proper.

The towne of Bewdley is governed with a bayliffe and a justice; he that is bayliffe this yeare is justice the next. Chosen out of twelve aldermen. Two bridgwardens.

The onely manufacture of this towne is making of capps called Monmouth capps. Knitted by poore people for 2d. a piece, ordinary ones sold for ijs., 3s., 4s. First they are knitt, then they mill them, then block them, then they worke them withe tasells, then they sheere them.

A grotto cut out of the quarry of stone within this parke towards the Severne.

Satterday morning the King &c. with his whole army marched back to Worcester.

Sunday, after sermon in the forenoone ended in the Cathedral at Worcester, his Majestie about xii. of the clock left Worcester and lay that night at Brodway, com. Gloucester [Worcester], going through Evesholme. His Majestie lay that night at Mr. Savage his howse there at Brodway.

BRODWAY Church.

West window ch.:

Azure, a fess gules between three garbs.
Ermine, two bends gules.

North window, crosse yle:

Quarterly, 1 and 4, Sable, a fess between three martlets argent; 2 and 3, Argent, two chevrons sable; impaling, Sable, a bend between two dexter hands, couped at the wrist, also in bend, argent.

Mantle sable, doubled argent.

East window, old:

Gules, three goblets or.

A small neate monument against the south wall of the chancel, with this:

Argent, six lions rampant sable, SAVAGE impaling (*blank*).

From Brodway, the King and all his army marched over the Cotswold Downes, where Dover's games[a] were, to Stowe in the Would, six myle. Then that night to Burford, in co. Oxon. being seven myles further, where his Majestie lay that Munday night at the George Inn in Burford. Where wee heard that the rebel Essex and his army followed the King when he first left Oxford, and on Thursday 6th of June lay in this towne, two or three nights, and then marched into the West to releive Lyme. Waller came hither too, but onely passed through, and so to Stowe, and after as far as Kidermister after his Majestie.

This night wee heard that Essex was then at Salisbury, Waller at (*blank*), following of his Majestie.

Tuesday, after his Majestie had beene at church and heard the sermon, and dyned, he marched to Witney that night, five myles.

There that night the foote which were left at Oxford came with the pikes and colours, for before there was none marched with the King this march, and (*blank*) trayne also.

Two myle short of Witney on the left hand, as wee came from Burford, stands Minster Lovel, an ancient howse of the Lord Lovel, worth seeing.

MINSTER LOVEL Church, co. Oxford.

" East window of the chancel broken."

The upper part of a shield, bearing, Sable, two locks or. Quarterly, 1, gone; 2, Argent, a chevron azure between three chaplets gules; 3, Gules, a lion rampant ermine; 4, Argent, a chevron between three

---

[a] For an account of these games, see the Annalia Dubrensia, concerning " Mr. Robert Dover's Olympic games upon Cotswold Hills," published 1636. See also Rudder's History of Gloucestershire.

lions passant sable. Impaling, Quarterly, 1, Sable, a chevron between three covered cups or ; 2, 3, and 4, gone.

" A collar of S with portcullises and roses about it."

These coates are painted very old on the chancel side, upon the boardes that divide the chancel and the body of the church, in a row, almost worne out:

Vert, a lion rampant argent.

A lion rampant.

Barry nebuly of six [or] and [gules,] [LOVEL]. Impaling, Barry of six debruised by a bendlet [? GREY of Rotherfield, DEINCOURT being omitted].

Quarterly, 1, LOVEL; 2, a fess indented between six billets [DEINCOURT]; 3, [GREY of Rotherfield]; 4, a lion rampant [? BEAUMONT or HOL-LAND]. The whole charged with an escocheon of pretence, bearing a lion passant, [? rampant for BURWELL ; see Vincent B 2, Coll. Arm.].

LOVEL, impaling (*blank*).

A fess between two chevrons.

A stag's head caboshed argent. " A kind of greene had spoyled the colours."

West window, under these coates thus written the remnant of the Saints are still:

Azure, a cross flory between four martlets or, Sanctus Edwardus Confessor.

Gules, a cross flory or, Sanctus Oswaldus.

In the south crosse yle of the church stands an altar tombe[a] of alablaster, which is adorned with four shields on each side, and two at the west end, for the east end joynes to the wall; on the south side is the statues of the Virgin Mary and another saint; on the north side, two bishops; at the west end St. Christopher; all handsomely carved. Upon the top lyes the statue of an armed knight, at his feet a lyon, under his head lyes his helmet, mantle, and upon a wreath a dog passant[b] like a lyon, his body compleate armour of woove worke, yet somewhat like the Black Prince.

[a] See an account of this monument in the Gentleman's Magazine, 1825, but the coats of arms are not mentioned. It is, in all probability, the monument of John Lord Lovel, father of Francis Viscount Lovel, who died 4 Edw. IV. The coat of Deincourt, his mother being an heir of that family, would seem to establish the fact.

[b] This is the crest of Lovel, viz. a talbot passant.

North side, these four:

> Quarterly, 1 and 4, LOVEL; 2, three padlocks; 3, two bars, debruised by a bend.
>
> 1, LOVEL; 2, DEINCOURT; 3, "gone;" 4, two bars debruised by a bend; 5, "gone;" 6, same as 1.
>
> " Third as the second."
>
> Three padlocks.

West end, these two :

> LOVEL.   Three padlocks.

South side, these:

> " Gone."
>
> LOVEL, impaling the three padlocks.
>
> GREY OF ROTHERFIELD.
>
> Gules, ten bezants, 4, 3, 2, and 1 [ZOUCHE].

In the north part of that yle lyes a large flat stone inlayed with brasse, sans pictures of bodyes, four shields, at each corner one, and one towards the upper end, with mantle, helme, and creast, a dog sejant, the shield gone; this motto is in divers severall scrowlls: " Mercy and Grace."

The one of the four shields remayne:

> An eagle displayed within a double tressure flory counter-flory [VAMPAGE.]

This inscription in the midst :

> Verbum fons venie Vampage miserere Joh'is
> Ad regis causas attornati primo juris
> Mater virgo Dei p'cor Elizabeth memorari
> Prima que vita felix sibi nupta
> —bus hos turbe jungat Deus atque beate
> Gratis quo cernant ipsos qui jura gubernant
> Et rogent in celis maneant ut quisque fidelis.

In the hall windowes of the hall which formerly had beene the seate of the Lord Lovel:

> LOVEL.   GREY OF ROTHERFIELD.

Rendesvouz of the King's foot neare Witney, with those that

came from Oxford ... June, Wednesday, 3910, besides officers, which are at least 1000.

All the howses in Witney and Burford are built of stone.

Friday the 21 of June. From Witney the King, &c. marched from thence to Woodstock playne, where the rendesvouz was of foot, with the Queenes regiment and officers, in all 6000.

The horse, 4 or neare 5000.

That night the King lay at Blechingdon at Sir Thomas Coghill's new howse. His troope was quartered at Islip, five myles from Oxford, two myles nearer Blechingdon to Oxford.

In the church of ISLIP, though large, is no armes in the windowes. A flat stone in the north yle [of the] chancel, of one Andrewes.

A new small one in the chancel, of [Henry] Norris, Esq. with the armes of Norris:

> Quarterly, Argent and gules, a fess azure; in the 2nd and 3rd quarters a fret or [NORREYS]. Impaling a cross moline.

A small brasse at the east end, with a coate and creast for Dr. Egliondby [Aglionby], parson of this church. Another in the chancel, four verses sans armes.

Jacet hic Vesey—a Churchman.

Westminster Colledge ownes the lordship of this towne. They have the guift of the living 200ʰ per annum at most: 36 yard-lands in this parish, 20ʰ a yeare land, betweene 30 and 40 acres in a yard-land.

From Islip, our quarters, wee wayted on the King, from Blechingdon, about six of the clock, to Bisseter, where, before wee came to the towne, on a greene playne was the rendesvouz.

In the church of Burcester [BICESTER], com. Oxon., north window north yle church, this old:—

> Ermine, a fess compony or and azure.

These three south window, church:

> Barry of six, ermine and gules, a crescent for difference [HUSEE], impaling, Argent, a cross sable. [? BANISTER; see pedigree of Husee of Shapwick.]

Blank, probably as in preceding, impaling, Argent, three "wolves or cats couchant" in pale azure within a bordure sable, charged with ten bezants.

Blank—impaling, Argent, three fleurs-de-lis azure.

Agaynst the north wall of the chancel is an altar-tombe of marble, and that part which is in the wall is inlayed in brasse with the pictures of a man with his surcoate and a woman with hers:

Two kneeling figures of a knight and his lady, the former apparently in plate armour, and his surcoat emblazoned with these arms: On a chevron, between three lozenges as many buck's heads erased, STAVELEY. Upon the lady's robe the following arms: A chevron between three eagles, displayed [FRANCEIS].

Between the figures, a shield of arms, but marked by Symonds as "behind the woman;" viz. Quarterly, 1, FRANCEIS; 2 and 3, a cross flory between four martlets [PLESSINGTON]; 4, a lion rampant, debruised by a bend.

This inscription in brasse following:

Orate p' aiābz Willī Staveley armigī quondam dnī de Bignell' et Alicie uxīs ejus filie un' hered' dnī Johīs Fraunces militis et dnē Isabelle uxīs ejus unice heredis dnī . : . . Plesington militis. Quiquidem Will's obijt 10 die Octobr' 1598 p'dcā vero Alicia obiit 20 die Octobr' 1500. Quor' aiābz p. d. a. [See Vincent's Oxon. f. 80, Coll. Arm.]

Against the south wall, right over against the former, is an old altar-tombe of stone, and in the wall is [a] brasse inlayed with three shields, mantle, helmes, and creasts:

Quarterly, 1 and 4, a fesse indented, between three mullets pierced [MOORE]; 2 and 3, a fesse between three annulets, impaling, Barry of six, ermine and gules, a crescent for difference or [HUSYE or HUSEE].

Blank, impaling the two coats quarterly as before.

Blank.

20 of Sept. 1551. Here was buried Roger Moore, esq., a second son of Moore, de la Moore, com. Oxon., and Agnes his wife, daughter and heire of John Husye, of Shapwick, com. Dorset, &c.

The boards at the east end of the north chappell were anciently painted and adorned with the coates of Stanley:

Quarterly Stanley and the arms of the Isle of Man, an inescocheon blank.

A small monument of brasse in the church, north wall neare the the chancel, this coate or like it:

A cross.

From this parish wee marched that night with the whole army and ten peices of battery, to Buckingham.

St. Peter's church in the towne of BUCKINGHAM, Satterday 22 June 1644.

This coate is often in the chancel and the north yle [of] church:

Azure, a chevron between three [wolf's] heads, erased.
A bend.

Both these coats are surmounted by mitres.

All may God amend, is painted on the wall.

All the windows are done with crescents and escallops.

Never were any windows more broken, in May, 1644, by the rebels of Northampton.

North yle were many coates, but all broken.

" Gone ;" impaling, Argent, three wolf's heads erased gules, within a bordure azure, charged with covered cups or.

[? Argent] on a bend gules three martlets argent, impaling, Ermine, on a bend or, three chevronels gules.

Fowler built this yle.

South window south yle, these very old:

Argent, on a fess, between three martlets gules, three fleurs-de-lis or.
Gules, three lions passant argent.
Blank [but ? same as the first, being marked " 1 "].

A poore towne, one church, Sir Alexander Denton [a] is lord of it, who lives at Hilsdon, two myles off. Parsonage his, was worth 1,000*l.* per annum; vicaridge 10*l.* per annum.

The bayliffe and the aldermen mett the King at the townes end,

---

[a] He died in 1644-5, having married one of the Hampdens of Hartwell, distantly related to the great Parliamentarian.

and there the bayliffe made a speech to his majestie.   And on Sunday morning went before the King to church.

Toward the north of this towne, half a myle off on the top of the hill, stands a village called MAIDES MORTON, co. Buck.

This shield is twice in old glasse in the south and north window of this church:

Argent, on a chevron gules three fleurs-de-lis or [PEYVRE].

In the church lyes a flat stone, with the former shield twice still upon it. The inscription and the pictures of two women, both stolne.

Two more flat stones in the chancel with the statues of women both gone and the inscriptions also.

Over the north doore [of the] church, is the former shield painted on the wall, with this under it:

" Sisters and maids, daughters of ye Lord Pever, ye honble founders and benefactors of this church." a

Over against this, on the north wall, is the same coate painted, and under written, Pever.

The inhabitants shew the feild next the church where the howse was where these virgin sisters lived.

This church belongs to Alsowles in Oxford.

HILSDEN, co. Buck.   The manor howse neare this faire and neate church is Sir Alexander Denton's, and by him made a garrison in winter 1643.

Taken by the rebels and burnt.   The church windowes spoiled.

An altar-tombe at the east end of the chancel next the north wall, divers matches of the family of Denton:

Argent, two bars gules, in chief three cinquefoils sable [DENTON, with an impalement left blank].

The statues of a man and woman which laye on the top of this tombe are broken and throwne downe there by the rebels.

Upon the north wall north yle of the chancel is a monument of

---

a The last heir male of this family died in 1382, leaving one daughter and heir, who married, and had issue ; consequently the tradition that this church was built by the maiden daughters of the last lord falls to the ground.

playne stone, with the quarterings of Denton, and inscribed; some of it I remember:

> Here lyeth Alex. Denton, son of Thomas Denton, Esq., by Ann [? Mary] his wife, daughter of [Roger] Martyn, Knight, who dyed A°D. 157[4].

This parish is two myles from Buckingham, southward.

Wednesday, 26 June. The King and the army marched from Buckingham to Brackley. His majestie lay there that night. Before you come to Brackley, is a large greene or downe called Bayards Greene, where often is horse-raceing, six myle long.[a]

The troope lay at Turson in Buck. alias Tary Weston, [Turweston] forty-five myles from Northampton. Thursday morning, wee marched to (*blank*) where the King lay. The troop lay at Throp Mandevile, all at Captaine Kirton's, the manor howse, where are divers matches of that family:

> KIRTON; Argent, a fess and a chevron in chief gules.

Friday, 28 June. From thence, wee marched towards Banbury, where, upon the hills at a faire howse of [Sir Anthony] Cope's, stood part of Waller's body. As wee faced the enemy on the windmill hill, and a comanded party of horse and foot, sent downe to make the passage good from beyond Banbury. (*Sic orig.*)

The enemyes horse endeavoured to passe the river on the right hand of Banbury, but were repulsed; one Captayne Martin of horse killed, after he had charged twice, his men did not follow. Some scowting beyond Banbury that evening; little or no hurt on neither side.

The King lay that night at a howse on the bottome of the hill neare Banbury.

Satterday morning, June 29, 1644. Betweene three and four in the morning, our whole army of horse and foot stood at the bottome neare Banbury. Waller and his comrades facing of us on the top of the hills beyond the towne. About eight the King's whole army marched by the Windmill towards a towne. When all the King's foot, ordinance and cariages were passt the two passes over the

---

[a] More anciently renowned for its tournaments.

river, viz., (*blank*) nearest to Banbury, and another passe at the parish of (*blank*)

A party of horse of the enemy came over the river and charged our reare of foot, about one or two of the clocke. The Lord Wilmott, who was behind them keeping of that passe next Banbury, fell upon them, and after divers skirmishes, horse against horse, some few of them killed, the enemy retreated, but ere they retreated the King's troope was drawne up by the Lord Bernard, very near the enemy. Whiles our troope faced them, newes came about four of the clocke that Sir William Boteler, a colonel of horse, and Sir William Clerke, another, [were] both killed at that passe next Banbury: the first by his owne trooper unfortunately, whome his comrades requited. Here was the Lord Wilmott shott in the arme, and small graze on his hand. Sergeant Major Panton killed of ours.

One blew ensigne of foot taken.

While our troope thus faced the enemy at the furthest passe, fourteen cannon shott was shott at us; some and most flew over us, some at last as much short. None of us hurt.

Then came the King about five of the clock, and drew us off on the top of the hill, betweene the two passes, our foot and theires all the while shooting.

An ensigne taken at the farthest passe, and three prisoners by one foot man of Colonel Penniman's regiment.

An ensign azure, on a canton a cross, issuing therefrom, towards fess point, a flame or ray of light wavy argent.

But before all this, at the nearest passe, we took eleven peices of the enemyes cannon, and all there horse belonging to them. The prisoners taken severally told us that Sir William Waller was killed, but it proved a lye.

The body of there horse and foot retreated up to the top of the hill ymediately after Lord Wilmot's horse had beate them from our reare; our horse and footstanding on the top of the hill, on (*blank*) side betweene the two passes.

At eight of the clock that night, the body of the King's army faced the enemyes body on the hill just over the first passe. The enemye shooting 10 or more great peices, some of them fell neare the King.

Sunday, 30 of June. The enemy lay in the same place that morning, as wee left him the night past.

Afore nine, the King, &c. went to prayers in the feild, and, sermon ended, we saw part of the body of the enemy march away towards Warwickshire, about xj. of the clock.

On Satterday before, 29 June, Mr. Robert Howard,[a] son to the Earle of Berks, and Leiftenant Colonel to his brother of horse, was knighted for his gallant service against the rebells [when] wee came over the passe.

Thirty commanders and officers of the enemy this Friday taken, whereof one was Weemes, Generall of the Ordinance to Waller, a man obliged to the King for his bread and breeding; a Scott.

This Satterday, at the first passe, one of Colonel Apleyard's ensignes tooke a guidon of dragoons of the enemy.

A trumpet and banner taken by a Frenchman of horse, with this coate upon it:

Argent, three snakes embowed vert.

Lieut.-Colonel Hooper, of Dragoons, knighted (per mistake. Thelwel [b] did the service.)   Sir Thomas Hooper.

That Sunday morning, the rebells shott 30 peice of cannon at a body of horse of ours which lay on the side hill, but did no hurt.

Nothing of any moment done all this day.

A spy hanged.

Munday morning, about four of the clock, his Majestie with all his army, drums beating, colors flying, and trumpets sounding, marched through Middleton Cheyney, from thence to Farmigo [Farthingho],

---

[a] The wit and poet.

[b] This was the fight of Cropredy bridge, of which Clarendon gives a good account, and mentions Colonel Thelwell.

where Sir Rowland Egerton hath a howse; from thence by Aynoe [Aynhoe] on the hill to [? Abberbury] where the Lord Wilmott hath a faire seat. Here a trumpett of Waller came and exchanged 60 and od prisoners of ours taken by them, which were all they tooke, wee having a hundred more.

The King lay at Dedington. From Dedington the army marched Tuesday morning, by [Great Tew], where the Lord Viscount Falkland hath a faire howse, com. Oxon.; thence that night to Morton Henmarsh [on the Marsh], where his Majestie lay.

From thence his Majestie with his whole army marched over the Cotswold hills, with colours flying &c., to Brodway; thence to Evesholme that night, where he lay.

His troope were quartered at Fladbury.

FLADBURY church in com. Wigorn.

This is a mother church to five or six hamlets. In the east window of the chancel the pictures, notwithstanding being broken about a fortnight before by Waller's men, these six following coates, very faire and old:

> Quarterly argent and gules, on the 2d and 3d quarters a fret or, over all a bend sable [LE DESPENSER].[a]
>
> Gules, a lion rampant, double queued, argent [MONTFORT.]
>
> Barry of six, on a chief two palets between two esquires, an inescocheon [MORTIMER].
>
> Argent, two bars gules, a canton of the last [Bosco or CORBETT].
>
> Bendy of ten, or and azure [MONTFORT].
>
> Gules, a fess company counter-compony argent and sable between six crosses flory or [BOTELER].

Upon a flat stone in the chancel, the picture of a churchman, and with this coate and inscription:

> Hic jacet magister Thomas Mordon utriusq' Juris Bacularius, Thesaurarius eccl'ie cathedralis S. Pauli, London. ac Rector istius eccl'ie, qui vero obiit ultimo die Aprilis, 1458, c. a. p. d. a.

In the middle yle of the church stands a faire altar tombe of

---

[a] These coats are so recorded by Nash, from Habingdon's MS.

blew marble; the top is inlayed with brasse, with the pictures of a man in armor, in the forme of the Black Prince, and a woman. Five shields, three on the west end, whereof two gone, and two at the east.

> [Gules,] on a chevron [argent] three bars gemels [sable, THROCKMOR-
> TON]: impaling a chevron between three crescents [SPINEY].
> The same, impaling a fess between six pears [BESFORD].
> The same, impaling on a fess three pheons.

The inscription was on the verge, circumscribed; this remaynes onely, north side:

> . . . . arius [a] Anglie, qui obiit 13 Apr. 1445, quor' a. p. d. a.

South yle of the church, a flat stone; the inscription was circumscribed in brasse; four shields, but gone. This remaynes east end:

> [uxoris] sue, filie et heredis Roberti Olney armig'i, quiquidem . . . . .

Under the three steps which ascend the east end is a faire charnel house with many bones.

Three myles from Evesholme towards Worcester.

Within the south wall chancel is an arch, old, with a shield, but no mention of a tombe.

This is newly written in the wall:

> In obitum Joh'is Darbey, defuncti 2° Martij, 1609, a° etat. sue 52.

This coate is painted in the old escocheons, Azure, a garb or.

Mr. Darbey now lives in this parish, where Lord Bernard lay. 100*l*. per annum.

These coates following are in old glasse in the hall windowe, and the dyning roome windowe of the parsonage howse neare the church of Fladbury, a faire large old and stately parsonage.

Hall window:

> Argent, ten torteaux, 4, 3, 2, and 1, [SEE OF WORCESTER].
> Paly of six azure and gules, over all, on a chevron argent three cross-
> crosslets gules, the chevron surmounted by a mitre or.

---

[a] Symonds here remarks "Justiciarius I suppose," but the monument commemorated John Throckmorton under-treasurer of England—the word was therefore *thesaurarius*.

Quarterly, I. quarterly, 1 and 4, Gules, a fess between six cross-crosslets or, [BEAUCHAMP]; 2 and 3, Chequy or and azure, a chevron ermine [EARLDOM OF WARWICK]. II. Quarterly, 1 and 4, Argent, three lozenges conjoined in fess gules [MONTACUTE]; 2 and 3, Or, an eagle displayed gules [MONTHERMER]. III. Quarterly, 1, Gules, a saltire argent, a label of three points [NEVILLE]; 2 and 3, a fret [? lozengy the old coat of NEVILLE]; 4, Gules, three chevrons or [CLARE]. IV. Argent and gules, in second and third quarters a fret or, over all a bend sable [LE DESPENSER].

Quarterly, France and England.

WARWICK EARLDOM and DESPENSER quarterly.

BEAUCHAMP.

Sable, three wolf's heads erased argent.

Erminois, a bordure argent.

Every one of the former coates held in the hands of an angel, and two little boyes of each side at bottome supporting them.

These are old as the former in the dyning roome windowes:

Quarterly, France and England.

Azure, three chevronels interlaced or, a chief of the last.

Azure, an eagle displayed argent, legged or, within a double tressure flory counter-flory of the second ?

Quarterly, 1, [BEAUCHAMP]; 2, [EARLDOM OF WARWICK]; 3, [MONTA-CUTE]; 4, gone; 5, [NEVILLE]; 6, [CLARE]; 7, [LE DESPENSER].

Quarterly, BEAUCHAMP and WARWICK; impaling, Quarterly CLARE and LE DESPENSER.

Quarterly, 1 and 4, A fess compony counter-compony between six crosses formée fitchy; 2 and 3, two bends; impaling, a fess between six martlets.

Sable, three hind's heads erased argent.

In most of the panes, written in a scroll: **Emanuel.**

Every Midlent Sunday is a great day at Worcester, when all the children and godchildren meet at the head and cheife of the family and have a feast. They call it the Mothering-day.[a]

The parson's wife of Fladbury, a young woman often carrying a milke-payle on her head in the street,—so far from pride.

---

[a] See Brand's Popular Antiquities.

Friday, July. The King and the army marched from thence thorough Brodway, then over the Cotswold neare Shudeley [Sudeley] Castle, the seate of the Lord Chandos, from whence the rebells gave us two great shott. That night, at one of the clock, the King got to his quarters, a poore howse in Coverley [COBERLY]. Mr. Dutton owes the manor howse, being a very old one. A small church with this coate in many of the windowes, old:

Argent, a fess between three martlets sable [BAYNHAM].

In the north wall of the chancel lyes the statue of a man cross legged; in the south yle a woman.

In the middle yle another, and a child by her; all cutt in stone, and lye flat on the ground.

This night wee lay in the wett feild without any provision. Wee made this march, from four of the clock in the morning to one the next night, without any bayte or rendesvouz.

In the hall windowes of Mr. Dutton's howse these coates:

Argent, on a cross sable a leopard's face or [BRIDGES].

Or, a pile gules within a garter [CHANDOS].

BRIDGES, impaling, Argent, a fess between three martlets sable.

BRIDGES, impaling, Azure, a lion rampant gules, armed or.

Quarterly, 1 and 4, BRIDGES ; 2, CHANDOS ; 3, A fess between three martlets sable [BAYNHAM], impaling, quarterly, 1, A chevron between three bull's heads cabossed ; 2, Gules, on a bend argent an eagle displayed sable ; 3, six gouts de sang ; 4, Or, a fess gules between six cross-crosslets.

Quarterly, BRIDGES, &c. ; impaling, Quarterly, 1 and 4, Barry of eight azure and argent ; 2 and 3, Quarterly, the charges gone.

Per pale argent and sable, a chevron per pale gules and or.

BRIDGES, impaling, Azure, a lion rampant or, charged upon the shoulder with a cross-crosslet fitchy sable [DARELL].

In a low roome:

Gules, a lion rampant or, within a bordure invected of the second, a label of three points azure.

Quarterly, 1 and 4, Azure, three bendlets gules; 2 and 3, Argent, a chevron between three eagles displayed sable.

A fess sable between three martlets; impaling a fess gules between six cross-crosslets or.

In a lodging roome very old, every coate thus underwritten in base French:

Azure, a lion rampant or, crowned argent, charged upon the shoulder with a cross-crosslet fitchy azure, DARELL; impaling, Azure, a lion rampant per pale wavy or and gules [LORTY].

Ces sont les armes de Elizabeth Darrel ap's decesse de Richard Heverynh cheveler.

(*Blank*) impaling, Per pale sable and argent, a chevron per pale or and gules [LOVNDRES].

Ces sont les armes Thome Calston' esquier ap's decesse de Richard Havering cheveler.

As last, impaling, Argent, four barrulets gules, in chief two lions rampant of the second [CALSTON].

Ces sont les armes Thome Calston esquier ap's decesse de Robert Londres cheveler.

As last, impaling, Three lions passant or [COMBE].

Ces sont les armes de Elizabeth Darrel ap's decesse de Thome Chelrey, esquier.

As last, impaling, Quarterly, 1 and 4, Argent, a bend wavy between two bendlets gules; 2 and 3, Argent, three annulets, one within the other, [CHELREY].

Ces sont les armes Thome Calston esquier aprez decesse de Lawrence Calston esquier.

Vide M. 2, p. 175.

As last, impaling, Sable, six lioncels rampant or, 3, 2, and 1 [ST. MARTIN].

Ces sont les armez Thome Calston, Esq. aprez decesse de Laurenc' Ouyn chiveler [a mistake for LAURENCE ST. MARTIN].[a]

---

[a] These armorial bearings may be referred to the marriage of Florence, one of the daughters of William Darell by his wife Elizabeth, who was daughter and heir of Thomas Calston of Littlecote, co. Wilts, and who married Thomas à Bruges or Bridges of Coberly. The old manor-house has been long since taken down, and every vestige of the stained glass destroyed or disposed of.

Satterday, July 12. His Majestie marched from Coverley, co. Gloucester, to Sapperton, and spent all the day in that short march, but six or seven myle. Sapperton is a small church, and the manor house being large, of free stone, belonging to Sir Henry Poole; a brave sweet seat and gallant parke. This family owes the royalty of seven hundreds in this county; eleven or twelve myle from Gloucester.

The King's troope quartered at Dagleworth, belonging also to Poole, two myle from Cirencester.

Sunday, the 13th of July, 1643. His Majestie and his army marched from thence to Badmington, a faire stone howse of the Lord Somerset's, now his daughter's, in the county of Wiltes, about twelve or thirteen myle.

In the middle way, at the rendesvouz, two foot-soldiers were hanged on the trees in the hedge-row, for pillaging of the country villages. The whole army of horse and foot marched by the bodyes. The troope was quartered that night at Nettleton, six myles from Malmesbury, a garrison of the rebels taken by Massye from his Majestie, whereof Mr. Henry Howard, son to the Earle of Berks, was governor. At the same time, about six weekes since, Massye tooke Beverston Castle, neare which castle the King's whole army marched this day. The owner of this castle is Sir Richard Ducie.

On Satterday night two of the King's captaynes of horse, viz. Captain Plowman and Captain (*blank*) fell out, and P. basely ran him thorough on horseback, but fled ymediately.

Wee heard that Waller was now about Daventry in Northamptonshire, very weake; Essex neare Exeter.

Monday, his Majestie marched from thence thorough Marsfield, co. Wilts; thence to Lansdowne famous for the beating of the rebels under the command of Waller, 1643; thence to Bathe that night, where his Majestie being mett at the bottom of the hill going downe into the towne by the Lord Hopton, Sir Thomas Bridges the governor and sheriffe of Somerset, and divers other gentlemen. His Majesty stayed till Wednesday morning, and thence he marched to

Mells, the howse of Sir John Horner. In this march two hanged for plundering.

The church at BATHE, being very large, hath not any ancient monuments. At the south yle is a large monument for the lady of Sir William Waller, his statue cutt in stone there too.

In the middle of the quire toward the north yle is a very large monument for Mountague, Bishop of Winchester, Prelate of the Garter, this badge on his upper garment, left shoulder [here a sketch is given of the ordinary badge]. A great benefactor of this church.

SHEPTON MALLETT, co. Somerset, four myles from Mells, six from Glastonbury, fifteen from Bristoll. In an inn without the towne, in old glasse in the hall and parlour, which formerly was the dwelling-howse of Sir Philip Fulford:

> Azure, three trouts interlaced.
>
> Gules, a chevron argent [FULFORD], impaling, Or, on a bend sable three bear's heads erased argent [FITZURSE].
>
> Quarterly, 1 and 4, [FULFORD]; 2 and 3, Gules, [Azure ?] three bird-bolts erect in pale argent [BOSOM].
>
> *Crest.* Out of a ducal coronet or, a demi-wyvern argent.

'Tis about one hundred years since this family lived heare, and hath beene an inne ever since, in Davies' possession. 'Tis the manor of Shepton, belonging to Prince Charles. Sir Edward Herbert hath the fee farm.

This coate in the howse aforesaid :

> Argent, a wyvern with wings erect sable.

Shepton Mallett church.

Within the north wall of the body of the church, under two arches, lyes the two statues of two Knights Templars, crosse-legged, in mayle, and shields upon there breasts. The roofe of the church is curiously carved. Against the east wall, north yle of the church, is a small neate monument with the picture of a man in armes. Captain Barnard, Esquire, 1640.

> Argent, a bear salient sable, muzzled, BARNARD.

This is a market towne.

Mr. William Strowd, one of the five members, married this Mr. Barnard's onely daughter and heire. (2000ᴸⁱ per annum.) Strowd lived at Barrington three myle from ILMISTER; another howse at Street; hath all the parsonages betweene this towne and Barrington.ᵃ He gott his estate by being a factor in Spaine. His father was a clothier in Shepton Mallet. His father left him 740ᴸⁱ in all. Bernard is descended of a clothier in this towne too.

This towne hath furnished the King with above 300 men since the beginning.

The King lay at Sir John Horner's howse in Mells, who is lord of the manor, a faire large howse of stone, very strong, in forme of a H, two courts. The church is very large and faire, adjoyning to the manor howse. Nothing in it, either monumental or other, but these two coates :

North yle of church, old:

Argent, a chief indented [gules ?].

South yle of church :

Quarterly, 1 and 4, Azure, a chevron ermine ; 2 and 3, [? bendy argent and gules].

Horners have lived here three or four descents. He is in rebellion, and his estate sequestered; 1000ᴸⁱ per annum.

6 myle from Shepton Mallett.

The Lord Hopton's chiefe habitacion is Witham, eleven myles from Bathe; was borne there. The Prynce dyned with the Lord Hopton. Woodhowse within two myles of Witham, belonging to Arundel, now kept by sixty-six rebells.

KILMERSDON Church, in com. Somerset.   July 18, 1644.

East window very old.   Church :

Argent, a chevron between three eagles displayed sable.

Argent, a griffin segreant gules, armed azure.

No armes else or monuments in this church, though a very faire and large one.

ᵃ This family was ancient and of good repute. See I. C. 22, f. 130, in Coll. Arm.; also the pedigree of Barnard, f. 362.

The Earle of Northampton is the lord of this parish, two myles from Mells, six from Bathe.

Here the King's troope quartered.

Friday the King left Mells, and his rendesvouz was neare Nunney, where is a faire neate church, and a pretty castle belonging to the family of Prayters, called Nunney Castle.[a]

A deepe moate and a wall without that.

Four square, a long square, very narrow, the towers at each end almost joyne; four towers.

NUNNEY Church, co. Somerset, about two myle from Mells toward Woodhowse.

East window of the south chappel, old:

Gules, three lozenges ermine conjoined in fesse between three martlets argent.

Quarterly, 1 and 4, Argent, a lion rampant gules; 2 and 3, Gules, three lozenges ermine conjoined in fesse between three martlets argent.

Azure, six sprigs of [? laurel] slipped, 3, 2 and 1, or.

North windowes, north yle of church, old:

Gules, two lions passant guardant argent, collared azure.

Argent, ten martlets sable, 4, 3, 2 and 1.

Against the north wall, north yle of the church, upon an altar monument, lyes the statue of a knight in compleate armour in the forme of the Black Prince, a lyon a this feet, under his head, upon a helme, a mantle and a leopard's head. Delamore, who temp. Edw. II. built the church and castle.

In the same chappel and neare the body of the church, stands a large white altar tombe, the statue of a man in armes with lyons gardant carved on his brest, a woman lying by him. These coates are round the sides:

Quarterly, 1 and 4, two lions passant gardant [DELAMERE]; 2 and 3, on a chief two mullets [ST. JOHN].

[a] He gives a rude drawing of this castle, from which it appears that the towers were then surmounted by conical roofs in the French style.

Quarterly, 1 and 4, three swords in pile, the points conjoined in fesse point, PAULET; 2 and 3, two lions passant guardant [DELAMERE].

A lion rampant, impaling three water-bougets.

Quarterly, 1 and 4, on a bend an annulet; 2 and 3, on a chief two mullets, impaling (*blank*).

Paulet's Monument at Melcombe Paulet [qu. this addition ?].

Neare the former and more in the midst of the chappel is another lofty altar monument, the statues of a man and woman, on the top divers children.   These armes on the sides.

Prayter's monument:

Three wolf's heads erased, on a chief a lion passant, PRATER.

Quarterly, 1 and 4, a trefoil slipped, between three mullets; 2 and 3, two lions rampant addorsed.

This is all the monuments and coates in this church.

Neare the church is a faire stone howse, wherein the said Mr. Prayter's sonne lives.

BATCOMBE Church.

A faire stone church, five bells, onely these [coates]:

Argent, on a bend sable three annulets or, a label of three points gules.

South window, south yle.   These two painted there on the wall, and carved on the out porch:

Sable, three escallops in pale argent, [BISS] impaling, Argent, a fret azure, on a chief sable a trefoil slipped between three mullets argent.

Same male coat as the last, impaling, Or, on a bend gules three saltires argent.

                    Sis Felix Bis.

A brasse in the north wall for Dr. Bisse, qui 28 Oct. 1613, aº etat. 72, mortuus, nunc regnat cum Cristo.

Non meritum, non missa juvat, non fictus et ignis;
Purgans sed Cristi mors mihi sola salus.
Sic docuit vixitque pie, sic mortuus omni
    Ævo Bis Doctor, quique beatus erit.
        PHILIPPUS BISS,
Archidiaconus Taunton, et hujus ecclesie pastor.

Two hands shaking, one from the clouds the other upon earth, over this brasse with this word—

> Farewell beloved till the Resurrection.

Biss hath a fayre stone howse neare the church, and lord of this towne.

That Friday night his Majestie lay at Brewton [Bruton] Abbey, the faire and noble habitacion of Sir Charles Berkley.[a] In the howse are divers quarterings and matches of this familie as impaled with Blount.

About a myle and halfe from Brewton, at Lamiat, co. Somerset, was the King's troope quartered, a small church without either armes or monument.

Captain Davies of the King's army is lord of the manor, and hath a pretty stone howse neare the church, 220ˡⁱ per annum.

In this march abundance of the country came to see the King, which was rare before. This Friday Woodhowse taken.

Satterday, 20 July, 1644. His Majestie marched from thence; the rendesvouz was on the hill, Queene Camel being on the left hand, the manor belonging to Sir Humfrey Mildmay of Danbury in Essex. Thence to Ivelchester that night, where his Majestie lay. The troope was quartered at Chilton, two myles off.

CHILTON church hath no armes in it.

A flat coffin monument, playne, lyes within an arch under the north wall of the north chappel. The Earle of Bristoll is lord of Chilton. These coates are depicted on the walls of the church:

Azure, a fleur-de-lis argent, DIGBY.

---

[a] The church here is well deserving of notice, especially for its beautiful tower. Symonds could not have seen it, or he would, undoubtedly, have mentioned it. See an account of it in Phelps's Somersetshire, the author of which has omitted several coats of arms in glass in the different windows, many of them however mutilated or reversed. The principal coats are Quarterly, BERKELEY, BOTETOURT, SOMERY, and ZOUCHE OF MORTIMER, the same as on the monument, of which the author speaks, in the chancel, but in noticing which he calls the coat of BOTETOURT erroneously MOHUN.

Azure, an ostrich argent, charged on the neck with a label of three points
gules. " Lord DIGBYE's Creast."

Tuesday, 23 July, 1644. His Majestie went to Kingsmore, a
myle from Ivelchester, where all the country people of Somerset
were, by the command of the Sheriffe, Sir Thomas Bridges, appointed
to meet the posse comitatus. Many mett, and there was appointed as
Colonels to command them Sir John Stowell, Sir Edward Rodney,
Sir Edward Berkley, and Colonel Biss: when they came to the point
whether they would goe in person to serve his Majestie, few stood
to it. Sir Edward Rodney had about 200, whome he had listed
before.

Wednesday, 24th, his Majestie marched from hence to Chard, co.
Somerset, a pretty faire towne. This morning was a duel *inter* the
Earl of Peterburgh[a] and Captain Willughby, whose father is
steward to the Earl of Northampton; Willoughby wounded in the
sholder and thigh, the Earl safe without hurt. Willughby challenged.

The King lay at Chard, his troope at Sir Robert Brett's howse, the
manor of WHIT STANTON, a fayre old stone howse. In the church
these, this coate twice in old glasse, north side church window :

Gules, five fusils ermine in bend.

Against the north wall of the chancel is a tombe of playne coarse
stone without any inscription. These escocheons are carved on the
sides, sans inscription, for one Birt:

Semée of cross-crosslets fitchy, a lion rampant, [BRETT] ; impaling, a che-
vron between three roses.
Three fusils conjoined in fess.
Fretty.
Three human heads in profile.

Upon a brasse in the south chappel in the chancel, these two
coates, and this [inscription]:

---

[a] Henry Mordaunt, second Earl of Peterborough, K.G., ob. 1697.

Quarterly, 1, BRETT; 2, three fusils in fess; 3, fretty; 4, an eagle displayed, impaling, a bend engrailed, a crescent for difference [RATCLIFF].

In this yle lyeth buried Margaret Brett, one of the daughters and coheires
of Hugh Ratcliff, Esq. and wife of John Brett, Esq. lord of this manor
of Whitstanton, who dyed 22 Feb. 1582.

In this yle lyeth buried Mary Morgan, eldest daughter of John Brett, Esq.
and Margaret his wife, lord of this manor, ob. 4 Jan. 1582.

Argent, on a bend cotised sable, a fleur-de-lis or between two cinquefoils
gules [MORGAN of Wells]; impaling BRETT.

In a little parlor in the howse these, very old:

Sable, an eagle displayed argent, impaling, Azure, a bend wavy argent,
between two bendlets or.

The same as the last; impaling, Gules, three eagle's heads erased or.

1, gone; impaling, three foxes passant in pale or.

In the kitchen these, as old:

1, gone; impaling, Gules, fretty or.

Three bull's heads caboshed; impaling BRETT, below which is a coat
checky.

Vair, argent and azure, impaling, the upper half of the shield BRETT, the
lower half checky.

Or, three torteaux, a label of three points azure; impaling BRETT above,
and a checky before.

Azure, a lion rampant argent; impaling as the last.

Argent, three fusils conjoined in fess gules.

An almes howse which the Bretts built. The family hath lived
here ever since the memory of the parish.

In the great parlour these, new:

Quarterly, BRETT [as at head of this page].

This in a lodging roome:

Or, a bend sable between six billets; impaling BRETT.

Thursday, 25 July, the King marched to Honyton, a market
towne, co. Devon, a very poore built towne. His troope lay three
myle farther nearer Exeter, at Fyniton [Feniton], where the foot
were all left.

On Friday 26, his Majestie went with his troopes leaving the horse quartered about Exeter. He lay that night in Exeter, at the Earle of Bedford's howse.

In the Meremaid Inn in Exeter, in old glasse, these:

> Quarterly, 1 and 4, Or, a lion rampant azure [REDVERS]; 2 and 3, Or, three torteaux [COURTENAY].
>
> Quarterly, 1 and 4, a cross engrailed between four water-bougets [BOURCHIER]; 2 and 3, a fess between eight — [confused].
>
> Quarterly, 1 and 4, Gules, a cross botonnée or; 2 and 3, Gules, four fusils in fess argent, each charged with an escallop shell sable.
>
> Quarterly, FRANCE and ENGLAND.

Two chests in this howse, wherein are writings belonging to the Earle of Bathe, opened by the Denhams. Here this forty yeare; his lordship doth not know of it.

In the Cathedral church of EXETER.

Vide lib. M. 2, the Visitation of this church.

On the south side in the yle by the quier lyes the statue of a knight crosselegged, and on his shield the armes of Bohun Earle of Northampton ; two others of the same forme. The rest of the monuments are for the most Bishops; two or three stately ones of the Caryes.

> Or, three lions passant sable.

Divers matches of that family. Judge Dodderidge's tombe, as I remember. In the north windowes of the north yle, this coate for Bishop Courtney :

> Or, three torteaux, a label of three points azure, the whole surmounted by a mitre.

The coate of Courtney Earle of Devon is often in these windowes.

In one of the north windowes behind the quire this coate, of one family, is thus variously borne:

> Argent, a fess sable within a bordure gules.
> Argent, a fess sable within a bordure gules, bezanty.
> As last.
> Argent, on a fess sable three trefoils slipped or, a bordure gules.
> A fess sable, a bordure gutty or.

This Satterday, 27 July, his Majestie went to see Prince Maurice his army, seven myles nearer Plymouth. His troope mett him on the way as he came back, and wayted on him to his quarters at Mr. St. Hill's howse, justice of the peace, at Brodenedge [Bradninch], a mayor towne, though almost all the howses be clay, without any timber in the wall, except the doores, roofe, and windowes, which is the fashion of the country. The troope went that night six myles farther to Halverton, more into the heart of the shire, twenty-one myles from Lyme.

This day the King knighted three in Prince Maurice his army. *Vide postea*, Aug. 12.

The King knighted the mayor of Exeter, Sir Hugh Crocker [a] a merchant, when he was there. Sir John Berkley being governor thereof.

One Mr. Ware lives at Halverton, a Colonel in Lyme, now in rebellion. Friday night last Lyme's forces tooke most of the horses of the Lord Percies regiment and two foot colours, by falling on our quarters. This Friday was the trayned bands of Devon summoned, and mett the King, and came into his service (few).

The Earle of Essex and his whole army now within seven or eight myles of Plymouth.

Newes this day that Basing howse had slayne many of the be-siegers, and had raysed the siege which had layne before to it long.

HALVERTON Church, com. Devon.

Argent, a cross gules.

No antient monuments. There be divers flat stones, and the inscriptions are round about in text letters, being the moderne fashion of this county, cutt in this and other parishes.

A small monument of Were, bencher of law, 1625.

Argent, a bend azure between six cross-croslets fitchy; impaling, Sable, a bend argent between two lions rampant.

This parish consists of clothiers that have land in their hands.

[a] Of a good family : see I. C. 1, f. 236, in Coll. Arm.

From thence on Sunday, 28 July, his Majestie and the whole army marched to Crediton, vulgo called Kirton, a great lowsy towne, a corporate towne governed by a bayliffe; the best howse in the towne belongs to a Justice of the Peace, where the King lay. Tuck-feild hath a great faire howse [a] neare this towne on the north side built by the Lord Cheife Baron Periam. In this march this day wee came over a high hill called Crisse-crosse Hill in the parish of Silverton, that survayes all the county round about, [and] lookes upon the maine by Ex. The King's troope lay at Newton St. Syres, [St. Cyrus,] three myles off Exon, betweene that and Crediton. Newes this day told by his Majestie that the Scotts in Ireland destroyed all that tooke not the Covenant.

In the church of NEWTON ST. SYRES, co. Devon.

East wall, this, old:

Gules, a sword argent, hilted or, and two keys argent saltire [SEE OF [WINCHESTER].

These three in the lower south wall of the church:

Quarterly, 1 and 4, Or; 2 and 3, Argent, three fusils conjoined in fess gules; 2 and 3, Gules, a saltire argent, a label of three points azure, upon each three plates.

Azure, a buck's head cabossed argent, pierced with a crosier [ABBEY OF BUCKFASTLEIGH].

Azure, three shoveller's heads erased argent.

These two very old, north wall: under each thus written:

Argent, three lions rampant gules, a bordure engrailed sable.

Orate pro bono statu Nicholai Kirklyn et Johan' uxoris ejus.

Or, three torteaux, a label of three points, each charged with three be-zants; impaling, Barry of six vair and gules [BEAUMONT of co. Devon].

Orate pro animabus Hugonis Courtenay [b] .... Matilde uxoris ejus.

These two east end north yle:

Quarterly, FRANCE and ENGLAND.
ABBEY OF BUCKFASTLEIGH.

---

[a] Now pulled down.

[b] Hugh Courtenay of Boconnoc and his second wife, daughter of ——— Beaumont.

Within the north yle chancel stand two faire and large monuments, both of one peice; the upper a man in compleate coloured armour and scarfe, his left foot standing on death's head, divers matches of the family about him, for Mr. John Northcote, who was a captayne of the trayned bands in this county; the other his son Sir John Northcott, now a prisoner in Exon. pour rebellion.

Sir John N. owes this manor.

Argent, three cross-crosslets bottony in bend sable. [NORTHCOTE].

In Devonshire they call the low grounds moores onely, and in Cornwall the highest hills are moores so called, because moores are there upon the top of the hills.

Essex and his army marched thorough Crediton[a] on Satterday last was seavenight. At that time was Prince Maurice and his army one myle from Exon. at Heavytree. None of the Prince's army went into Exon. and when Essex was gone nearer Plymouth the Prince came on the hither side of Exon.

When Essex's army was here, some of his troopes came to Newton St. Syres church, gott the key, went into the church with their horses, and broke up the chest, and tooke out the communion cup worth 5^{li}. and broke up the poore man's box and tooke out all, being 8^s. 2^d. ob.

The same company, or such like, went to Whitstone, a myle off, and tooke away a pall for buriall of black velvet, worth seven or eight pound, or rather 10^{li}.

Others of them burnt a great reake of oates at Darverton [Thorverton] parish, five myles from Crediton; the reake consisted of 500 dozen, 12 sheaves to the dozen, the accompt of this shire; and in the same parish found 1700 pound in money in the parson's howse under the pavement; tooke 200 from Mr. Tuckfeild.

Munday, 29 July, to Bow [Nymet Traci], where the King lay at an alehowse; his troope at Stretton [Spreyton] three myles distant. This day a soldier was hanged at the rendesvouz for plundering.

[a] It is remarkable that Symonds makes no allusion to the fine church at Crediton.

STRETTON [SPREYTON] Church, co. Devon.

East window chancel, old:

> Vair, on a chief or three mullets gules, pierced of the second.
>
> Sable, three lilies argent, on a chief per pale azure and gules, in the dexter a fleur-de-lis, in the sinister a lion passant, both or.
>
> Sable, a crosier and a mace in saltire argent, on a chief of the last three mullets sable.

This old, south window, church.

> Argent, a chevron between three talbots sable; impaling, Or, on a bend argent three torteaux.

Not one flat stone.

Tuesday, 30 July, to Okehampton, co. Devon, where his Majestie lay; his troope at a village belonging to the towne on the top of the hills. Neare this towne stands the remnants of an old castle, on a hill, but commanded by two far higher hills, a small black brooke running by it.

In the howse where the King lay are many coates of the Courtneyes, old. I saw them not.

Wednesday, 31. To Lifton, in com. predict. three myles short of Lanceston in com. Cornub. The King lay at the parsonage, neare the church.

LIFTON Church, co. Devon, 11 myles from Okehampton.

East window chancel:

> Or, on a bend azure three mascles of the field.

This twice, old:

> Argent, a human heart gules, on a chief azure three mullets argent [DOUGLAS].

This [alluding to the coat of Douglas] is in the north window, chancel, with the garter about it.[a]

This [coat of Douglas] is carved on the seates, chancel; old, with the garter.

East window, south yle chancel:

> Gules, a chevron argent between three salmons naiant.

---

[a] ? James Earl of Douglas, elected 3 Edw. IV.

South window, chancel:

Argent, three torteaux, a label of three points azure, each charged with three torteaux [COURTENAY].

North window, chancel, these:

Or, on a bend azure three mascles of the field.
DOUGLAS, within a garter.
Quarterly, 1 and 4, Argent, a chevron between three heath-cocks sable; 2 and 3, Or, on a bend sable three bear's heads erased argent.

First north window, chancel, these three, very old:

Barry vair.
Gules, a saltire or.
COURTENAY, with a label of three points azure, each charged with three torteaux.

Second window:

Quarterly, 1 and 4, Per chevron azure and gules, three greyhound's heads erased counter-changed; 2 and 3, Gules, a bend engrailed sable.
Gules, a chevron argent between three lion's paws erased ermine; impaling, Per pale azure and or, a chevron wavy between three lions salient counter-changed.

Belfrey, these three:—

This in a south window, very old:

Gules, a chevron argent between three lion's paws erased ermine.

West window north yle, this againe, thus impaled:

Per chevron, azure and gules, three greyhound's heads erased counter-changed; impaling, Per pale azure and or, a chevron wavy between three lions salient counter-changed.
Per pale azure and or, a chevron wavy between three lions salient counter-changed.

Against the north wall of the chancel is a large monument, three statues, two of men, the other of a woman kneeling, over theire heads this:

Piissimæ Memoriæ sacrum ornatissimi Viri Gulielmi Harris de Hayne, Armigeri, 23 die Feb. anno 1590, etat. 66, vita functi.

And this shield:

> Sable, three crescents within a bordure argent [HARRIS], impaling, Sable, a cross within a bordure or [GREVILLE: the wife was a daughter of Sir Fulke Greville.]

Middle, a man in armour:

> M. S. Venerabilis Viri Arthuri Harris de Hayn, Ar. et Montis Sancti Mich'is in com. Cornub' pr'fecti Regij, 16 Maij, 1628, etat' sue 71, vita functi.
>
> HARRIS, impaling, Argent, a chevron sable between three fleurs-de-lis [? DAVILL].
>
> M. S. Florencia Harris Joannis de H. ar. uxoris, de vetusta familia Johannis Windhami, com' Somerset, militis, ob. 1631.
>
> HARRIS, impaling, Sable, a chevron between three lion's heads erased or [WINDHAM].

Under every of them are verses, thus: Anagram for Arthur H.
Arturus Harriseius.
Ephes. i. 14.   *Tu ruris Arrha Jesus.*

Round about a flat stone this, the letters cutt in:

> Four fusils conjoined in fesse, [DYNHAM,] impaling HARRIS.
>
> Here lyeth the body of John Dynham, Esq. who married Margaret the da. of Arthur Harris of Hayne, Esq. buried 2 Dec. A.D. 1641.

This evening his Majestie with his troop, Prince Maurice and his troop, went to see the passes of the river which divides Cornwall and Devon. Two bridges pulled up.

This night the troop quartered at Haynes, the ancient seate of Harris, a myle from Lifton more into Devonshire; round about the howse many rowes of sett tall oakes in brave order. This Harris that now owes it married the Lord Mohun's daughter; sans children, both ◯, but she the cause. His estate is about 1000*l.* per annum.

Some of us quartered in the parish of Stoford, [Stowford,] two myles short of Lifton. In the howse of Haynes are divers matches of the family of Harris, old:

> HARRIS.
>
> The same, impaling, Argent, a chevron gules between three birds sable.
>
> The same, impaling, Argent, a chevron between three [? billets] gules.

This evening his highnes Prince Maurice his army marched after the King's army thorough Lifton.   On Wednesday some of his horse and foot entered into Lansdon [Launceston] in Cornwall; all Essex his army being gone thence, and no resistance.   This day came a messenger to the King from Sir Richard Grenvill to the rendesvouz, and told that Sir Richard was 8,000 strong, and desired his Majestie to make hast towardes him.   The King bid the fellow tell him he was coming with all possible speed with an army of 10,000 foot, 5,000 horse, and 28 piece of cannon.   Prince Maurice his army consisting (out of this number) of 5,000 foot, five-and-twenty hundred horse, 11 piece of cannon.

STOFORD [STOWFORD] Church.

Mr. Harris is lord of it.   Upon a flat stone in the chancel this coate and inscriptions cutt into the stone; the one circumscribed with text letters; that in the midst is printed.

Hic jacet Gulielm' Darrel filius natu minim' Ed. Dar. nup' de Ilmere in com. Buck' gener', qui ob. 18 Oct. anno 1630, etat' 86.

Was parson of this parish.

Three bars, thereon six cinquefoils, 3, 2 and 1, an annulet for a difference [DAYRELL] ; impaling three demi-lions passant guardant [HAMOND].

Hic jacet Phā ux' Gulielmi Darell filia et una de heredibȝ Ric'i Hamond de Prytwell in com. Essex, gen', qui obiit 1° Sept. 1633, etat' 70.

On a wreath a goat's head erased.   [The crest of DAYRELL of Bucks.]

Harris his coates are painted on the walls.

Thursday, 1 Aug., his Majestie marched to Trecarell, in the parish of Lysant [Lezant], and lay there at the howse of Mr. Manaton, in com. Cornubiæ.

The whole army lay this night round about this howse in the feild.

These are antient in the hall windowes of the howse of Mr. Manaton aforementioned:

Sable (imperfect) impaling, Argent, a lion rampant.

Argent, two chevrons sable, a crescent or for difference [ESSE alias TRECARREL] ; impaling, Sable, two fish naiant.

Three fish naiant, impaling, Sable, on a bend a "holy lambe."

Three "like crosiers," 2 and 1, or.

TRECARREL; impaling, Argent, on a bend cotised azure three crosiers or.

Same as impalement of last shield, impaling, three crosiers.

Quarterly, 1 and 4, TRECARREL; 2 and 3, two fishes naiant.

Quarterly, 1 and 4, TRECARREL; 2, two fishes naiant; 3, on a bend cotised azure three crosiers.

Quarterly, 1 and 4, TRECARREL; 2 and 3, Per saltire sable and argent.

Quarterly, 1 and 4, TRECARREL; 2 and 3, Per saltire or and argent, four "pynes" proper.

These following on the right side windowes coming into the hall:

A chevron sable between three estoiles or, and a chief "imperfect," impaling, Per pale argent and sable, a cross compony of the same.

TRECARREL; impaling, Per saltire argent and sable.

Per saltire argent and sable; impaling, a chevron sable between three estoiles or, a chief "imperfect."

Per saltire, four "pynes proper;" impaling, Argent, a fesse gules, a label of three points sable.

TRECARREL; impaling, Argent, a pair of glazier's irons in saltire sable, between four "pynes, rather peares" [STOFORD].

This last is carved over the doore.

This day a fellow that was carrying letters from Essex was taken and hangd below the rendezvous, that all the army might see him as they marched by.

Friday, 2 Aug. 1644. Newes that Essex was at Foye, [Fowey,] and had taken it; his army most at Bodman in Cornwall. His Majestie, &c. marched about 4 in the morning and came that night to Liskard, com. Cornub. A mayor towne, large, the buildings of stone covered with slate, one church. He lay at Mr. Jeanes howse. At the rendezvous 2 captaynes of Essex men were brought prisoners. One was Will of the West, a famous wrestler and carpenter in Chancery Lane; the other a pewterer, of London. At night, 2 other of their captaynes taken of horse and 12 troopers at St.

Clere. Newes that Essex was at Bodman, 10 myles off, and marching towards us.

The King's troop lay in Mynhenet [Menheniot] parish 2 myle from Liskard, at the villages of Beloytha [Belitho] and Curtether [Cartether].

Trecarrel built the howse where his Majestie lay the night before, temp. Hen. 7.

Tre signifyes towne, and carrol, merry or song in Cornish. Most of the gentry of this county live toward the South sea. This part of Cornwall which wee have seene they account barren. The people speake good and playne English here hitherto. Divers of the country people came to the King with much joy to tell him of his enemyes where they lay, " and please his worship."

LISKARD church. South window, south yle, chancel these, old:

Argent, three fusils conjoined in fesse gules.
Argent, a cock gules, on a chief three torteaux. "The cock is carved on the seates."
Chequy or and azure, a bend vert.

The seates of the south yle of the church have escocheons with severall bearings alluding to the passion, of the scourge, whip, &c. dice, lanthorne, garment.

South yle window, below.

Or, a chevron azure between three roses argent.

West window, south yle, this:

Argent, three nails erect in pale sable.

North yle of the church, these:

Quarterly, Or, a chevron gules between in chief two roses and in base a fish naiant azure [ROSCARROCK]; 2, imperfect; 3, Gules, two lions passant guardant argent ; 4, Per saltire argent and sable.
Quarterly, 1 and 4, Argent, a chevron between three [? portcullises] sable ; 2 and 3, Gules, a chevron ermine between three dolphins embowed or.
The four preceding coats, quarterly, impaling, Or, three wolves passant in pale azure.

North window, north yle, chancel:

Quarterly, FRANCE and ENGLAND.
COURTENAY with a label.
Quarterly, FRANCE and ENGLAND, a label of three points argent.

Divers flat stones in the chancel, the inscriptions round about cutt in text; most of them write " gent."; noe armes on the stone.

In the windowes of Mr. Harris his howse, a myle from Liskerd sowthward, called Curtether, a large old howse.

Quarterly, 1 and 4, Argent, a cross-flory engrailed sable, charged with an escallop argent, between four martlets; 2 and 3, Quarterly, 1 and 4, Sable, a lion rampant or ; 2 and 3, Sable, two lions passant argent.

Quarterly, 1 and 4, Sable, semée of cross-crosslets fitchy or, a fesse of the last between three boar's heads couped [BECKET]; 2, Argent, a fesse azure between three estoiles sable [CARTETHER] ; 3, Sable, a chevron between three covered cups argent [TOTWELL].

CARTETHER.

'Tis the manor of Curtether, anciently belonging to the family of Becket till this two yeares; 200*l.* per ann., a great estate in this county.

On the east end of the towne of Liskerd stands the ruines of walls of a castle, belonging say they to a duke. The Prince of Wales now keepes court there at a house adjoining; 'tis his manor.

Satterday, 3 August. Divers prisoners of Essex his army brought into the King; among the rest two women tooke one.

Sunday 4. Some of the country people came and complained to the King that the enemy was a plundering of the country and desired ayde. The King sent a party of horse of Colonel Nevil's regiment, commanded by Sir Bernard Gascoigne, an Italian, who troopes with Colonel Nevil, and the colonel went with him as a volunteir. They mett with a boy who told of a many of gay men at the Lord Mohun's howse. Notwithstanding they had eighty musque-teires to guard them, as they were caressing they forced the doores upon them, killed the man that locked the doore, broke up the howse, took Colonel Aldridge who was governor of Aylesbury, the Leiftenant-Colonel, Captain, and one Ensign of Essex his life guard, another Leiftenant-Colonel, without the losse of any one of his Majesties party. This howse was within two miles of Essex his head quarters. Dalbeir, a Dutchman, Quartermaster--General of Essex his army and engineer, was in this howse with those rebels, but putt off his sword and hatt and pretended to be servant to the house of my Lord Mohun, and so escaped.

Munday his Majestie went unto the heath, Caryton Downe, towards Launceston, and met those soldjers which were raysed by his warrants of those that escaped Essex his search. Their commanders were most of them gone to Sir Richard Grenvile. There were in all about 100. xx prisoners more taken this day from Essex.

Wednesday his Majestie with his army went to Brodock Downe or Heath, the place where the Lord Ruthin Gray [Grey de Ruthyn] was beate in Cornwall: this was within three myles of Essex his head quarters, being at Listithell: some scouts of both sides mett, four of our foot killed in fetching in provision, one more killed that was sent to fetch in the rambling soldjers.

His Majestie and his troope, with the Prince, faced on the top of the hill from 12 to 5; the foot army lay short of the hill all night. The King returned to Liskerd, where wee watcht on horseback: the horse in this night marched towards the foot, which were before, being about four myles from Liskerd.

Thursday, 8th August. The whole army of the King's lay upon Brodock Downe, about 16,000 horse and foot. Some scouts of the enemyes seene about 11 of the clock. The forlorne of 1,000 foot, commanded by Colonel Apleyard, went off the heath through a lane between inclosures to another heath called by the same name, nearer the enemy. Some bodyes of our horse followed about 12 of the clock.

This morning the Lord Willmott, Leift.-General of the horse, was comitted.

Goring was made generall of the King's horse this morning.   Lord

Wentworth was Serjeant-Major of the Horse before and now too. The King's army, besides Prince Maurice, of horse, consisted of five brigades—Lord Willmott's, Lord Northampton's, being taken out of the Lord Willmott's, Lord Cleveland's, Lord Wentworth's, Colonel Bennet's. Divers great parties of our horse beate the enemyes horse quite off the hills within view of Listithiel, the head quarter of Essex. Wee took some prisoners, five or six killed on both sides in piquering. Some of their foot was seene this day neare this towne of Listithiel in the closes; parties onely of their horse mett some of ours.

Toward night the body of the King's foot were moving toward the enemy nearer, but, growing night, returned halfe a myle back to the bottome of another hill.

Friday 9th. About 8 of the clock the body of our foot moved toward Listithiel.

Newes from Oxford this morning, that the Lord Rich was renegaded to the rebells at London, though not considerable. Ben Holf. dead at Exon. That Waller was at Abingdon on Tuesday last was sevenight.

About 10, some of their foot came out of the towne and hill. They shott two peice of cannon at halfe an howre after 10 at ours.

Prince Maurice his army had the van this day, and marched towards my Lord Mohun's howse in the parish of Boconock, and .... between this howse and the Lord Roberts [Robartes] his howse called Lanhedriack [Lanhydrock], both howses being but four myles distant.

Boconnock Church.

West window, churche, old:

> Azure, three fishes in pale naiant argent; impaling, Gules, on a bend or three buck's heads cabossed argent.
> Azure, six demi-fishes in pale, three and three, naiant from the centre of the shield argent. " Six fishes hariant, their heads looking *ut hic* both ways."

East window south yle, these, old:

> Quarterly: 1, France and England, quarterly, within a bordure; 2 and 3, Courtenay; 4, Redvers; the whole within a garter.

Quarterly, 1, Or, a cross engrailed sable [MOHUN]; 2, Vert, three ram's heads or, " horns downwards;" 3, quarterly, COURTENAY and REDVERS; 4, Azure, three bendlets or [BREWER]; 5, Azure, three bull's heads or; 6, Azure, a bend or, a label of three points gules [CARMINOW].

Argent, a chevron between three eagles displayed sable ; impaling, Gules, on a bend or three buck's heads cabossed argent.

East window this, old:

Quarterly, 1, gone [MOHUN no doubt]; 2, Vert, three ram's heads or; 3, BREWER; 4, Gules, a dexter arm habited in a maunch ermine, holding in the hand a fleur-de-lis [a coat of MOHUN]; impaling, quarterly, 1 and 4, quarterly COURTENAY and REDVERS; 2 and 3, CARMINOW.

Against the north wall of the chancel is a faire monument, the picture of a man and two women, six sons, three daughters.

Here lyeth the body of Sir William Mohun, who dyed 6 April, 1588.

This quartering in the midst.

Quarterly, 1, MOHUN; 2, BREWER; 3, Ermine, a bull passant gules [CAVELL]; 4, COURTENAY and REDVERS quarterly, quartering CARMINOW; paling, quarterly, 1, three bendlets [FITZWILLIAMS]; 2, three ram's heads; 3, three bull's heads; 4, a chevron between three birds.

Gules, two lions passant or, " John Lord Strange ;" impaling, MOHUN.

Quarterly FRANCE and ENGLAND, a label of three points argent, each charged with three [? torteaux]; impaling MOHUN; " Edward Duke of York and Philippa Mohun."[a]

Divers matches of this family, and over the head of the sons, the coates of Mohun and his wife impaled. Over the daughters their names and the coates of their husbands.

Another monument at the east end, with pictures of three children and the coate of Mohun.

MOHUN; impaling, Ermine, three lions rampant gules [CHUDLEIGH. She was third wife of Sir Reynold Mohun].

Here lyeth interred three children of Sir Reynold Mohun, Knt. and Baronet, whome he had by his wife, the Lady Dorothy Mohun.

This Reynold was grandfather to the now Lord Mohun.

[a] She was third daughter and coheir of John Lord Mohun, one of the founders of the Order of the Garter, and sister of the wife of John Lord Strange.

Another, the picture of a woman married to William Drew, of the Mohuns.

Another of an infant of this family.

Another, the picture of a woman.

The monument of Margaret the daughter of Martin Trewmard Esq. widdow of John Lanton, Esq. who dyed the 13 March, 1616.

These two are cutt in stone over the chimney in the parlor.

MOHUN; impaling, a bend fusilly ermine [? HELE].
MOHUN; impaling, a tower, issuing therefrom a demi-lion rampant.

Amongst the rest these verses :

> And yonder innocent transcends death farr,
> For of a Moun shee's cutt into a starr.

A chevron between three birds ; impaling MOHUN.

Among the rest these verses are upon the monument of Penelope daughter of Sir Raynold Mohun, wife to William Drew of Broad Henbury, com. Devon, Esq.

Ermine, a lion passant gules [DREWE] ; impaling MOHUN.

> My name was Mohun, my fates like various were;
> My short life's often changes makes it cleare.
> A virgin star on earth a wife I shind
> With noted splendor cheifly of the mind,
> Till my Will. Drew me to his nuptiall bed,
> Then soone by God's high call to heaven I fled,
> Not without hope in Christ to live agen,
> Set in the walls of his Jerusalem.

Twenty-five quarterings of the Mohuns in the great parlour of the Lord Mohun's howse, where the King quartered this night, supported with two lyons [rampant] gardant crowned.

Motto—Generis revocamus honores.

The army of foot quartered on the hills northward neare this towne.

The head quarters of our horse was this night at St. Neot's.

This Friday in the open feilds a commanded party of our horse mett with some of the enemy, but loosely retreated without charging. No buisnes of noate done; some soldiers came in, some taken.

This evening his highnes Prince M. and the Generall the Earle of Forth sent a lettre (subscribed likewise by the chiefe officers) to Essex for a treaty by a trumpeter.

Sermon on Sunday before the King at this church, speaking against popery; that one of the greatest arguments against them is the denyall of reading the Scriptures: for how can that be an honest guardian that will not suffer the heire looke into his father's will ?

Satterday morning about ten of the clock came the King's trumpet back from Essex, and brought a letter directed for his highnes Prince Maurice and the Earle of Forth:

My Lords,

In the beginning of your lettre you express by what authority you send it. I having no authority to treat without the Parliament who have entrusted me, cannot doe it without breach of trust.

Your humble servant,

ESSEX.

From Listithiel, Aug. 10, 1644.

Newes about night that Sir Richard Grenvile was with his army at Bodman and had forced his entrance into the towne. This afternoone the King and his cavaliers went on to the hills upon Brodock Downe, where he saw many of the insolent rebells braving upon the adjoyning hill betwixt him and Listithiel: many horse mett on both sides, in piquering; none killed, few wounded, many of the rebells were.

Sunday, 11 Aug. This morning came newes that the Lord Hopton, who had about 2000 men with him, mett with Sir Richard Grenvile and his whole army. About 3 in the afternoone Sir Richard came to court; left his army at or about Bodman, raysing up workes as if they would fortifie the towne, but in the night left it, and all lay on the Downe. When Sir Richard came to Bodman he found about 100 troopers plundering there; seven of them were killed and taken prisoners. One Ramsey a Scott with Sir Richard killed three, but afterwards taken prisoner. This night the rebels left Resprin Bridge, neare the Lord Roberts his howse. So by that meanes there was free passage from Sir Richard Grenvile's army to ours.

Munday his Majestie went on to the hill where he was on Satterday before, where he saw many of the rebels scouts vaunting on the foresaid hill, but our horse beate them off awhile, but after an howre they possesst it agayne. When our horse had the hill, some of our men by the King's command scattered some papers, that if any would come in that were in rebellion, they should be pardoned and received into grace, signed by Mr. Walker ᵃ as the King's express pleasure. Some of our horse shott and some of theirs, few killed. This afternoone by reason of the want of provision his Majesties troops went to quarter at Liskerd.

At Crediton, (*vide retro,*) Sunday, 28 July, when his Majestie came from Oxford, he knighted Sir Thomas Basset, Generall of the ordinance to Prince Maurice, and Sir Joseph Wagstaffe, Serjeant Major Generall to the Prince, Sir Henry Carye who had a gallant regiment in the Prince his army. These were knighted when the King went from Exon. to see the Prince's army, it being the first time he saw it, being Satterday, 27 of July.

Tuesday, 13. Sir Jacob Astley tooke two butts of sack, much tobacco, and horseshoes, &c. coming from Foye to the enemy.

M. [? mem.] whether the Lord Hopton fell on the enemy and killed many.

Wednesday, Aug. 14. Sir Richard Grenvile made approaches nearer the enemy on the west side of the river, 2000 of the Prince's foot joyning with him. This day Lord Percy quitted his place of Generall of the Ordinance, and his Majestie gave it to the Lord Hopton.

This night the King's army stood to their armes all night. Commanded by Prince Maurice, that one of his soldiers should be hanged, and a ticket written on him, for plundering the Lord Roberts his howse. It seemes a protection was given to the howse and a strict order. In the howse was found many bowes and divers

ᵃ Afterwards Sir Edward Walker, Garter King of Arms.

quivers of arrows, and 6, 7, or 8 of the Lord Mohun's horse there too. This was wett weather.

Thursday. A blustring cold day, and the evening very wett: above 40 prisoners brought to Liskerd from the army, but they escaped out of prison.

Friday, 16 Aug. The King's army of foot removed the leaguer wider, and at more distance. (A wett day.) This night the enemy gave an alarm to the King's army and to head quarter at Boconnock. The King this day went on the other side of the river to the Lord Roberts his howse. Two of Essex's men came in to us this day, and told that provisions were very scarce with Essex.

Satterday, 17. His Majestie attended with his owne troope, Queenes troope, commanded by Captain Brett, and sixty commanded troopers, went to Cliffe, a parish on this side of the river that runs to Listithiel, where Colonel Lloyd the Quartermaster Generall's regiment lyes to keepe the passe. The enemye keepes the passe on the other side at the parish of Glant. From thence his Majestie went to Lantegles to the manor howse belonging to the Lord Mohun just over against Foye, where his royall person ventred to goe into a walke there, which is within halfe musket shott from Foye, where a poore fisherman was killed in looking over, at the same time that his Majestie was in the walke, and in the place where the King a little afore passed by. A little below are some of our great peices that command the towne of Foye, and beyond that a fort of ours that commands the entrance into the mouth of Foye haven in the parish of Perwyn: this howse, walke, &c. being gotten by the vigilant care of Sir Jacob Astley, Major-Generall of his Majestie's army, three or four days before, which now is mainteyned by 200 commanded foot of ours under Sir Jacob's command. At night his Majestie, &c., returned to their quarters. 'Tis twelve myles from Listithiel to Foye.

A gentleman of this county told me the original of the Lord Roberts his family. His great-grandfather was servant to a gentleman of this county, his hynd. Afterwards lived in Truro, and traded in wood and fferzen: got an estate of 5 or 6000*l.*; his son was so bred, and lived there too, putt out his money, and his debtors paid it him in tynn. He, engrossing the sale of tyn, grew to be worth many thousands (300,000*l.*). His sonn was squeezed by the court in King James his time of 20,000*l.*: so was made a Baron, and built the house at Lanhedriak, now the seate of this Lord Roberts.

Sunday, 18 August. Some of the rebel horse came within the Lord Mohun's parke, but theire boldnes was presently forced to fly.

Munday.

Tuesday. Proclamacion that all stragling foot presently repair to their colonels, upon payne of death.

Wednesday, 21 August. The King's troope and Queenes troope marched in the night from Liskerd to the leaguer at Boconnock. About five in the morning, being very misty, the King's army and Prince Maurice's was drawne out, and about seven they marched on to the top of the high hill that lookes into Listithiel. The body of foot and cannon lay all this day on this and the adjoyning hill, being on each side flanked with horse, and a reserve of horse consisting of the earl of Cleveland's brigade behind the foot.

A commanded party of 1000 foot, led by Coll. (*blank*) of Prince Maurice army, gott a hill this side the river neare the towne, where at bottome was a passe. The small cottages which were on this hill next the towne were all this forenoone a burning. Our foot and theirs pelting one at another all day: small harme done to ours. The enemy shott a many great peices of cannon at them and at the left wing of our horse; little or no hurt. Thus stood both armyes all this day on this side. But Sir R. Grenvile with 700 men on the other side pelted the rogues from their hedges betweene the Lord Roberts his howse and Listithiel and neare Trinity (Restormyn) castle, in the parish of Lanhedriack or Listithiel, which castle was this morning surprised by Sir Richard Grenvile's men and some thirty of the rebells taken and divers barrels of beefe. This day Major Smyth, that commanded a party of horse neare this castle, who did most gallantly, was shott with a musket bullet, yet living.

At night Sir Richard Grenvile's men retired. Towards night the body of the King's foot gott into the closes on the hills of the left and right side of the playne that goes down to Listithiel, and in the night planted many peices of our cannon. That hill on the left hand neere the chappel of St. Neeton's [St. Nighton] in the parish of St. Twynoe [St. Winnow], was commanded by a commanded party of about 1000, led by Colonel Apleyard. The hill opposite was kept by Prince Maurice his army.

Thursday, August 22. This day wee mainteyned in all parts what wee had gott in the night, many of the enemies great shott of 9lb. being shott at our men. One of our cannon shott luckily at a party of the enemyes horse, and killed two horse and one horse leg shott off at once. Most part of this day the King's and Queenes troopes faced the enemy of the top of the playne, doing duty. This night upon the top of the highest hill, and in the middle between our hedges and the enemyes hedges, our men made a worke twenty yards square, notwithstanding many of the enemyes shott. Rostormyn [Restormel] castle was the ancient seate of the Duke of Cornwall.

Friday, 23. The worke on the top of the hill aforesaid next the said chappel seemed in the mysty morning to the enemye to be a body of horse, as some of their centryes were heard to say. They shott a piece of 9lb. many times at this worke, killed one and hurt another; that was all the hurt was done to us this day at the worke. On Sir Richard Grenvile's side Colonel Champernown of Devon, colonel to the Prince Maurice, leading up his foot neare Trinity castle, was shott in the neck; his owne men tooke off his sword and cloake and left his body, which the enemy tooke. Since by a drummer we heare that his wounds is not mortall.

This halfe of the day fine, four in the morning till twelve. The King's troope and Queene's with Prince Maurice's faced on the plaine the day before. All the afternoone, a commanded party of both troops wayted on the King there till night. Then we returned to our quarters in the field, as the two nights before; mornings and evenings being very mysty; through the night starlight.

Satterday, 24 August, being the day of Saint Bartholomewe, the forenoone was spent in great shott from them to our battery. No harme: wee gott many of their bullets. About xii. of the clock his Majestie went downe to court to dinner; his troop and the Queene's drew off then too, having been there ever since the day began. In the afternoone about three of the clock the King went upon the hill, and divers came and told him the enemy was gone towards Foye, for indeed none or very fewe of them could be seene; about two of their cannon played some time, and some muskets; almost all that were there besides the King and Prince Maurice were of opinion they were gone.

Sunday, 25 August. His Majestie went into the feild upon the hill at three in the morning, attended as before, the morning being very wett and wyndy: presently sends word to the Prince his army to know if they were marching, and to tell them he was here and ready, and that he conceived it a fitt morning to doe the buisines; likewise he sent the like to Sir Jacob Astley to tell his owne army so. Preparacions on all parts of the King's side: his horse are come into the feild, half of them gone over to Sir Richard Grenvile's side. An [?hourly] expectacion of our rediness to fall on: Prince Maurice about twelve of the clock comes armed and tells the King he was ready, and asked the King if he were so: ymediately their resolution altered, and our troops were sent to Liskerd. Long before this 'twas evident enough that the enemy was not gone, onely was hid from the danger of our battery, but was *toute preparé* to receave us. 'Twas appointed for the Westerne army to fall on first.

Munday. This day 2,000 horse and 1,000 foot of the King's went to westward behind the enemy to stopp their landing of provisions by sea, and to hinder their foraging westward by land. Also this day came to us 100 barrels of powder, &c. from Pendennis Castle, and much from Dartmouth.

BRODOCK [BROADOAK or BRADOCK] Church, com. Cornub.

In the south-west of the church are many coates in allusion to the Passion—Argent, three nails sable; ladder in bend; and divers more cutt upon the seates in escocheons.   This of Courtney is cutt on the seates:

> Three torteaux.

Courtney did owe this land and Boconnock also.   Sir William Mohun, father to Sir Reynold Mohun, bought Boconnock of the Queene Elizabeth: it fell by attaynder to her from Courtney, who was beheaded in the beginning of her rayne.

Mr. Williams, of Ivy Bridge, in com. Devon. is patron of Brodock.

Munday morning the King's and Queen's troopes removed from hence to Lanreth, 3 myles nearer the south sea.

[LANRETH Church, com. Cornub.]

In the south windowes of the chancel these coates, pretty old:
East window south yle these three:

> Ermine, impaling, Sable, a bend or between six "fountayns" [STOURTON].
> As last, impaling, Sable, three swords, points towards the base, argent, hilted or [PAULET].
> As last, impaling, Or, a chevron between three escallops.

South window that yle these two, older:

> Per pale or and argent, two lions rampant regardant counterchanged.
> Argent, a chevron wavy gules.

The partition between the church and chancel, which was the foundacion of the roodloft, is carved and guilt.

Against the south wall of the chancel is a pretty neate monument, fairely colourd and guilt, the effigies of a man and woman, 3 sons and 4 daughters: these coates and inscription:

> Or, a bend and two bendlets enhanced gules, GRYLES or GRYLLS; "This is often."   Crest, On a wreath a porcupine passant argent, armed or.
> GRYLES, impaling, Argent, a chevron sable between three gournets haurient gules, " The coate of TUBB of this county."
> GRYLES, a crescent for difference, impaling, Gules, a chevron vair between three crowns or [MAYOW.]

GRYLES, impaling, Azure, a bend engrailed argent, cotised or, a crescent for difference [FORTESCUE].

GRYLES, a martlet for difference.

Argent, a chevron sable between three [? eagle's] heads erased, a crescent for a difference, impaling GRYLES.

Azure, fretty argent, a fesse gules; impaling GRYLES.

Gules, on a bend wavy argent 3 "choughs;" impaling GRYLES.

Quarterly, 1 and 4, GRYLES; 2 and 3, Argent, a bear salient sable, muzzled gules [BERE].

Here lyeth yᵉ body of Charles Gryles, Esq. counsellor-at-law, who was buried the 2nd day of March, 1611. Also the body of Agnes Gryles his wife, who was buried 13 day of June, 1607, by whom he had 4 sons and 4 daughters, all which daughters are departed this life, and one sonne. In memory of whome this monument is erected, by John Gryles, Esq. their son and heire. 1623.

(Two flat stones in Tavistock, with the coates of Gryles.)

These escocheons are often carved on the seates of the south yle belonging to this family, and coloured:

Quarterly, GRYLES and BERE.

GRYLES, impaling MAYOWE.

Upon the old seates in the church these are carved:

COURTENAY, with a label of three points, impaling in chief [? two fleurs-de-lis].

COURTENAY; impaling three roundles, in chief a lion passant.

These alluding to the Passion:

Five shields charged with the emblems of Christ's Passion.

In this county they call the church clerk the bed-man or grave-maker.

By tre, pol, and pen,
You may know the Cornish men.ᵃ

The seates and habitations of the gentlemen in Cornwall at this present as followes.

ᵃ Camden's version is :—

By Tre, Ros, Pol, Lan, Caer, and Pen,
You may know the most Cornish men.—Remaines, p. 142.

TOWARDS THE NORTHERNE SEA.

At Stowe, Sir John son to Sir Bevil Grenvyle lives, being the antient seate of that family.

Lanherne, belonging to the family of Arundel, who has a vast estate in this county.   Sir John Arundel, being a ward, knighted at Boconnock, and that freed his wardship.

Ruscarick, belonging to the family of Ruscarick, very antiently. 500*l.* per annum: had more.

Carminow, Esq. an antient family, and had much possessions, now poore; lives in St. Eth [? St. Erth].   200*l.* per annum.

WEST PART OF CORNWALL THESE.

Tredurfe [Trethurfe], in the parish of Lasick, [Ladock, vulgo Lassick,] the seate of Sir Peter Courtney.   700*l.* per annum.

Godolphyn, tyn myne.   Colonel of a foot company in Prince Maurice his army.

Sir Richard Vivian [Vyvyan], of Trelawarren, neare Helston.

Sir Charles Trevanion, knighted now at Boconnock, of Carhese. 1500*l.* per annum.

John Trefuse [Trefusis], Esq. lives at Maylor [Mylor].

John Arundel, of Trerice, now Governor of Pendennis Castle.

Sir Francis Basset, of Tehiddy, in the parish of [Illogan], now Sheriffe of Cornwall, this yeare, 1644, brother to Sir Thomas Basset, Generall of the Ordinance to Prince Maurice.   This Sir Francis was knighted at Boconnock.

EAST PART OF CORNWALL.

Sir William Wraye, of Trebeth [Trebigh], in the parish of St. Ives; his son, a colonel of the foot, with 700*l.* per annum, was knighted at Bristol 1643, under age.

Peirs Edgcombe, of Mount Edgcombe, in the parish of Maker, neare Milbroke.   30,000*l.* [? 3000*l.*] per annum.

John Conock, of Trewergey, neare Liskerd.

William Glyn, Esq. of Glyn, in the parish of Cardinham.   600*l.* per annum.

William Coryton, of Newton, Esq.

John Harrys, of Stoake, Esq. and of Curtether, in the parish of Mynhennett.

SOUTH PARTS OF CORNWALL.

Warwick, Lord Mohun, of Boconnock. 2,000*l.* per annum.

Sir John Trelawney, of Trelawney, in the parish of Pelynt. 1,000*l.* per annum.

Walter Langdon, Esq. of Keveryn [Keverell], in the parish of St. Martin's. 600*l.* per annum.

John Gryles, Esq. of Court, in the parish of Lanreathe. 700*l.* per annum.

Mr. Trefry at Foye.

Saturday, Aug. 31. The night before the King had notice (being at Boconnock,) (his troopes at Lanreath,) that the enemy was marching away. General notice was given thereof at one of the clock in the night. His troop and the Queen's troop came to Bocconnoc, whither came newes that the enemyes horse were then upon the downe and coming up betweene the hills where our whole army's leaguer was, but most of our foote were stragling, 3 parts of 4. The Earle of Cleveland, with those of his brigade, viz. most of his colours, but not above one hundred of 400 men, faced the enemy on the hill, but did not, nay dare not, charge them, as Leiut.-Colonel Leake tolde us. When the King came up wee saw most of their body of horse on the hill, neare Brodock, upon that downe: ymmediately the Earle of Cleveland's brigade and the Queen's regiment followed them and charged their reare. The King, supposing they would goe thorough Liskerd and Launceston, sent 2 messengers of our troope, Mr. Brooke and Mr. Samuel West, with a letter to Sir Fr. Dorington, (who hath 1,000 horse in Devon.) to stop theire march. But the enemy went not neare Liskerd this day, but went right to Saltash, to ferry their horse over into Devonshire.

In this interim his Majestie lost no time, but with those foot he had (which God knowes were very few, most of them being stragled abroad the country for provision,) and with his owne troope and the Queenes, marched towards Listithiel. On the hill next beyond the towne were bodyes of the enemyes foot with colours left in their reare to make good their retreate: their baggage, artillery, and the rest of Essex his foot army having marched all the night towards Foye. At 7 in the morning, the King's forlorne hope of foot, consisting of about 1,000, entred Listithiel, without much opposition, their foot still retreating. And after that his Majestie had commanded 2 or 3 pieces of cannon to be placed in the enemyes leaguer to command the hill where their foot reserve stood, the enemyes reserve marched away, our forlorne following them in chase from feild to feild in a great pace. About 8 of the clock his Majesty with the two troopes passt over the river on the south side of Listithiel, where the enemy had left a cartload of muskets, besides many more in the durt a little higher, 5 pieces of cannon in several places, 2 of them being very long ones. With this small force his Majesty chased them 2 myles, beating them from hedge to hedge. Being come neare that narrow neck of ground betweene Trewardreth [Tywardreath] Bay and St. Veepe passe, the rebells made a more forcible resistance; then about 11 of the clock Captain Brett led up the Queenes troope, and most gallantly in view of the King charged their foot and beate them from their hedge, killing many of them, notwithstanding their musquets made abundance of shott at his men: he received a shott in the left arme in the first field, and one of his men, La Plunne, a Frenchman killed, yet most gallantly went on and brought his men off; his cornett's horse shott, with 2 other horses, and 2 more wounded: he retreated to be dresst, and the King called him and tooke his sword which was drawne in his hand, and knighted Sir Edward Brett on his horse's back. This was just at 12 of the clock. About this time wee tooke 7 or 8 prisoners, whereof one was a captayne of foot, who was taken by Captain Brett's men, and another tooke one of their canoneirs, who was pitifully drunke, having shott off his cannon but once. Now the King's foot came in apace and increased much. Shooting continued much on both sides, more on theirs, wee still gayning ground.

About 4 of the clock some of the rebells' horse (they having 2 or
3 troopes with them,) charged our foot, but the Lord Bernard
ymediately gott leave of the King to draw up his troope, who were all
ready, and drew up to the rogues, standing their musket shott a long
time; but, because their horse retreated and their foot lay so close
under the hedges, which are all cannon proofe and have no avenues
wider then one or in some places 2 horse can approach at a time, and
likewise because his Majesty sent to draw us off, wee fairely retreated:
one of the Queenes troope here was killed. More of our foot coming
up to releive the rest. By this time Colonel Goring, Generall of his
Majesties horse, came to the King, having not heard of the enemyes
march till 10 of the clock. Now was our foot in great bodyes gott
upon the high hill just in the narrowest passage of land betweene
Trewardreth parish church and the passage over the river which runs
by Listithiel. Just at 6 of the clock the enemy made a very bold
charge both of cannon, muskets, and horse, to gaine this hill, as
likewise the passe neare St. Veepe, but were valliantly beate off, and
our men not onely keeping both but gott some ground also: this
heate lasted about an howre; at first it was so hott that the Lord
Bernard drew out his Majesties troope with the colours (for the time
before wee left them with the King) to charge the rebells, but
Generall Goring mett us and told him the roome was too little for
horse and our troopers to charge too, and advised he would please
to face a little and draw off to the King. Here was of the Queenes
troope one shott in the sholder. With our troope was drawn up
the Queenes, Prince Maurice his life guard, commanded by Arundel,
and the Lord Hopton's, which was comanded by Sir Thomas Wilford,
of Kent: these made a brave body of about 200, all well armed.

The King sending for us to come to him, and the enemyes vollyes
abating and ceasing, wee were drawne in the next close but one
where his Majesty was. And this was the cheife of the buisines of
this day. Now did many of the enemyes cannon give fyre at our men,
till darke night. I saw a fellow of ours dresst, a musketeir who was
shott in the chin, the sholder, and the hand by cannon at one shoot.

This night the King lay under the hedge with his servants in one feild. The troopes of life guards lay in the next, it being very wyndy, and crosse wind for Essex shipping of his men, and rayned much and great stormes. I saw 8 or 9 of the enemyes men dead under the hedges this day.

Some shooting continued all night.

Sunday, primo Septembris. This morning our army was in the same place it lay in the night, and small or no shooting on either side.

The 4 life guards about 7 of the clock were sent to quarters; wee to Lanreth; for all the pasture in those feilds was eate up very bare by the enemyes horse, whome wee had in this time of stay almost starved.

This morning, about seven of the clock, Generall Goring was sent with the horse to pursue the enemyes horse, who as the King was informed were gotten into Saltash. Sir Edward Walgrave, de com. Norfolk, colonel of horse, tooke above one hundred of the rebells horse in the pursuite on Satterday, and told the King that if the country had brought in intelligence but an howre or two sooner, where and which way they went, he believed they might have cutt off and taken all their horse, they were such cowards and so ferefull that eight (sayd he) would make twenty cry for quarter. Essex his life guards, commanded by (*blank*) Doyley,* went away with the horse as wee heard. He himself was with the foot.

This Sunday, the rebells being within but a little compasse of ground, (being surrounded by sea on three parts, and our army on the land,) and because their rebell Generall the Earle of Essex, Robert Devereux, and their Field Marshall the Lord Roberts, with many others of their cheife commanders, had left them, and went by sea as they supposed, or they knew not which way, Skippon, now left in cheife, being Major Generall, sent propositions of treaty to his sacred Majesty, who out of his abundant mercie, notwithstanding having them all in so great advantage, was pleased to give them leave to march away with these condicions:

* ? Colonel Edward Doyley, afterwards Governor of Jamaica.

Leaving all their cannon, which were in all 42, and 1 morter. All their musquetts and pikes, which were (*blank*). All their cariages except one to a regiment. To march away with their colours, and foot officers with their swords. Those officers of horse with swords, hatbands, and pistolls.

A waggon full of musquet arrowes, 100 barrels of powder.

Munday, 2° Septembris, 1644.

His Majesties army of foot stood on the same ground or there-abouts as before, the several regiments by themselves, and the colours stuck in the ground flying. His Majestie in the feild accompanied with all his gallant cavaliers dispersed in severall places.

While about 10 of the clock, Major Skippon, first or in the front, marched with all that rowt of rebells, after the colours of their several regiments. These regiments I tooke a note of after three or four had passt.

Colonel Lord Roberts.

Colonel Bartlet.

Colonel Aldridge, blew colours with lions rampant or.

Colonel Davies, white colours, Citty London.

Colonel Conyngham, greene colours.

Colonel Whichcote, greene, Citty London.

Colonel Weare, A. [? argent] Governor of Lyme.

Colonel Carr, potius Karr, xj ensignes or, distinctions b. [*sc.* blue.] These are Plymouth men. They had more foot.

Colonel Layton, a regiment of horse, b. cornets. All their ensignes and cornets were wound up. veloped.

It rayned extremely as the varlets marched away, a great part of the time.

The King himselfe ridd about the feild and gave strict command to his cheife officers to see that none of the enemye were plundered, and that all his soldjers should repair to their colours which were in the adjoyning closes. Yet, notwithstanding our officers with their swords drawne did perpetually beate off our foot, many of them lost their hatts, &c.

Yet most of them escaped this danger till they came to Listithiel, and there the people inhabitants and the country people plundered some of their officers and all, notwithstanding a sufficient party of horse was appointed by his Majesty to be their convoy.

They all, except here and there an officer, (and seriously I saw not above three or four that looked like a gentleman,) were strucken with such a dismal feare, that as soone as their colour of the regiment was passt, (for every ensigne had a horse and rid on him and was so suffered,) the rout of soldjers of that regiment presst all of a heape like sheep, though not so innocent. So durty and so dejected as was rare to see. None of them, except some few of their officers, that did looke any of us in the face. Our foot would flowt at them and bid them remember Reading, Greenland Howse (where others that did not condicion with them tooke them away all prisoners), and many other places, and then would pull their swords, &c. away, for all our officers still slasht at them.

The rebells told us as they passt that our officers and gentlemen carried themselves honorably, but they were hard dealt withall by the common soldjers.

This was a happy day for his Majesty and his whole army, that without losse of much bloud this great army of rascalls that soe triumphed and vaunted over the poore inhabitants of Cornwall, as if they had bin invincible, and as if the King had not bin able to follow them, that 'tis conceived very few will gett safe to London, for the country people whome they have in all the march so much plundered and robd, that they will have their pennyworths out of them.

One of their actions while they were at Listithiel must not be forgotten. In contempt of Christianity, Religion, and the Church, they brought a horse to the fount in the church, and there with their kind of ceremonies did as they called it Christian the horse and called him by the name of Charles, in contempt of his sacred Majesty.

Another was done by their Provost Martiall, who put his prisoners in the said church. The night they marched away, two of the prisoners, being rich men of Cornwall, gott up in the steeple and pulled up the ladder and called to the marshall, jeering at him. " Ile fetch you downe," saide he, and sett mulch and hay on fire under them, besides they shott many muskets into the belfry at them; all would not doe. Then he fetcht a barrel of powder and gave fire to it, thretning to blow them up, and that blew into the church and blew off most of the slate and yet did no hurt to the prisoners.

They had a strong hold and a hill, where was an old dowble trenched fort, wherein they had planted many of their great peices. It would have bin difficult to beate them out of it; and then Foye was fortified, and when his Majesties forces were in Foye, before Essex his men tooke it, it was governed by Mr. Trefry, who lives in it and hath a very faire all [old?] seate there.

Tuesday, 3° Sept. The King and all his army rested; wee at Lanreath.

Wednesday, 4°. The King marched from Boconnock to Liskerd; his Majestie lay at Mr. Jeanes. The troopes of life guards marched 6 myles farther to Southill. Lord Bernard quartered at Mr. Manaton's, of Manaton, in this parish. This coate, old, in the hall window:

Ermine, a saltire vair between four cross-crosslets fitchy or.

Cronogramma made at this time.

VIVat reX. CoMes effeXIVs DIssIpatVr.
Anno Domini 1644.

These coates and writing are painted, old, in the parlor of Trefray House. Visited Munday, 1° September, 1644.

Quarterly,[a] 1 and 4, A chevron between three hawthorn-trees argent [TREFRY]; 2 and 3, Argent, a fret raguly sable.

Thomas Trefry married Elizabeth daughter of Robert Boniface.

Quarterly, 1 and 4, TREFRY, 2; Sable, three wings argent [MICHEL-STOWE]; 3, blank.

Thomas Trefry married Amicia daughter of John Mighelstowe [Michel-stowe], of Rescasu [? Rosecossa, in the parish of Tonkin].

[a] This and the two following coats ought clearly to be impaled and not quarterly.

Quarterly, 1 and 4, TREFRY ; 2 and 3, Argent, a saltire sable [LUCOMBE].

The armys of Sir John Treffrye, knight, and yᵉ lady his wife the daughter of Lucom.

TREFRY, impaling, Argent, a cross between four mullets gules [FLAMANK].

John Treffrye married Ivot, yᵉ daughter of Nicholas le Flamāck of Erreglothnow, knight.

And 9 matches more in this roome, some imperfect.

Neare the church of Foye is a large old howse of stone belonging to Mr. Trefry.

In the hall windows, these, old:

Quarterly, 1 and 4, Azure, three fleurs-de-lis or ; 2 and 3, Argent, a chevron between three falcon's heads sable [? SAWLE or SCAWEN] ; impaling, quarterly, 1 and 4, Sable, a pheon argent [? NICHOLL] ; 2 and 3, Argent, a chevron between three birds sable.

Quarterly, 1 and 4, TREFRY ; 2, gone ; 3, quarterly, 1 and 4, Argent, a fret raguly sable ; 2, and 3, MICHELSTOWE.

"Last four" impaling, quarterly, 1 and 4, three fleurs-de-lys ; 2, and 3, a chevron between three birds.

1 "gone," impaling, Azure, three fleurs-de-lis or, the "band sable, charged with three roundles."

These newer, in the hall:

Quarterly, 1 and 4, TREFRY ; 2 and 3, Azure, three fleurs-de-lis or.

Argent, on a fesse azure, between two chevrons gules, three escallops or [TREVANION], impaling the preceding coats [JOHN TREVANION and JENNET his wife].

Argent, three chevrons sable, with the same impalement.

FOYE Church, com. Cornub.

The church is Langode in the parish of Foye: the old towne of Foye is on the river nearer Listithiel.

Chancel window east, these two, very old:

Quarterly, FRANCE and ENGLAND.

Gules, three demi-lions passant gardant or ; conjoined in pale with as many [? ship's sterns] or. [Arms of the CINQUE PORTS.]

South yle windowes of the chancel, belonging to the family of Trefry:

A rose gules seeded argent, supported on the dexter side by a lion rampant, on the sinister by a wivern.

Quarterly, FRANCE and ENGLAND; impaling, quarterly, 1 and 4, CASTILE and LEON; 2 and 3, ARRAGON and SICILY [JOHN OF GAUNT].

Argent, on a fess azure, between two chevrons gules, three escallops or [TREVANION]; impaling, Gules, on a bend argent cotised or three boar's heads couped of the second [EDGCUMBE]. Supporters, dexter, a lion rampant gules; sinister, a buck argent, attired or.

The kneeling figures of a man and woman, the surcoat of the former emblazoned with the male coat, the robe of the latter with the female coat [SIR WILLIAM TREVANION and ANNA his Wife].

TREFRY.

South window, south yle:

Argent, five lozenges conjoined in fesse gules, in chief a lion passant sable.

South window, south yle of the church, these two:

Quarterly, FRANCE and ENGLAND.

This old and fayre and large:

Quarterly, 1, Quarterly, FRANCE and ENGLAND; 2, Or, a chevron gules [STAFFORD]; 3, Azure, a bend argent cotised or between six lioncels salient of the last [BOHUN]; 4, the same as 3 [? EDWARD STAFFORD, Duke of Buckingham].

Second south window this:

Argent, a chevron bottony at the point azure, between three left hands couped at the wrist gules.

West window south yle, this, old:

Quarterly, 1 and 4, quarterly, 1 and 4, [erroneously sketched] Gules, three birds argent; 2 and 3, Argent, three billets gules; 2 and 3, Argent, a chevron gules between three escallops azure.

In the south yle of the chancel, the picture of a man and woman in brasse, and this inscription, two shields gone (temp. Edward II. at least):

Orate pro animabus Thome Trefry senioris armigeri et Avisie uxoris ejus et omnium benefactorum suorum.

Another with the pictures of a man and woman, two shields, top gone:

Orate pro animabus Thome Trefry armigeri filii Thome Trefry et Elizabeth uxoris ejus et omnium filiorum.   (Temp. Edwardi 2^{di}.)

A flat stone there, the picture of a man in armes scratcht in the stone; the inscription is round about   imperfect: dyed 1590, 28 January.   Trefry, esquire.

TREFRY, impaling, a cross engrailed.

Quarterly, 1 and 4, TREFRY ; 2 and 3, a chevron between three roses [TRESITHNEY].

Another huge large stone, three pictures of men in armes scratcht upon the stone, these two shields, and the inscription circumscribed:

TREFRY.

Quarterly, 1 and 4, TREFRY ; 2 and 3, three fleurs-de-lis.

Here lyeth the bodyes of Sir John Trefry, Knight, William Treffry and Thomas Treffry, Esquiers, bretheren : they dyed in the moneth of September, the said Sir John in the 16th yeare, the said William in the 20th yeare of the reighne of King Henry ye 7, and the said Thomas Trefry the first yeare of the reighne of King Henry ye 8.

Another flat stone there:

Quarterly, 1 and 4, TREFRY ; 2 and 3, three lozenges, a crescent for difference.

Quarterly, 1 and 4, TREFRY ; 2 and 3, quarterly, 1 and 4, four lozenges; 2 and 3, a lion rampant.

Quarterly, 1 and 4, TREFRY; 2 and 3, on a chevron between three [roundles] as many [? annulets, or roundles].

Here under lyeth buried the body of Thomas Treffry, Esq. and of Elizabeth his wife, daughter of John Killigrew, Esq., the which Thomas dyed the yere 1563, the 24 of Jan. for whose godly departing the Lord be praysed.   Amen.

A course [*sic orig.*] monument against the east of the said yle:

TREFRY ; a mullet for difference.

Quarterly, 1 and 4, TREFRY ; 2 and 3, MAYOW.

Here lyeth the body of Thomas Trefry, Esq. Councellor at Law, who
  tooke to his wife Katherine one of the daughters and heires of Thomas
  Hellyer, Esq,. who dyed the 1 of March, 1635.

Dum Deo placuerit.

In an escocheon on the wall over this monument aforesaid :

TREFRY, impaling, Gules, three human arms conjoined at the shoulder,
  in the fesse point, the fists closed, argent [TREMAYNE].

This is also in a paper [*sic orig.*] on the wall :

A shield of nine coats, viz. 1, TREFRY ; 2, Argent, an eagle displayed
  sable within a bordure [KILLIGREW] ; 3, Argent, a fret raguly sable ;
  4, MICHELSTOWE ; 5, A chevron between three eagle's heads erased ;
  6, Gules, three fleurs-de-lis or : 7, Vert, on a bend three [? doves
  volant] ; 8, Gules, three mascles or [? argent] ; 9, TRESITHNEY ; impaling, quarterly, 1, TREMAYNE ; 2, Or, a chevron azure between three
  escallops ; 3, Argent, a saltire azure between four cross-crosslets fitchy ;
  4, Argent, on a chevron between three " hogs " sable three " roses " of
  the field [WILLIAM TREFRY and URSULA his Wife].

There hangs two pennons, mantle, helme, and crest, old :

On a wreath, an eagle's head erased sable, holding in the beak an oak
  branch slipped vert [Crest of TREFRY].

In the north yle of the church lyes a fayre alablaster monument,
the picture of an old man in a round cap :

A cross, in dexter chief a sea-gull, in sinister a text T, in base two
  crescents, on the cross a crescent for difference [RASHLEIGH].

A ship in full sail, on a chief a cross, thereon a lion passant.

RASHLEIGH ; impaling, 1 and 4, a castle, issuing therefrom a bird rising
  [LANION] ; 2 and 3, Per pale, two bucks trippant counter-changed.

John Rashleighe lived yeares threescore three,
    And then did yeild to dye,
He did bequeath his sowle to God,
    His corps herein to lye.

The Devonshire howse, the Rashleighes hight,
Well shewes from whence he came :
His virtuous life in Foye towne
Deserveth endlesse fame.
Lanion he did take to wife, by her he had children store.
Another in memory of John R. Esq. 1631.

This following is the coppy of a noate found in the quarters of the Commissary Generall of Essex his army in Cornwall : viz.

Anno 1644.   The number of Officers and Troopers mustered at Tiverton and other places.

		Officers.	Troops.		Officers.	Troops.
1	Sir Philip Stapleton	13	100	Captain Pymm	11	80
	Major-Gen. Skippon	11	74	Captain Lukeman	9	48
	Major Hamelton	11	72			267
	Leiut.-Col. Graves	12	98			
	Captain Draper	11	96	Colonel Sheffeild	11	84
	Captain Copley	9	68	Captain Shefeild	10	73
	Captain Chute	11	76	Captain Hayle	10	70
	Captain Abercromy	8	55	Captain Fynnis	11	71
			639	Captain Robotham	9	63
2	Sir William Balfour	14	100	Captain Wogoone	10	53
	Major Balfour	9	77			414
	Sir Sam. Luke	10	72	Sir Robert Pye	11	82
	Captain Rainsborow	9	57	Captain Scrope	11	80
	Captain Semple	10	61	Captain Pyle	10	46
	Captain Boswell	10	65			208
			432	Colonel Harvey	19	97
	Colonel Baheer	14	74	Major Manering	11	75
	Major Bosa	10	77	Captain Hacket	11	56
	Captain Buller	10	80	Captain Blackwel	10	44
	Captain Flemyng	9	68	Captain Norwood	11	65
	Captain Carmighill	11	72	Captain Washburne	10	52
			371			389
	Colonel Dalbeer	12	67	Captain Abercromy,		
	Captain Salkeild	11	72	9 Officers, Dragoons 65		

Toto of both sides : Troopes 39, Officers 420, Troopers 2785, toto 3205.

EDWARD DODSWORTH, Commissary-General.

* Cornish Language.

English.	Cornish.	English.	Cornish.
A howse	chy	A foot	troos
A tree	guetheine	An eye	lagesse
A man	dene	A nose	frigo
A child	flo	A pig	cal
A hog	ragamo	—	gous
A horse	marh	An arme	breach
A mare	casick	A mouth	ganno
A dog	kie	A boy	mao
A saddle	deeber	A girl	mose
A bridle	frodin	A sword	clitha
A hand	dorne	A scabbard	gooz
A leg	gar	A towne	tre

Numbers.

1	onein	12	doathac
2	deu	13	carthat
3	try	14	pedgwarther
4	padger	15	pemthac
5	pemp	16	whetstarck
6	whe	17	sitack
7	sith	18	ithac
8	ath	19	nounjack
9	naw	20	ygaus
10	deag	21	kaub.
11	idnac		

English.	Cornish.
God save you.	Deu ragges blessye.
I thanke you.	Gad marshe.
God be with you.	Bed me tew thew.
I wish you well.	Dieu new grace thew gilda.

This language is spoken altogeather at Goon-hilly [? Gunwallo] and about Pendennis, and at Land's-end they speake no English. All beyond Truro they speake the Cornish language.

PELYNT, *vulgo* Plynt Church, com. Cornub.

Against the north wall a monument of black stone, handsome for a country monument:

On a wreath, a fox passant.   [Crest of TRELAWNEY.]
TRELAWNEY with a crescent for difference ; impaling, Per chevron [azure] and ermine, in chief two buck's heads caboshed [or] [ARSCOTT].

Edward Trelawnye, June 7, 1630.

Anagr.

Wee wander, alter, dye.

---

* Between the preceding list of officers, &c. and this vocabulary, a leaf appears to have been torn out before the volume was acquired by the Museum. An extensive vocabulary of the Cornish language is given by Borlase.

Oh what a vapour, bubble, puffe of breath,
A neast of wormes, a lumpe of pallid earth,
Is mudwald man : before we mount on high
Wee cope with change, wee wander, alter, dye.

Causidicum claudit tumulus (miraris) honestum,
Gentibus hoc cunctis dixeris esse novum.

Here lyes an honest lawyer, wott you what,
A thing for all yᵉ world to wonder at.

Another far larger on the north wall, but more clownish, many impalings and quarterings.

Sable, on a cross argent, pierced of the field, four eagles displayed sable [BULLER].
The same, impaling, Argent, a chevron azure between three lozenges sable [STALEY].
The same, impaling, Per fess argent and gules a fess counter-changed between three "greyhound's heads."

Abundance more of assumed matches, false.[a]

Francis Buller, of Tregarick, within this parish 1611.

A late family.

Another monument in the south yle, a statue of a man in armour :

Quarterly, 1 sable, a maunch between eight cinquefoils, [ACHYM]; 2, 3, and 4, not given.
William Achym, Ar. ob. Nov. 17, 1589.

A captain of foot in the county.

[a] This assertion, so entirely destitute of proof, may be attributed to the prejudice of the writer against his opponents. Sir Richard Buller of Shillingham, the son of Mr. Francis Buller, was one of the members of the "rebel" Parliament. The Visitation of 1620 contains the family pedigree, from which it appears that, although the grandfather of Sir Richard became seated in Cornwall by his marriage with a coheiress of Trethurffe, he was, nevertheless, descended from a long line of ancestors (eight generations are given) in Somersetshire, and these "matches" so flippantly pronounced to be "false" are recorded in that pedigree.

In the south yle, belonging to Trelawny, a monument and picture of a child:

> To the memory of El: daughter of John Vivian the younger, Esq. and Ann his wife, daughter of Sir John Trelawny, Knight and Baronet, ob. 13 Feb. 1640.
>
> Or, a chevron azure between three eagle's heads erased gules, a chief of the last [VIVIAN] ; impaling, TRELAWNEY.

In the north window, north yle, chancel, lyes an old statue in compleate armour, fashion of the Black Prince.

> Rude sketch of a knight in armour, and cross-legged.

> [The following verses occupy a page by themselves:]
>
> Farewell fond Love, under whose childish whip
> I have served out a weary prentiship,
> Thou that hast made me thy scorned property,
> To dote on those that love not, and to fly
> Love that woo'd me: goe bane of my content
> And practise on some other patient.
> Farewell fond Hope, that fann'd my warme desir
> Till it had raysd it to unruly fire,
> Which nor sighes could nor thoughts extinguish can,
> Although mine eyes outflow'd an ocean.
> Forth of my thoughts forever, thing of ayre,
> Begun in errour, finisht in despaire:
> Farewell fond world, upon whose restles stage,
> Twixt Love and Hope, I have foold out an age;
> Ere I will sue to thee for my redresse,
> Ile woo the wynd and court the wildernes,
> And buried from the dayes discovery
> Studdy some slow but certayn way to dye:
> My wofull monument shalbe a cell,
> The mourning of the purling brooke my bell,
> And for my epitaph the rocks shall groane
> Eternally; if any aske the stone
> What wretched thing doth in that concave lye,
> The hollow eccho shall reply, 'Tis I.

A coppy of a commission for constituting a provost marshall.[a]

By the generall of his Majesties forces imployed against Plymouth.   To Josias
Hearle, of Liskard, in the county of Cornwall.

These are to certifie all whome it may concerne, that I doe hereby constitute
and appoint you to be Provost Marshall Generall for the county of Cornwall,
to take and safely keepe in your custody every such person or persons as you
shall from time to time receave order for, from Captayne Symon Cottell,
treasurer to the said army for the county of Cornwall, or any of his troope, and
them not to release without speciall order from me, or the sayd Captayne Cottell :
and for the doing thereof this shalbe your sufficient warrant.   Given under my
hand and seale this 25 day of July, 1644.

RY. GRENVILE.

---

[a] This Commission occurs in the original some pages back, but is inserted here in order
not to interfere with the narrative.   In one corner is a shield bearing three chevrons, the
coat of Grenville, with an inescocheon.

A Continuation of the Actions, Moovings, and Marches of his Majestie with his Army, from the time they left Cornwall, Sept. 5°, 1644.

Thursday, Sept. 5°. His Majestie marched from Liskerd in Cornwall, to Tavestock, com. Devon, neare Plymouth. Two tr[oops] at Peter Tavie parish, three myles farther. This day Sir Richard Grenvile, by the King's appointment, sent a trumpet in his Majesties name to Plymouth to render the towne.

Friday 6°. The trumpeter returned with this answer, but first abused and imprisoned: that they would send an answere by one of their drummers.

TAVESTOCK Church, com. Devon.

East window, south yle, chancel, this, not old:

Quarterly, I. quarterly, 1 and 4, a lion rampant, on a chief three escallops [RUSSELL]; 2 and 3, a castle [DE LA TOUR]; 2, three fish haurient [HERING]; 3, a griffin segreant [FROXMORE]; 4, three chevronels, a crescent for difference [WYSE]; impaling, quarterly, 1 and 4, three dovecotes [SAPCOTE]; 2 and 3, On a cross a fleur-de-lis between four mullets; the whole within a garter. "RUSSELL, Earl of Bedford" [JOHN 1st EARL, grantee of the Abbey].

Against the south wall, chancel, a faire and stately monument with the statue of a judge: [a]

Azure, three saltires or, a mullet for difference [GLANVILLE].

1, Probably the last coat; impaling, Azure, a chevron or between three martlets argent.

A saltire engrailed ermine; impaling [? GLANVILLE].

Honoratæ sacrum memoriæ Johannis Glanvil unius quondam Justiciariorum de Com. Banco. Qui merito factus Judex summo cum labore administravit justiciam, justicia conservavit pacem, pace expectavit mortem, morte invenit requiem 27 die Julij, 1600.

[a] Engraved in the Gentleman's Magazine for September 1844.

Statutum erat hoc monumentum, A. D. 1615, impensis Dominæ Aliciæ
Godolphyn viduæ, prius uxoris ejusdem Johannis Glanvil, renuptæ vero
Francisco Godolphyn Militi jam eciam defuncto, quæ peperit eidem
Johanni viro suo 7 liberos, videlicet,

1. Maria, defuncta, nupta Edwardo Estcourt Ar. postea Militi.
2. Franciscus, qui duxit in uxorem Elizab. filiam Will'i Grymes Ar.
3. Dyonisia, nupta Thomæ Polwheile.
4. Johannes, qui duxit in uxorem Winifredam filiam Will'i Burcheir Ar.
5 Alicia, defuncta innupta.
6. Johanna, nupta Sampsoni Hele Ar.
7. Thomas.

These two are in the north yle window, east end:

Quarterly, 1 and 4, Argent, a cross gules, "FAYS"; 2 and 3, Sable, three
battle-axes argent; impaling, quarterly, 1 and 4, A chevron between
three "rams" passant; 2 and 3, Argent, a chevron between three
human "legs" sable.

Quarterly, 1 and 4, Ermine, on a chevron three buck's heads caboshed;
2, a mallet; 3, Sable, three arrows in pale, the heads pointing to the
dexter side, argent; impaling, quarterly, 1 and 4, Ermine, on a chief
wavy gules an eagle displayed or; 2, "gone"; 3, Azure, three lions
rampant argent.

Against the north wall, north yle of the chancel, is a faire white
monument, two statues of men and this shield, no inscription, not
painted, one statue of a woman.

Quarterly, 1 and 4, Gutty de sang, a cross engrailed [FITZ]; 2, three
battleaxes erect; 3, three fleurs-de-lys; impaling, quarterly, 1 and 4,
three rams passant; 2, a bend lozengy; 3, a bend between six fountains,
a mullet for difference [? STOURTON].

" Sans inscription."

It was for Sir John Fays [Fitz], who hath a faire howse in this
parish, standing on the west side of towne called Fays [Fitz] Ford.
Now Sir Richard Grenvill owes it in right of his wife.

Neare the church, and upon the bank of the Stony [Tavy] river,
stands the remnants of the abbey of Tavestock, now belonging to the
Earl of Bedford.

This coate and crest are carved upon the roofe of the porch going
into the hall of the abbey:

Vaire argent and sable, on a chief argent two mullets pierced sable, " TAVESTOKE ABBEY ARMS."

A Crest, on a wreath a demi-eagle displayed, charged on the breast with a quatrefoil, and holding in its beak a [? laurel-sprig].

These are painted, old, over a doorway in the hall:

A chevron between three [owls], a chief or, " Olden bishop of Exeter."[a]
A pastoral staff and crosier in saltire.

WHITCHURCH [Whitechurch] Church, com. Devon, one myle south of Tavestock.

Third north window, north yle of the church, these, pretty old, in small:

Sable, three crescents argent, a bordure engrailed of the last, " HARRIS ;" impaling, Azure, a bend engrailed argent, cotised or, " FORTESCUE."

Per pale indented gules and argent, a bend sable ; impaling, A saltire argent between four eagles displayed.

" Gone," [sc. the blason of the field,] a fess embattled between three Katharine wheels or.

West window in the belfray, these, older:

Quarterly FRANCE and ENGLAND.
THE ABBEY OF TAVISTOCK.

In the churchyard, two tombes for the Radfords, lately buried, no great estate.   This coate is carried on both:

Three lions [with human faces] passant in pale, " tayles cowed" [RADFORD].

Three myles from Tavestock is a small village called Samford [Sampford Spiney]; in the church nil.   The manor belongs to Sir Francis Drake, nephew and heir to Sir Francis D. the seaman.

Munday the 9° Sept.   His Majestie with his troopes of guard, &c. and foot army went to Rubert [Roborough] Downe neare the Beacon, four myles from Plymouth.   The Queenes regiment of horse, commanded by Sir John Campsfeild their colonel, was sent to face the towne.   Parties of the rebels' horse came out and followed his reare, when he drew off at night all to quarters: Lord Bernard's troope to Beere parish [Beere Ferrers, vulgo Ferris], an island in Devonshire.

[a] These are the arms of Hugh Oldham, Bishop of Exeter.   He had frequent disputes with the Abbot of Tavistock, whom he excommunicated, and died in 1519.

BEERE Churche, com. Devon.

In the church and chancel windowes, this coate is often, exceedingly old:

Or, on a bend sable three horse-shoes argent, "FERRARS."

Neare this church is an old stone howse, which antiently was very large; a towre imbattayld standing, now habitable; 'tis the manor howse.

Mountjoy Blount, Earle of Newport, is owner of this island, worth 1000*l.* per annum.

In this island of Beere are many silver mynes: none els knowne but in this place. The other mynes round about in Cornwall and the adjacent part of Devon are all tynn. These tinn mynes have not been used since Queene Elizabeth's time; they are of vast depth.

Tuesday, 10 Sept. His Majesties army and Prince Maurice's of foot, and some horse, marched towards Plymouth, and with the Queenes regiment of horse, Earle of Northampton's regiment, and the 3 troopes of the life guards.

At 12 of the clock both armyes of foot marched with drums beating and colors flying and tooke possession of the ground neare the workes, under mercy of the enemyes cannon, which played upon them as they went. Wee planted many of our cannon under a hedge within little more then halfe cannon shott. Many great shott on both sides.

Wednesday kept the same ground. In the morning the King sent one of his owne trumpets with propositions of treaty, whome they kept that day.

At night the King sent a drummer for the same purpose.

Thursday the returne of those two was expected. At night the trumpet returned, much abused, and would have taken away his horse, and told him they would hang him if he came agen.

Friday came newes to the leaguer that Barnstaple, a garrison of the rebells in this county, of their yeilding to his Majestie, leaving their armes, &c. and marche away with colors, &c.

Satterday 15° September. In the night our soldjers gave the

enemy strong alarmes and cryd, Fall on, fall on the enemy. Shott thousands of musket, and many pieces of cannon, as was the severall night before. Betweene 6 and 7 morning his Majesties army, &c. with drums beating, and colors flying, marched off, leaving the seige. But Sir Richard Grenvill, with 30 or 40 Cornish, is appointed to lye at Plymton and make workes to stopp them from foraging into the country.

This morning the rogues followed the reare commanded by Lord Northampton; little or no hurt, onely the basest language.

The King's regiment to their quarters at Peter Tavie. His Majestie to Tavestock that night in Mr. Glanvile's howse in the towne.

Munday, 17° September. The King with his troopes of guard, (over whome the Lord Bernard Stuart is made Captain Generall, and of all his Majesties horse guards, by commission dated at Boconnock Aug. 20, 1644,) marched by Lidford this day, where the water runs so low and deepe under the bridge before you come to the towne as 'tis scarce to be seene unles in one place betweene two craggy rocks.

In this towne is the Stannary Court, kept properly for the tyn myners, but brings in all. A court of vast priviledges. A maior towne, about 16 or 18 howses in it.

His Majestie lay this night at Okehampton, the howse he lay in as he came into the West. Rattenbury, an attorney, owes it. The troope at North Tawton, 5 myles farther.

OKEHAMPTON Church, com. Devon.

East window, chancel, old:

> Quarterly, FRANCE and ENGLAND.
> Azure, three shoveller's heads erased argent [LACY].
> COURTENAY, with a label of three points azure.

South window, church, this:

> ABBEY OF TAVISTOCK.

A flat stone in the south yle of this chancel this coate:

> A fess embattled upwards between two escallops [NEWCOMBE]; impaling,
> A saltire engrailed between four mullets [? cinquefoils, NAPPER].
> Will'm Newcombe, of Okehampton, ob. 8 April, 1626.

A shelfe for bread like a monument: this coate and a long inscription against the north pillar of this church:

> Or, a bend gules, a crescent for a difference [COTTELL].

> George Cottell, of Holborne, a gentleman, gave by his testament, dated 1621, to Okehampton, where I was borne, 50*l.* to be layd out as followes. [The rest omitted.]

Tuesday, Sept. 18, 1644, his Majestie dyned at Crediton. That night to Exeter in greater state then ordinary.

His troopes to Brod Clist, 4 myles distant.

At this place wee rested till Munday following.

The King's army of ffoot marched by Colhampton [Collumpton].

The Coates of Armes and Monuments within the antient Cathedral Church of EXETER, 20 Sept. 1644.

These are in old glasse, about the age of the armes in the cathedral at Worcester.

South [? north] chappel, above the quier, where Bishop Careyes monument is:

> Ermine, a cross engrailed gules [NORTHWODE].
> MORTIMER.
> Argent, three fusils conjoined in fess gules [MONTACUTE].
> BOHUN.
> COURTENAY, with a label azure; impaling, Or, three piles azure [BRYAN].[a]
> Quarterly, 1 and 4, Gules, a lion rampant or [FITZALAN]; 2 and 3, Checky or and azure [WARREN]; over all a label of three points.
> Paly of six argent and azure, on a bend gules three eagles displayed or [GRANDISON].
> NORTHWODE; impaling GRANDISON.[b]
> Same as last, but in place of eagles in the impalement are roses or.
> GRANDISON.

[a] Sir Hugh Courtenay, one of the founders of the Garter.

[b] John, Baron Northwode, married the sister of Bishop Grandison.

What remain of these coats are noted in the Transactions of the Exeter Diocesan Architectural Society, vol. iii. p. 105. For the "rebels sacrilege" at Exeter see Ryves's Mercurius Rusticus, p. 158, &c. 5th edition, and which, if not exaggerated, must have been on their second occupation of that city.

These coates stand in this manner in the top of the window, north yle of the quier:

> Argent, a fess sable within a bordure gules, charged with twelve bezants [WESTON].
>
> Same as last, but the bordure engrailed.
>
> Same as last, but without the bezants.
>
> Argent, on a fess sable three trefoils slipped or, a bordure engrailed gules.
>
> Argent, a fess sable within a bordure gules, charged with twelve guttes or.

These and the reste of the painting are both of an age.

At the bottome, the picture of a blew preist with a bald pate and beades, and this under him:

> 𝔚illielmus de 𝔚eston me fecit.

South yle windowes of the body of the cathedrall.

First window:

> Ermine, three lions rampant gules.
>
> MONTACUTE.
>
> Argent, a bend wavy sable within a bordure sable, charged with ten pairs of keys, the wards outwards, or [BISHOP STAPYLDON].
>
> Paly of six argent aud azure, on a bend gules a "mytre" between two eagles displayed or [BISHOP GRANDISON].[a]
>
> "By this coate yᵉ age of these windowes may be found."
>
> Gules, a chevron between ten crosses potent [? pattée] argent [BERKELEY].
>
> COURTENAY, with a label of three points azure.

Second window:

> Azure, on a chevron gules, between two birds rising or, three lions passant argent.

Aloft these:

> Gules, a saltire vair between thirteen cross-croslets fitchy argent.
>
> Argent, on a bend sable three buck's heads caboshed or.
>
> Argent, a chevron azure between three wyverns gules.
>
> Argent, a chevron couped sable, a label of three points gules.

Third window:

> COURTENAY, with a bend compony argent and azure.
>
> BOHUN.
>
> Azure, three quatrefoils argent, 2 and 1.
>
> REDVERS.
>
> Argent, on a fess sable three trefoils slipped or, a bordure engrailed gules.

---

[a] He became Baron Grandison on the death of his brother, and died in 1369.

Second window:

Quarterly FRANCE and ENGLAND, a label of three points argent.

Argent, three fusils conjoined in fess gules.

COURTENAY, with a label of three points azure.

Gules, fretty or.

Or, three lions passant in pale sable [CAREW].

Fourth window:

Or, a chevron between three escallops azure.

Argent, two bendlets wavy sable [STAPYLDON].

Ermine, three chevrons gules.

Azure, three bends argent.

Per chevron gules and sable, three keys erect, wards facing the dexter side, or.

The picture of a monke:

𝔐𝔞𝔤ʳ. 𝔗𝔥𝔬. 𝔡𝔢 𝔥𝔞𝔯𝔱𝔢𝔩𝔢𝔶 𝔪𝔢 𝔣𝔢𝔠𝔦𝔱.

Fifth window:

Quarterly, FRANCE and ENGLAND.

The same with a label of three points argent.

Gules, three lions passant or, a label of three points each charged with three fleurs-de-lis or [EARLS AND DUKES OF LANCASTER].

Or, a chevron between three escallops azure.

Azure, three quatrefoils argent.

FERRERS.

Per fess gules and azure, three crescents argent.

Sixth window:

A similar coat to the last.

Argent, three fusils conjoined in fess gules, a bordure sable.

Or, three lions passant sable.

Gules, threë fusils conjoined in fess ermine [DINHAM].

These are aloft in the north side of the body of the church:

A chevron between three keys erect, the wards pointing to the dexter side or.

GRANDISON.

Argent, three chevrons sable.

MONTACUTE.

Argent, three bars gules.

Second window, beginning eastward:

MONTACUTE, with a bordure sable.

Argent, a fess sable, a bordure gules.

Argent, on a fess sable three trefoils slipped or, a bordure engrailed gules.
Same as last, the bordure charged with ten guttes or.[a]

Third window:

GRANDISON.
BRYAN; impaling, Argent, three fusils conjoined in fess gules.
COURTENAY, with a label of three points azure.
Argent, three fusils conjoined in fess gules.
Argent [? or], three piles azure.

Fourth window:

COURTENAY, with a bend compony argent and azure.
Argent, two bars gules, in chief three lozenges of the last.
Argent, a griffin segreant gules.
The same; impaling, Gules, four fusils conjoined in fess argent [DAUBENEY].
DAUBENEY.

Fifth window, small, these:

Or, a lion rampant gules.
FERRERS.
Argent, a saltire engrailed, charged with nine plates.
Argent, a " bull " passant sable, a bordure of the last charged with nine
bezants.
Argent, a chevron sable between three billets gules.
Sable, three chevronels ermine.
Per fess indented argent and gules.
Argent, on a bend sable three roses argent.
Argent, a saltire gules [imperfect].
Argent, two chevrons sable between three roses gules.
Quarterly, FRANCE and ENGLAND.
Quarterly, FRANCE and ENGLAND; impaling, 1 and 4, "imperfect;" 2 and
3, Or, a lion rampant gules.
Quarterly, REDVERS and COURTENAY.
Argent, two chevrons sable.
Gules, two chevrons argent.

Lowest window:

Or, a lion rampant gardant gules.
Azure, three " imperfect " or, a chief of the last.
Per fess gules and azure, three crescents argent.

These in the low window, north side of the body of the church.

---

[a] These seem to be variations of the coat of Weston. *Vide antea.*

First window next the quier:

GRANDISON.

Argent, two bendlets wavy sable within a bordure of the same charged with nine pairs of keys, the wards facing outwards, or [BISHOP STAPYLDON].

BERKELEY.

Second window:

Per fess gules and azure, three crescents argent.

COURTENAY, with a label of three points azure.

COURTENAY, with a bend compony argent and azure.

Gules, four fusils conjoined in fess ermine [? for DINHAM].

First window, below the doore:

NORTHWODE.

Gules, four fusils conjoined in fess ermine, DINHAM.

Second window:

BRYAN.

Per fess gules and azure, three crescents argent.

Argent, on a bend sable three buck's heads caboshed or.

Third window:

Barry nebuly argent and gules.

Barry nebuly argent and gules, a label of three points azure, the whole within a bordure sable charged with ten bezants.

Argent, two bars gules, a bordure engrailed sable.

Barry nebuly argent and gules, a bend azure.

GRANDISON.

Barry nebuly argent and gules, on a bordure sable 14 mullets or.

Same as last, but bezants instead of mullets.

North windowes aloft:

NORTHWODE.

GRANDISON; impaling, Gules, two bars or "imperfect."

NORTHWODE; impaling [GRANDISON].

Window below the doore, aloft:

COURTENAY, with a label of three points azure; impaling BOHUN.

COURTENAY.

Or, on a bend gules three [imperfect] argent.

Or, on a bend gules three "imperfect" argent; impaling, COURTENAY.

Same as the last; impaling, Gules, three clarions or [GRENVILLE].

COURTENAY.

BRYAN.

[Field not given], on a chevron sable, between two keys in chief erect, the wards pointing to the dexter, argent, and a broken spear, the points reversed in base, three [? cinquefoils] or.

BISHOP GRANDISON.

Sable, a cross engrailed or.

Argent, three bars sable.

Third and lowest:

Sable, a bend ermine.

These in the west window:

Gules, on a fess between six martlets or, a mullet sable pierced or.

Or, three piles azure.

BISHOP GRANDISON.

MORTIMER.

Quarterly, FRANCE and ENGLAND, a label of three points azure.

ENGLAND, with a label of three points azure.

Paly of six or and gules, on a chief in canton a mullet.

NORTHWODE.

Betweene the pillars of the south yle in the body of the quier [? nave] stands a lofty altar monument, very faire; on the top the effigies of a man and woman; she on the right hand, he like Black Prince. On his breast three torteaux, and a label of three points.[a]

Neare this in the body of the quier lyes a flat large stone inlayed with brasse, a picture of a man in complete armour, chayned at the necke; these coates; the inscription is circumscribed.

COURTENAY, a label of three points.

COURTENAY impaling BOHUN.

COURTENAY impaling (blank).

Under his head a helme, and forth of a crowne a bunch of ostrich feathers.[b]

South yle, againste the partition of the quire, an old marble altar tombe; written over it,

" Leofricus, ye first bishop of Exeter, lyes here."

Divers verses.

North [? same sc. south] side of the quire, these monuments:

[a] Monument of Hugh 2nd Earl of Devon, and Margaret Bohun.

[b] Monument of Sir Peter Courtenay, son of the Earl, K.G.

One lying crosst-legged, drawing a sword, and a shield on his left arme painted.

Checky gules and or, a chief vair [CHICHESTER],

for Chichester, who had a brother, bishop of this church.[a]

Next him another of the same forme.

BOHUN.

A cap, like a helme, lying under his head; no creast.

Epitaphium D. Bohunni illustrissimi quondam Comitis Herefordensis.

A faire neate chappel; on this south side a bishop fairely and costly entombed.

Hic jacet Hugo Oldom Epis' qui obiit 25 die Junij 1519, c. a. p. d. a.

Sable, a chevron or between three owls argent, on a chief of the 2nd three roses gules.

"Founder of Corp. Chr. in Oxon."

This lookes into the church, but stands out of the church, because he was excommunicated.

Another, south chappel; a faire monument; statues of a man and woman.   Sir John Gilbert.

Argent, on a chevron sable three roses of the field [GILBERT]; impaling, Ermine, three lions rampant gules [CHUDLEIGH].

Another, the statue of a bishop, and this coate; onely this inscription:

In memoriam Valentini Carey, olim hujus eccl'e Ep'i, qui obiit 10 Junii, 1626.

Two keys in saltire, over all a naked sword in pale erect [SEE OF EXETER]; impaling, Argent, on a bend sable three roses of the field [CAREY].

He was buried in St. Paul's church, as the verger tells me.

Another bishop's picture on a faire tombe.   South side these coates; no name:

A stag's head caboshed.

Two eagles displayed in fess.

Or, on a chevron sable between two keys in chief, and a naked sword erect, in base, of the second, three quatrefoils or.

North side these, upon this monument:

SEE OF EXETER.

a The Bishop was of earlier date.   He died in 1150.

A chevron gules within a bordure azure, charged with ten mitres or [BISHOP STAFFORD].

Three shoveller's heads erased, "LACY."

Azure, a bend engrailed argent, cotised or, " FORTESCUE."

In the Lady chappel beyond the quier a stately faire monument, the picture of a judge.

To ye memory of Sir John Doderidge, Knt. ob. 13 September, 1628.

Argent, two pales wavy azure between nine cross-crosslets gules [DODDER. IDGE].

On a wreath a lion's head erased, murally gorged [crest of DODDERIDGE].

Another monument for

Dorothea ux' Joh'is Doderidge, ob. 1ᵒ Martii, 1614.
Filia Amisii Bampfeild, Militis.

On a lozenge shield, Or, on a bend gules three mullets argent [BAMPFIELD].

Under the south wall in an arch lyes a statue cutt in marble, very are work : a bishop, very old.

Another right over against it, ill done, in the like stone.

A very stately monument of alablaster, the statue of a bishop :

Hic jacet Edm. Stafford.

Lord Chancellor of England.

Arms of BISHOP STAFFORD.

These coates are painted on the monument :

Or, a bend gules, a bordure engrailed sable [STAFFORD].

Gules, in bend two pair of keys, the wards facing outwards or, each saltire-wise with a naked sword, hilted argent.

Or, a chevron gules between three martlets sable, " STAFFORD."

Vair, or and gules.

Quarterly, 1 and 4, STAFFORD ; 2 and 3, "imperfect."

Quarterly, 1 and 4, Barry of four argent and azure, on a chief three roundles ; 2 and 3, Quarterly, 1 and 4, a maunche ; 2 and 3, a fess.

Or, a lion rampant gules.

Quarterly, Gules, three maunches or ; 2 and 3, Or, a fess gules between two [? barrulets].

These I beleive were contemporaneans, whose coates are painted on his monument.

Quarterly, 1 and 4, Azure, a fess or between three leopard's faces argent, " DELAPOOLE ;" 2 and 3 not given.

Against the north wall in a chappel, a stately monument ; a man and woman, he in armes:

> Gawinus Carew, Miles, filius Edmundi Carew, ob. 1584.

Under him in armes a knight lying crosse-legd drawing a sword, and this with the bearing carved on his left arme:

> Or, three lions passant sable [CAREW].
> Sir Peter Carew, knight, elder brother to the Lord Carew, Baron of Clopton.

His coate over his armes, gules, turned up ermines; which Sir Peter was slayne in Ireland.

Very many matches and quarterings of the Carewes upon this monument; among the rest this :

> "CAREWES 21 quarterings, "impaling, quarterly, COURTENAY and REDVERS ; and with a second impalement, Gules, a chevron or between three leopard's faces.

A small chappel, north yle, neare the Ladyes chappel.

The statue of a man in armes.

These armes in the window of the chappel: [viz. COURTENAY, with a label.]

> Barry of eight, azure and argent, over all a double-headed eagle displayed gules [SPEKE]. " Supported by two bears argent. *Creast,* Upon a wreath azure a hedg-hog argent " [crest of SPEKE].
> The same ; impaling, Checky argent and sable, a chief vair.
> " For Speke."

On the outside Speke's eagle is carved, and this coate too:

> Quarterly, "COURTENAY " and REDVERS ; impaling, quarterly, "FRANCE and ENGLAND."

Against the north wall an armed man crosse-legd, drawing a sword, a shield on his left arme, these two bends wavie sable are painted:

> Epitaphium Stapulduni Gualteri Exoniensis Episcopi fratris.

The picture of a cripple holding a horse, cutt by him.   Vide Stow in Cripplegate.

Another neare the former.

[Anthony] Harvey, Esq. [died 1564].

> Quarterly, 1 and 4, Gules, on a bend argent three trefoils slipped vert [HARVEY] ; 2 and 3, three lions rampant.

Bishop Lacyes playne monument; this coate over it:
LACY.

Against the said monument of Stapleton is a faire monument for his brother, a bishop, between this and the quier:

Epitaphium Gualteri Stapledoni Exoniensis
Episcopi ejus nominis secundi.

Divers verses.

Annos Eduardus ter senos ille secundus, &c.
Vide Speed's Chron. p. 574, vita Edw. 2di.

Another small one, divers matches of the Carewes.

Peter Carew, Eq. Aurat. ob. in Hibernia, 27 Nov. 1575.

A monument of one consumed to nothing but skin and bones: brother to Bishop Lacy; this coate:
LACY.

Divers flat stones both in the quier and body of the church; as also rownd about in the yles and east chappell are divers flat stones whose inscriptions are cutt into the stone of text letters, divers with coates of armes cutt also.

None that I observed had any inlayed brasse in them but onely Courtney.[a]

The story of the Old and New Testament, especially of Our Saviour, is very anciently and curiously painted on the outside of the portion of the quier next the body of the church.

Much abused by the rebells when they tyrannized in Exeter.

Another monument in the north crosse yle between the body of the church and quier, of a bishop consumed to skin and bones like a skeleton.

The east end of the quier is painted very curiously with a temple, Moses and Aron, &c.

In this steeple is one of the biggest bells in England.

The rebells when they had this citty digged up a monument in the south chappel where Bishop Carye lyes, and they found a coffin of stone with the bones of a man whole togeather. Upon the breast lay a silver chalice, which they tooke away.

[a] There is one other still remaining, viz. that of William Langeton, 1413.

This coate is under the picture of a king at the west end on the outside of the cathedrall :

Per saltire argent and gules, over all a cross flory issuant from a globe.

and upon the south porch also.

Upon the pulpit in the body of the church are divers coates of the nobility, lately painted.

Argent, a chevron engrailed gules between four water-bougets sable.

" CECILL."

Cornets making at Exeter for a Danish lord raysing a regiment for Prince [Charles *erased*] :

A standard sable bearing for device an open book with clasps, " upon the booke 'Inseparabilia,' " over all a crown enfiled by a sceptre in bend dexter and a naked sword in bend sinister, saltire-wise, the whole within a circular label with this motto, " Dieu comforte mon cœur, et console mon ame."

A standard sable, bearing for device, on a mound vert a column erect proper, surmounted by a crown enfiled by a sceptre in bend dexter and a naked sword in bend sinister, saltire-wise, hilted or, on the dexter side and near the staff this motto, " Hoc medio."

A standard sable, bearing for device, on a mound vert a pyramid reversed argent, surmounted by a ducal crown or ; on either side, the letters placed singly from top to bottom, the words CONSTANTIA CORONATRICE.

Over the doore of the howse right anent the west doore of the cathedral these carved in stone :

Hugo Oldon, Ep'us Exon.   Coat of OLDHAM surmounted by a mitre.

Quarterly ENGLAND and old FRANCE (semée of fleurs de lis).

Lord Hopton's cornet for his troope of guard.

A standard gules, bearing for device a cannon discharging or, above this motto, " Et sacris compescuit ignibus ignes."

BROAD CLIST Church, in com. Devon, 4 myles north-east of Exon.

A very faire neate church. These very large and faire in the east window south yle, about the age of Henry 7.

> Quarterly, COURTENAY and REDVERS.
> The same; impaling, quarterly, 1 and 4, Gules, a cross or; 2 and 3, MORTIMER, surmounted by a crown or.

Upon the crowne or, a bunch of ostrich feathers or, thereon a falcon, as I remember.

North window of church:

> Ermine, three lions rampant [CHUDLEIGH].

Divers other matches of other families, which I remember not.

Against the north wall of the north yle is a faire large monument, the body of an armed knight lying along sidewayes, the monument of Sir John Ackland, father to Mr. Ackland now sheriffe of this county, lives at Colum John, a howse in this parish so denominated from the river Colum.

Another monument in the south yle for Sir John Drewe, of Killerton, in this parish. Now Mr. Ackland owes it.

Upon the gallery in this church are the armes of all the contributors to that building, lately done.

A priory in this parish.

A great howse by this church built by the Chidleyes.

Between this parish and Exon is a faire parke paled in belonging to Sir John Bampfeild; an ancient seate and faire howse belonging of a long time to that family in the parish of Poltimore.

East window chancel these two:

> Gules, two keys addorsed in bend sinister or, a naked sword in bend dexter, saltire-wise, argent, hilted or [? See of WINCHESTER].
> On a cross between four crosses pattee sable, each charged with five bezants, a crosier in pale or.

South window, chancel, aloft, old:

> Gules, a saltire vair between sixteen billets or.

COURTENAY, with a label of three points azure.

The same coat, each point of the label charged with three fleurs-de-lis or

These following are very large and faire in the east window south yle chancel:

Quarterly, 1, Quarterly FRANCE and ENGLAND, within a bordure also quarterly gules and azure, charged in the first and fourth with six lioncels, three and three, and in the second and third with six fleurs-de-lis, three and three, all or ; 2 and 3, COURTENAY ; 4, REDVERS : the whole within a garter. Supporters, two boars argent crined or. *Crest,* On a helmet affrontée argent, barred or, an earl's coronet, issuing therefrom a tuft of feathers proper. A " mantle gules doubled ermine," tasselled or. On either side the helmet a " falcon " rising from a billet of wood, raguly or.[a]

Quarterly, FRANCE and ENGLAND within a garter, and surmounted by a crown or, jewelled gules.

Quarterly, 1, quarterly FRANCE and ENGLAND ; 2 and 3, Or, a cross gules ; 4, MORTIMER. The whole encircled by a " wreath " or and azure, and surmounted by a ducal coronet or, issuing therefrom a " falcon " rising from a billet of wood or.

Quarterly, COURTENAY and REDVERS ; impaling the preceding coats, all within a wreath as last, and, above, the falcon rising as before.

North window, north yle chancel, these :

CHUDLEIGH.

Same ; impaling, Argent, a fess per fess indented vert and sable between two cotises sable [HUDDY].

Azure, three escallops or, a mullet for difference ; impaling, Gules, two demi-lions passant guardant or.

(Blank) impaling the preceding male coat.

The last impalement ; impaling, Azure, three escallops or, a mullet for difference.

CHUDLEIGH, impaling STOURTON.

Middle north window of the church these two :

Gules, three demi-lions passant guardant or.

Azure, a pair of wings in lure argent, over all a fess gules.

Next window adjoyning these two, very old :

CHUDLEIGH.

[a] Henry Earl of Devon, created Marquess of Exeter 1525, K.G.

Gules, four fusils conjoined in fess argent, each charged with an escallop sable [CHEYNEY].

Within the south wall in a faire arch chancel, lyes the statue of an armed knight lying along *modo* Edward b. pr. [*sc.* Black Prince]. Under his head a helme, forth of it a lyon's pawe, at his feet a lion. Divers shields, but all the painting gone; no embossing.

Rownd about a flat stone, chancel, in text letters, cutt in, and this coate cutt also:

CHUDLEIGH.

Hic jacet Will's Chudlegh, Armiger, qui obiit 29 die mens' Jan. 1515; cujus aīe pp. d. a.

Two flat stones adjoyning, one for Thomas Chappel, of Brockhill, gent. ob. 1611.

Another Chappel, buried 1605.

Against the north wall a faire monument for Sir John Ackland, sans inscription:

Checky sable and or, a fess gules charged with a crescent of the second, [ACLAND].

Same; impaling, Or, on a fess indented counter-indented between three billets azure, each charged with a lion rampant or, three bezants [ROLLS].

Same; impaling, Or, a fleur-de-lis azure [PORTMAN].

Upon his seates these also are carved.

South yle chancel, 2 statues.   On a monument:

Ermine, a lion passant gules [DREWE].

Argent, a chevron sable, charged with a mullet or, a label of three points gules [PRIDEAUX].

Sable, a chevron between two "dolphins" haurient, embowed argent [FRENCH].

"Edw. Drew serviens ad leg: Reg: Elizabeth, ob. 1622."

In the window of the chancel:

Three shields bearing for device the instruments of our Lord's Passion.

Against the north wall, chancel, a small monument:

Ermine, a falcon's head erased azure between three fleurs-de-lis or [BOROUGH].

Henr. Borough, Gent., ob. 12 December, 1605. Elizabeth his wife, daughter of John [? George] Reynell, who founded twelve almes-howses in Broadclist.

An old paire of organs now used in the church.

This is carved, old, in the roofe of the south porch:

Ermine, three lions rampant, " CHUDLEGH."

Munday September 24, 1644. His Majestie marched to Chard in com. Somerset, being twenty myles; his troope to *(blank.)*

This night wee heard that Waller was about Bridport in Dorset-shire, raising the Posse Com. with 2,000 horse and 1,500 dragoons.

This is a copy of the late Earle of Essex his march from St. Albon's into Oxford, &c. 1644, as it was found in one of the pockets of there soldjers at Listithiel.

Hertfordshire:—

From St. Albon's to Beconsfield.

From B. to Henley.

From H. to Reading.

From R. to Wickham com. Oxon.

From W. to Bradfeild in com. Berks.

From Bradfeild to Blubery.

From B. to Abingdon to my Lady Powel's howse: from thence wee faced Oxford, and so to Islip, where Sir Ralph Hopton's army lay within two myles of us, and the next morning, being Holy Thursday, we had a skirmish with them untill the next Munday.

Oxfordshire:—

From Islip to Woodstock.

From W. to Chipping Norton.

From C. to Barfoot [? Burford].

Berkshire:—

From B. to Faringdon, June 8.

From F. to Lamburne, June 10.

From L. to Bedding [? Bedwin], June 11.

From B. to Amfeild [? Amport], June 13.
From A. to Compton, June 14.　[? Compton Chamberlain].
From C. to Blanford.
Dorsetshire :—
From B. to Dorchester, June
From D. to Bridport.
From B. to Crewkerne, June 23.
Somersetshire :—
From C. to Chard, June 24.
From C. to Axmister, June 30.
From A. to Honyton, July 1.
Devonshire :—
From H. to Colhampton, July 2.
From C. to Teverton, July 3.
From T. to Kirton, July 20.
From K. to Bowe, July 21.
From B. to Okehampton, July 22.
From O. to Tavistock, July 23.
From T. to Horsebridge, July 26.
Cornub :—
From H. to Linkolnhorne, July 27.
From L. to Bodman, July 28.
From B. to Listidwell, August 2.　[Lostwithiel].
From thence like rogues to the Divell.

The troop at Knoll, a myle from Chard; afterwards wee removed to Southpetherton.

SOUTHPETHERTON, com. Somerset.

These two, old, in a howse window where wee quartered :

Or, two ravens in pale sable [CORBET] ; impaling, Or, on a chevron sable three mullets argent.

Argent, a chevron sable between three bird-bolts azure, feathered or.

In Mr. Sands his howse, (parlor,) old:

"Vert, 2 batt's wings argent conjoyned by a chayn or."

CASE his coate, was owner of this howse called Cassells, 150 yeare since.   In the hall there, these, as old:

Azure, on a fess or, between six arrows bendwise, the barbs pointing upwards, [? downwards in bend or] argent, three blackamoor's heads proper in profile [? WATTS].

Azure, three fishes in pale naiant argent, " vide Boconnock church."

Sable, a cross between four lion's heads erased argent.

Gules, a lion rampant argent attacking a wyvern or [DAUNTESEY].

Argent, a chevron between three owls gules.

Argent, two bars azure, over all an eagle with two heads displayed or, " SPEKE."

Chancel window,[a] old:

Argent, four fusils conjoined in fess gules [? BLONVILLE].

Argent, a chevron between three owls gules.

DAUNTESEY.

Quarterly, 1 and 4, Sable, six [? ducks] argent; 2 and 3, Azure, a bend or [SCROPE].

Sable, a cross between four lion's heads erased argent.

Gules, a dexter arm in fess, habited in a maunche ermine, holding in the hand a fleur-de-lis or [MOHUN].

East window of the chancel these, at bottome, large:

Or, a cross engrailed sable [MOHUN OF BOCONNOCK].

MOHUN.

Quarterly FRANCE and ENGLAND, within a bordure compony argent and azure [BEAUFORT].

Gules, four fusils conjoined in fess argent [DAUBENEY].

Sable, a bend argent between six fountains proper, " STOURTON."

Or, three eagles displayed purpure [RODNEY].

Argent, three hurts each charged with as many chevrons gules, "CARRANT."

---

a All the armorial glass here, as generally elsewhere, has been destroyed or abstracted.

East window, cross yle of this church, for the steeple is in the middle like a cathedral; the church every way answerable in fairenes of structure.

> Argent, three fusils conjoined in fess gules [? BLONVILLE].
>
> Quarterly, 1 and 4, Azure, three cinquefoils between six cross-crosslets argent; 2 and 3, Azure, four bars gemel or, a chief of the last.

South window, south crosse yle:

> Gules, four fusils conjoined in fess argent [DAUBENEY]; impaling the preceding coat.

In the east window, north crosse yle, these, exceeding old and large, at bottome of the window, under pictures of saints:

> Argent, a griffin segreant gules, armed azure. "Broken much by the rebels."
>
> DAUBENEY; impaling, Argent, a fess gules between three "hawks or martlets" or.
>
> DAUBENEY.
>
> Same, with a label of three points or.
>
> Same, debruised by a bendlet azure.

These of the same age, north window, same north yle, not so large:

> Same, without the bendlet; impaling, Argent, three fusils conjoined in fess gules [? BLONVILLE].
>
> Same, without the impalement.
>
> Same, with a label of three points or.

The picture of a woman over this last, **Dna Kat'ina [Dau] beney.**

> Argent, a griffin segreant gules, armed azure.

Uppermost, north window, north yle:

> Quarterly, 1 and 4, Azure, three cinquefoils between six cross-crosslets argent; 2 and 3, Azure, four bars gemels or, a chief of the last.
>
> Gules, four fusils, &c.
>
> Or, a chevron gules within a bordure engrailed sable [STAFFORD].
>
> Same, the chevron charged with a mitre [STAFFORD, bishop of Bath and Wells].

Second north window:

Argent, a cross gules.

DAUBENEY.

Argent, a chevron gules.

Upon a flat stone in the south crosse yle, the picture of a woman and this inscription in brasse, two shields, both gone.

Hic jacet Dnā Maria Daubeney ux' Egidii Daubeney Militis, quondam filia Simonis Leek Armig'i de Comitatu Notingamiæ, quæ ob. 17 Feb. 1442. c. a. p. d. a. [Still remaining.]

In the middle of the same south yle stands a large altar tombe, two foote high, four shields carved round about the sides; the top is fairely inlayed with brasse, the picture of an armed knight, under his head the creast following, and a woman. Arched over thear heads. Four shields, the two first gone; on the west end over thear heads:

DAUBENEY; impaling, Quarterly, 1 and 4, Azure, three cinquefoils between six cross-crosslets argent [? DARCY]; 2 and 3, Azure, three bars gemel or, a chief of the last.

Quarterly, 1 and 4, Azure, three cinquefoils between six cross-crosslets argent; 2 and 3, Azure, three bars gemel or, a chief of the last.

They call him Earle of Bridgwater.[a]

The inscription which was circumscribed is gone.

Sketch of the head of the male effigy resting upon a helmet, surmounted by a crest, apparently of jewelled feathers, " gay worke."

These verses under their feete [still remaining].

<blockquote>
Sis testis xpē q'd non jacet hic lapis iste
Corpus ut ornetur set spiritus ut memoretur;
Quisquis eris qui transieris sta perlege ploro,
Sum q'd eris fueramq' q'd es, pro me precor ora.
</blockquote>

Against the east wall, south yle, a large clownish monument:

The Lady Penelope Hele, and Mrs. Elizabeth Harris.

Sable, three helmets, two and one, within a bordure argent [COMPTON]; impaling, Or, two crescents sable, on a canton of the last a crown or.

Another playner though handsomer monument, north yle, church.

Memoriæ æternæ Jacobi Ayshe, Generosi, qui cum ad 28 pie vixisset annū in Domino placide ob. Maii 5, 1626.

[a] Henry Lord Daubeney, created Earl of Bridgewater 1538.

Quarterly, 1, Argent, two chevrons sable [AYSHE]; 2, Vert, a lion rampant argent; 3, Gules, a cross ermine; 4, Argent, a fess sable, in chief two mullets of the last; impaling, Argent, two bars or, between three martlets, two in chief and one in base, sable.

The monuments, organs, made eight years since, &c. were torne by Essex his horse a fortnight since.

Lord Arundel of Wardour is owner of this towne.

'Tis a market towne, 6 myles from Evill [Yeovil].

Now the family of Dawbeny live at Crewkerne.

Colonel John Fleetwood's regiment of horse of the Earle of Cleveland's brigade, September, 1644.

Leiftenant-Colonel John Stuart, Scot; Major Cornelius Calakan, Irishman.

First Captain, John Lowe, Nottingham.

Second Captain, John Bill, fil. imprimat.ᵃ [*sic orig.*]

Third Captain, William Alford, Major of the late Earle of Cleveland's brigade. Standard gules, 160 men.

Earle of Cleveland's brigade consists of 6 colonels.

Colonel Earle of Cleveland, which was Colonel Caries	200
Colonel Sir Nicholas Crispe . . .	80
Colonel John Fleetwood	160
Colonel ——— Hamilton	160
Colonel Richard Thornhill	100
Colonel ——— Culpeper, who was Leiftenant-Colonel to Sir William Clerke.	100
	800

MARTOCK Church.

East window, chancel, very large and old, these four following:

Quarterly FRANCE and ENGLAND, within a bordure compony argent and

---

ᵃ The Editor is indebted to Sir F. Madden for the suggestion that this officer was the son of Mr. John Bill the King's Printer.

azure; Supporters two "greyhounds" sejant argent, "collared or"
[BEAUFORT].

ARMS OF THE CONFESSOR; impaling, FRANCE and ENGLAND quarterly.
Supporters, two white harts gardant, ducally gorged, with chains passing
between the fore legs and reflexed over the back or. [RICHARD 2d.]

DAUBENEY. "This is supported by two griffons argent."

[*Field blank*] on a chief sable two crescents argent; "Swans supporters."

South yle chancel.

Quarterly gules and or, over all a bendlet argent.

The See of CANTERBURY; impaling, Or, a chevron gules charged with a
mitre of the field, within a bordure sable [ARCHBISHOP STAFFORD,
translated from Bath and Wells 1443].

Quarterly, 1, gone; 2 and 3, three fusils conjoined in fess; 4, Or, a double-
headed eagle displayed vert.

Quarterly, 1 and 4, Sable, six mullets, three and three, argent; 2, "gone;"
3, Gules, three lions rampant, two and one, or.

South window, same yle:

Argent, two bars wavy gules, over all a bend compony or and azure.

Azure, six mullets, 3, 2, and 1, or.

North window chancel:

Quarterly, 1 and 4, Gules, a fess between six cross-crosslets or [BEAU-
CHAMP]; 2 and 3, Checky or and azure, a chevron ermine [EARLDOM
OF WARWICK].

Quarterly FRANCE and ENGLAND, within a bordure compony argent and
azure [BEAUFORT].

North yle, church:

Gules, an inescocheon within an orle of martlets argent [? ERPINGHAM].

Or, three chevrons azure.

DAUBENEY.

Sable, six mullets, 3, 2, and 1, pierced of the field, argent.

The same, with a label of three points gules.

Argent, a fess embattled counter-embattled gules between two bugle
horns sable, stringed or.

Paly of six, vert and or.

South yle, church:

DAUBENEY.
Quarterly, 1, Gules, seven "fusils" [? mascles], 3, 3, and 1, or ; 2, Sable, a
fret argent ; 3, Sable, six mullets, 3, 2, and 1, argent; 4, Azure, a
cinquefoil ermine.

This very old, south yle window:

Argent, two bars wavy gules, over all a bend compony or and azure.

The south and north windows of this church aloft, middle yle, are
full of escocheons, about ten in a window, six windows on a side, *toto*
about 120 coates.   These are some of them.

Quarterly, 1 and 4, Quarterly "imperfect ;" 2 and 3, Quarterly per pale
and per fess indented argent and gules counterchanged ; the whole
within a garter.
Or, a pile gules [? CHANDOS].
COURTENAY, a label of three points azure.
BEAUCHAMP.
DAUBENEY.
Gules, three battle-axes erect, 2 and 1, argent.
HUDDY.

This is carved in stone at the foot of the studd, [? corbel] that
supports the roofe:

Two bars wavy, over all a bend compony ; impaling, Six mullets, 3, 2,
and 1.

This is a very large faire church as ever I saw in·this county.
A large paire of organs north side of the chancel.

This parish of Martock is a hundred of itselfe.

The howses are built of a brave ffree stone, colour of umber, here
growing.

No gentleman lives in this parish, a low deepe rich grownd.
The richest parish in this county.

No flat stones or monuments with any inscriptions in this church.

In the churchyard, east end of the chancel, two monuments; the surface is the statue of a woman, old.

Another the face of a man, and a crosse on his breast, carved.

These six shields are in old glasse in an antient howse in South Petherton:

Argent, a chevron sable between in chief two roses gules, and in base a talbot of the second.

DAUBENEY; impaling, Quarterly, 1, Sable, seven martlets, 3, 3, and 1, argent [ARUNDELL]; 2, Azure [imperfect]; 3 and 4 "imperfect."

Gules, a chevron between three roses argent; impaling "gone."

Gules, a saltire vair between four mullets argent; impaling, Argent, a chevron sable between in chief two roses gules, in base a talbot of the second.

Argent, two bars wavy sable.

Azure, a chevron engrailed sable between three pears or; impaling, Sable, a chevron between three fleurs-de-lis or.

KINGSBURY Church, com. Somerset.

A myle north-west of Martock.

Is a faire handsome church. On the outside of the east [end] is built a vestry, the whole breadth of the chancel, no higher then the bottome of the east window, yet very stately.

Here in the chancel, north side, stands a new and neate paire of organs.

Upon the steeple are divers statues of kings sitting in armour crosst-legged. These coates are carved on the south side in stone:

Paly wavy of six; impaling, A chevron between three lions passant. "Sett up 1640."

A chevron ermine between three leopard's faces.

A . . . . . . between three crescents; impaling, Paly wavy of six.

A chevron between three lions passant.

East window chancel, being fairely painted, not old, as also the north and south windowes:

Sable, a cross moline argent.

North window, north yle, chancel, these, not very old, in small, aloft :

Quarterly, FRANCE and ENGLAND, a label of three points argent, each charged with three fleurs-de-lis [EARLS and DUKES of LANCASTER].

Quarterly, FRANCE and ENGLAND.

MORTIMER.

STOURTON.

Or, on a chevron gules, within a bordure engrailed sable, a crescent argent. " STAFFORD."

Quarterly, 1 and 4, Azure, three bars wavy argent ; 2 and 3, Sable, a fret or, a label of three points ermine [MALTRAVERS].

Argent, a chevron between three lion's heads erased gules.

Argent, three hurts each charged with three chevrons gules.

Azure, a dolphin embowed argent between three mullets gules.

North window, over north doore :

Joh'es Storthwayt, Cancel' Well' hanc fenestram [fieri fecit].

West window, north yle, this coate, old :

Argent, on a cross gules five escallops or.

South windowes, south yle :

Or, on a chevron gules, within a bordure engrailed sable, a mitre, " BISHOP STAFFORD " [of BATH and WELLS].

Sable, six mullets pierced argent, 3, 2, and 1.

On a cross gules five escallops " sans color."

STOURTON, a mullet for difference.

The Earle of Berks is lord of this towne.

August 8, 1644.

THE HUMBLE PETICION OF YOUR MAJESTIES OLD HORSE,[a]

Humbly sheweth,

That whereas they have had the honour long to serve your Majestie under the command of the Lord Wilmott, of whose just loyall intentions they conceive they have had some demonstracion, but now to their great amazement and almost to distraction find him fallen to your Majesties displeasure and sus-

[a] This and the two following documents are alluded to, and commented upon, by Clarendon ; and one sentence of this somewhat mutinous petition is quoted. The editor is not aware that they have, hitherto, been printed at length.

pition.[a] And, although they intend not to arrogate unto themselves a liberty of searching into your Majesties designes or disputing your commands, yet they most humbly beg your pardon if they beleive it a right they owe themselves and your Majesties service to request they may receive some present light of this buisines from your Majestie, that they may not have reason to suspect themselves partakers of his crymes, having ben by your Majesties order executors of his commands. And wee hope for such a satisfaction from your Majesties justice in this particular as may encourage your Peticioners to goe on with the same zeale to your service as they have hitherto expressed in the hazard of their lives and fortunes, and in their prayers for your prosperity, which shall ever be continued by

Your Majesties most humble, &c.

August 12°.

OUR ANSWERE TO THE OFFICERS OF OUR OLD HORSE.

Charles R.

Wee have considered your Peticion and receive it as a thing very well becoming you to expresse to us a sence of the misfortune of a person who hath so long commanded you, as the Lord Wilmott hath done, in so eminent a charge as that of Leiftenant-General of our Horse, Sithence wee assure you that the occasion wee had to sett so great a marke of our displeasure upon one so highly trusted and favoured by us, is an affliction to ourselfe not inferior to the greatest which his best freind can conceive by the effects of it. And wee shall expect that you will be so kind to us in your beleife either of our justice, or prudent care at least of our owne interest, as to be confident that at a season when the cheerfulnes and unanimity in our service (wherewith all of you have hitherto so eminently obliged your King,) is so much more necessary then it hath bin almost at any time, wee should not have done an act that might hazard the discontenting many had wee not bin forced to it by the assurance that it was absolutely necessarie to the preservation of us all. And though in such cases, wherein a Crowne lyeth at the stake uppon the decision of a battaile, a small suspition is grownd enough for Princes to remove any person but doubted from such a trust, whereby he had power so easily to destroy all, yet so desirous are wee to give full satisfaction unto you whose meritt of us hath bin such that we must ever profes no king did ever owe more to gentlemen and officers, that wee have thought fitt to annexe hereunto a declaracion of the causes of the Lord Willmot's removall from our trust, being onely sorry for this, that we are urged by your desires to publishe more then perhaps we ever intended to the unfaithfulnes and ingratitude of a person whome

---

[a] See before, p. 49.

we had not onely trusted so long and so far, but also so highly and so many severall wayes obliged, that it is a great improvement of greife and trouble to us, that, when it shall please God by your meanes to restore us to our rights, wee can scarce ever hope for power to doe it proportionablie to the rest of you.   Given at our Court at Boconnock, Cornwall.

THE CHARGE.

That the Lord Wilmott hath endeavoured principally these three moneths last past to possesse the officers of his Majesties army with a disvalew and contempte of his Majesties person; and secondly with prejudice against the sincerity of his Majesties intentions for the good of his people; and thirdly an endeavour as far as in him lay to draw men to revolt from their allegiance, and particularly hath used discourses and persuasions to this effect, and to persons of charge, power, and creditt in the army.

1. That the King (he saw) would putt all the power into his nephewes hands.

2. That rather then suffer it they should (for his part he would) make him submitt to the Parliament.

And to others to this effect :—

1. That the King was afraid of Peace.

2. That he was not a man ever to goe thorough with these buisinesses.

3. That there was no way but one, which was, to sett up the Prince, who had no share in the causes of these troubles.

4. That he (the Pr.) should declare against those about his father, wherein all honest men would stick to him and so putt an end to all.

5. That the said Lord Wilmott hath without his Majesties knowledge sent secret messages of dangerous nature unto the Earle of Essex, particularly, 1. It being resolved by his Majestie that a privat message should be sent to the Earle of Essex from a person of honour, to whome the said Earle professeth respect, inviteing him to send two persons of most trust with him to meet and confer with the said person of honour and another of whome the said Earle was beleived to have a good opinion; and the instructions to the messenger, one who had a free excesse to the Earle of Essex, being punctually drawne at a private counsell, (at which the Lord Wilmott was present,) with precise directions that the messenger should know no more of the buisines, or deliver any thing concerning the publique but what was sett downe by unanimous consent of that counsell and attested by the Secretary of State; the said Lord Wilmott notwithstanding desired the said messenger to commend him kindly to the Earle of Essex, and to tell him from him that he had many good freinds

in the army. 3. That he should lay hold of this oppertunity ; and, 4. that then they should shew themselves ; and, 5. that the courtiers should not have power to hinder or to carry it as they had done, or words to this effecte.

By which secret message from him, being leiftenant-generall of his Majesties horse, unto the generall of the rebells' army, he did not onely forfeit his duty and allegiance, but hath, by giveing the Earle of Essex such assurances, (though most false of a partie in his Majesties army and of such division betwixt that and the Court,) bene probably the cause of that insolent returne which the said Earle hath made unto his Majesties most gracious lettre, which he vouchsafed to write him with his owne hand to invite him to peace, and so frustrated the great hopes which his Majestie had raysed to himselfe, by such a letter, of saving a further effusion of bloud and procureing a happy accomodacion, whereof, had there bene the least hopes left, his Majestie hath declared that he would have connived at these of W., yea, at greater crymes.

An Answere to a Declaracion and Charge against the Lord Viscount Wilmott.

I doubt not but my actions, and the losse of what I have in his Majesties service, might satisfie the world of my integrity and respect to his Majesties person and dignity, if I should onely insist on that ; but, since my accusers intends to prove the contrary by the averment of persons of charge, power, and creditt in the army, I am confident 'tis a right I owe my owne innocence and a civility to men of their quality, wholly and absolutely to refer myselfe to the justice and integrity of their testimonies, without endeavouring to assure the world from myselfe of my owne innocencie, though I dowbt not, whensoever it shall please the King to call me to publique triall (which I am promised will be speedily), I shall be able to make that appeare with as much clearnes to the whole world, as I now find in the private satisfaction of my owne conscience. But, since some persons have interested themselves in my justificacion, I conceive myselfe obliged to satisfy their desires in this generall accompt. For the present, I must in the first place rejoyce with them that the malice it selfe of my accusors can suggest nothing of practice against me. The height of my pretended offences (were they confessed by me or proved by them) reacheth noe farther then words, though of such nature as are as disagreable to my loyalty and duty, as they were alwayes distant either from my intentions or expressions. Till my adversaries find out a way to make good as well as to accuse, I must require from the justice of all persons (since my here in all points fully contradicted these pretended accusacions) a suspension of judgment, and desire they would not put the forged suggestions of mine enemyes in equall ballance to the endeavors of my whole life, and often hazard of it, which, if his

Majestie had thought fitt, he might have found would have bene still continued in as full and faithfull a degree in his Majesties service as ever. The truth is, my affections have alwayes enclyned to peace, but (I take God to witnes) such a one as might have agreed with the honour of the King and the happines of the countrey. And though my intentions are not to recriminate, yet, in order to mine owne justificacion and acquitement, I must take leave to say, I doe more then feare that it agreeth not with the inclinacion of some persons so fully as I could wish, which I take to be the principall cause of my present condicion. But I have onely undertaken to cleare myselfe; may each man's particular faults light on his owne head! Whosoever shall abstract the substance from the copiousnes and subtill aggravacoins of language, I am confident will find, whatever dresse they may be able to putt upon it, the groundworke of their accusacions to bee cleerely nothing but a too violent expressing mine inclinacion unto Peace. Whether I have ever sought further then my allegiance and duty to his Majestie allowed of, or my obligacion to my countrey might exact from me, I must refer to my publique answere. In the meane time, I desire and doubt not that all good men will be satisfied with this profession and protestacion:—

That I never had a private treaty, nor ever spake anything to the prejudice of the publique cause. That if there could be a meane found out to reconcele the just interest of the King and Kingdome, such as might become an honest and well affected man to appeare in, I am sure I should be very forward to engage all myne assistance, and shall thinke it an action I may very well justifie to God, my King, and all honest men; In which resolucion I meane to live and dye.

Munday, 1° Octobris. The King left Chard and kepte the roade; dyned at the Lord Paulet's, and went that night to South Porret [Perrott], the first parish in Dorsetshire, leaving Crewkerne two myles short of it, a little on the left hand.

HINTON ST. GEORGE Church, com. Somerset.

East window, chancel:

Sable, three swords, the points conjoined in base, argent [POULET.] STAFFORD, BISHOP of BATH and WELLS.

Argent, on a fess azure, between in chief three buck's heads caboshed or and in base as many fleurs-de-lis sable, a mitre or.

Azure, on a chief argent a demi-lion rampant gules, "ST. GEORGE" [an error—DENEBAND].

South window, chancel:

POULET; impaling, quarterly, 1 and 4, Argent, a chevron gules between three [? trefoils] erased vert; 2 and 3, Per fess gules and azure, three crescents argent [AUMERELL].

Quarterly, 1 and 4, probably POULET; 2 and 3, Gules, a pair of wings conjoined ermine [RAYNEY]; impaling, quarterly, 1 and 4, DENEBAND; 2 and 3, Argent, three chevrons sable, the upper one charged with an annulet [ARCEDECKNE].

South yle church these:

Quarterly, POULET and RAYNEY; impaling, quarterly, 1 and 4, Gules, a cross flory or [LATIMER]; 2 and 3, Gules, a wyvern argent, "BRENT."

Quarterly, 1, POULET; 2, AUMERELL; 3, DENEBAND; 4, ARCEDECKNE; 5, RAYNEY; 6, "gone;" 7, LATIMER; 8, "gone." [Confused.]

West window, south yle church:

DENEBAND.

POULET; impaling, Argent, on a chief gules two mullets or [ST. JOHN].

POULET; impaling, Argent, a pair of glasier's nippers in saltire sable, between four "pears" or [KELLOWAY].

West window in the church, the same.

East window, north yle chancel, old:

DENEBAND; impaling, Gules, a cross flory or, charged with four escallops sable [LATIMER].

DENEBAND; impaling "BRENT."

The same; impaling, Or, three eagles displayed vert [? for RODNEY.]

North window, north chappel, old:

POULET.

RAYNEY.

Quarterly, 1, PAULET; 2, RAYNEY; 3, AUMERELL; 4, A chevron gules, between three trefoils [? garbs] vert [Bosco].[a]

POULET; impaling, Azure, six mascles, three and three, argent, "not conjoyned."

POULET; impaling Bosco.

POULET; impaling DENEBAND.

[a] For the quarterings of Poulet see Fun. Cert. I. 31, f. 23, Coll. Arm.

Quarterly, 1, DENEBAND ; 2, "gone ;" 3, LATIMER ; 4, Or, three eagles displayed vert [? for RODNEY].

Argent, on a bend sable three roses of the field ; impaling POULET.

Argent, three escallops, chevron-wise, vert, between two chevrons sable ; impaling POULET.

Or, on a cross azure, voided of the field, four fleurs-de-lis or ; impaling POULET.

Betwene the body of the church and the north yle stands an altar tombe ; upon that lyes the statue of a knight in compleate armour, neare the fashion of the Black Prince. A lyon at his feet.

Under his head lyes a helmet with this creast :

Rude sketch of a portion of a recumbent knight, his head resting upon his helmet, surmounted by the crest, viz. a demi-lion rampant gules, issuing from a plume—"like feathers." [Crest of DENEBAND.]

The inscription was written rownd about on the verge in black letters, some words remayning.

Upon shields at the west end, one and two, south side, are painted these coates, worne off :

DENEBAND.
The same, impaling BRENT.
(Blank) an impaled coat, "seates cover it."

In the north chappell lyes a blew flat stone with five shields, all gone, as also the brasse letters, which were in old caracters round about :

YCI : GIST : AnesTEISE : ÐE : SAINT : QVENTIN :
Fille : SIRE : IOÞAN : MVTRAVERS : feme :
ÞERBERD : DE : SEYNT : QVENTYN : PRIES :
PVR : LI : KE : DV : DE [s'] AlmE : EYT : MERCY : ⊠

Sketch of a flat tombstone, having a small blank escocheon at each corner, and another near the centre.

Against and within the north wall, north chappel, lyes the statues of a knight in compleate armour and a lady ; this atcheivement carved over them, and two playne coates of the Poulets at the side :

POULET impaling KELLOWAY.

The coat and crest of POULET with supporters, a "wild man" and a "wild woman." Motto, GARDES LA FOY.

Hic jacet Amisius Poulet Miles, qui obiit decimo die Apr. 1537.

This is cutt in these letters over the statues.

Another joyning to the former, of playne white stone, the statues of a man and woman, he in compleate armour. The same atcheve-ment and the same fashion. These two on the side:

POULET.

POULET, impaling, quarterly, 1 and 4, A chevron between three escallops [POLLARD]; 2 and 3, A chevron between three mullets pierced.

Hic jacet Hugo Poulet, Miles, qui obiit sexto die Decembr. An° D .. [1570] "blotted out. 80 yeares since."

Between the chancel and this yle another monument, more costly, arched over, of white stone too, the statue of a knight, armes, and a ruffe, and gathered breeches, and a lady by him; these two coates often carved:

POULET.

Quarterly, in the 2nd and 3rd quarters a fret, over all a fess [NORREYS].

The statues of four sons:

Joh'es P. filius et heres; Amos [sc. Amias] P. filius 2^{dus}; Henr. P. filius 3; Tho. P. f. 4, obijt 14 July, 1611. Phillipus P. f. quintus.[a]

This inscription also north side:

Hic jacet Antonius Poulet, Miles, et Dux Insulæ Jersey, qui ob. 22 July, 1600.

This coate also carved on the north side over the statue of him :

POULET, quartering 1, REYNEY; 2, six fusils conjoined, three and three ; 3, Barry of ten, over all a bend; 4, a chevron between three garbs ; 5, DENEBAND; 6, Three lions passant, a label of three points ; 7, a fess between three cinquefoils.

"Creast as before, sans supp."

---

[a] Collins gives only two sons.

This coate next side to the chancel over her picture :

> POULET, with the previous quarterings, and for ninth, on a bend three trefoils slipped [HERVEY]; impaling, a coat prepared for sixteen quarterings, only two of which are given: viz. 1, NORREYS, and 16, three cinquefoils.
> Two crests, viz. POULET and NORREYS.

> Hic jacet D'na Katherina Poulet, uxor Antonij P. Militis, filia unica D'ni Norreis Baronis de Rycot, quæ obijt 24 die Martij, 1601.

The statues of 5 daughters :

> Elizabeth filia, Anna 2, Margeria 3, Susanna 4, Margarita 5. [a]

Round a grey flat stone in black letters, chancel:

> Hic jacet Amos [? Amias] Poulet, Miles, filius 2ndus.
> Antonij P. Militis, qui obijt 1° die Maij, A°.D. 1626.

A small neate monument against the east wall, south yle, chancel, the pictures of a man and five sons in brasse, a woman and five daughters; theire names written over their heads. Colors and the inscription in alablaster. This coate and Latine verses :

> Argent, two bars gules, the upper one charged with a crescent [MARTYN].

> Adamus et Elizabetha Martyn. About thirty years since.

This is now the seate of the Lord Poulet.

Munday. The King lay this night at Mr. Gibbs his howse, the manor of South Barret [Perrott], com. Dorset. The troope that night 6 myles off, at Overshott [EVERSHOTT].

These coates are old in the hall window, where the King lay at Mr. Gibbs :

> Gules, four fusils conjoined in fess argent [DAUBENEY].
> DAUBENEY; impaling, quarterly, 1 and 4, ARUNDEL; 2 and 3, SCROPE.

Tuesday, 2° October. Most of this day was spent at the generall rendesvous on Newton-Downe, neare where the King lay, being

---

[a] Collins gives only two daughters.

Mayden Newton. The troope at Kingcome [Kencombe], &c. This day Prince Rupert came to his Majestie from Bristoll.

Wednesday. The King, &c. marched to Sherborne, and lay at Sherborne Lodge, the brave seate of the Earle of Bristoll.

The troope at [Lewston] the faire seate of Mrs. Fitz-James: her son with the rebells [Sir John Fitz-James, ob. 1670]. In the dyning-roome wyndowes these, newly sett up:

Azure, a dolphin embowed argent [FITZ-JAMES].

FITZ-JAMES; impaling, Sable, three palets argent [meant for TRENCHARD]. The same; impaling [? TRENCHARD].

Quarterly, 1 and 4, [? TRENCHARD]; 2, Ermine, a dexter arm embowed, habited gules, holding in the hand a fleur-de-lis [MOHUN]; 3, Semée of cross-crosslets, a lion rampant or.

Gules, three battle-axes erect argent [LEWSTON]; impaling, Argent, a bend engrailed gules [COLEPEPER].

FITZ-JAMES; impaling, COLEPEPER.

Quarterly, 1 and 4, FITZ-JAMES; 2 Sable, a cross flory between twelve billets, 4, 2, 2, and 4, or; 3, Argent, a cross engrailed sable.

FITZ-JAMES; impaling, Per pale gules and azure, a lion rampant argent holding a tree eradicated vert [WINSTON].[a]

SHERBORNE Church.

In the south low windowes of the chancel yle:

Azure, three crowns or.

Quarterly, FRANCE and ENGLAND.

ENGLAND.

Azure, three crowns or.

2 window:

Argent, three hurts each charged with a like number of chevrons gules, "CARRANT."

Or, three fusils in fess gules.

Or, a chevron gules within a bordure engrailed sable [STAFFORD].

Barry wavy argent and azure [SAMPFORD or BRUNING].

---

[a] Eight other shields of arms as then existing "in Mr. Lewston's house" are given Harl. MS. 1427, fol. 43 b.

3 window :

> Gules, three lions passant argent, debruised by a bend azure ; impaling,
> Sable, fretty or [MALTRAVERS].
> Same as dexter of last shield.
> MALTRAVERS.

These in the south windowes aloft, south side, chancel :

> STAFFORD, within a bordure engrailed sable.
> Gules, a cross flory or.
> Gules, a saltire argent [NEVILLE].
> Azure, a cross flory within an orle of martlets or.
> Gules, a chevron vert between three roses argent.
> CARRANT.

3 window :

> Azure, three pair of keys indorsed the bows interlaced or [ABBEY OF
> ABBOTSBURY].
> STAFFORD, within a bordure engrailed sable.
> Argent, a " Cornish chough " displayed sable, armed gules.
> The dexter coat "gone ;" impaling, Argent, five birds sable.
> Argent, a chevron per pale gules and azure, in chief two annulets sable.

North side windows aloft, chancel, these :

1 window :

> STAFFORD.
> ENGLAND, within a bordure azure, charged with fleurs-de-lis or.
> Quarterly, FRANCE and ENGLAND, within a bordure argent.
> Quarterly, FRANCE and ENGLAND.
> STAFFORD, within a bordure engrailed sable, a crescent for difference.
> The same coat without the crescent.

2 window :

> The same.
> Quarterly, 1 and 4, quarterly, 1 and 4, Gules, three fusils in fess argent
> [DAUBENEY] ; 2 and 3, a lion rampant vert ; 2 and 3, a saltire argent, a
> label of three points [NEVILLE].
> STAFFORD.
> Quarterly, FRANCE and ENGLAND, within a bordure gobony argent and
> azure [BEAUFORT].

Azure, an ostrich argent, within a bordure ermine.

Argent, on a bend azure three mullets of the field.

CARRANT.

(Blank.)

3 window:

STOURTON.

Sable, an orle of mullets argent.

STAFFORD.

Or, three lions passant in pale sable [CAREW].

Sable, two bars argent, in chief three plates.

Barry of six ermine and gules, a chief or.

Azure, a chevron between three cross-crosslets or, within a bordure engrailed of the last.

Or, three bends azure.

STAFFORD.

South window, south yle, west end:

STAFFORD.

Gules, an inescotcheon within an orle of martlets argent [CHIDIOCK].

Argent, on a bend azure three garbs or.

CARRANT.

These following are in the south window, aloft, in the body of the church, older then the former:

1 window next the east end:

Quarterly, FRANCE and ENGLAND, within a bordure gobony argent and gules.

Quarterly, FRANCE and ENGLAND, a label of three points argent.

The same, without a label.

The same, within a bordure gobony azure and ermine.

The same, within a bordure argent.

Gules, four fusils conjoined in fess argent [? intended for DINHAM].

Quarterly, 1 and 4, quarterly, 1 and 4, A cross sable between four water-bougets "BOURCHIER"; 2 and 3, A fess between seven billets, 4 above and 3 below [HANKFORD]; 2 and 3, Quarterly per fess indented argent and gules, "FITZWARREN."

Quarterly, 1 quarterly, 1 and 4, Sable, a cross or; 2 and 3, Argent, a cross potent sable ; 2, Gules, a cross flory or ; 3, Sable, a fess indented ; 4, Sable, a chevron gules [the two last very indistinct].

Quarterly, 1 and 4, Gules, four lozenges conjoined in fess argent [should be ermine, for DINHAM] ; 2 and 3, Gules, three arches argent [ARCHES].

2 window :

Or, three bends azure within a bordure engrailed gules.

Gules, a cross flory or, charged with five escallops sable.

POULET.

Quarterly, 1 and 4, Sable, a cross engrailed or; 2 and 3, Gules, a cross moline argent.

Azure, a chevron between three garbs or [? HALTON].

Gules, three buck's heads caboshed or.

" CARRANT."

Gules, on a bend argent three escallops sable.

Sable, two lions passant in pale, paly of six argent and gules, " STRANG-WAYES."

3 window :

STOURTON.

Azure, a dolphin embowed argent between three mullets gules.

Azure, three horse's heads bridled or [HORSEY].

Sable, semée of cross-crosslets, a lion rampant argent [LONG].

Ermine, a cross flory gules.

Ermine, on a fess gules three bezants.

4 window :

Argent, a fess dancetty sable and vert, within a bordure engrailed sable.

Vair, on a chief or three mullets gules.

Argent, three lion's heads erased gules.

West window :

Argent, a chevron per pale gules and azure, in chief two hurts.

Gules, a pair of wings in lure argent, over all a bend sinister azure.

North windowes aloft, body of the church, older than the last : 1 window beginning west end :

Argent, on a chevron between three eagle's heads erased sable three [? acorns] slipped or.

Azure, three covered cups gules.

Per fess indented azure and or.

Ermine, a bend engrailed gules.

2 window :

Or, a cross engrailed vert.   Another shield " old and gone."

3 window, all old :

Sable, three [? dovecotes] argent.

Or, a bend sable between six martlets.

Gules, two crescents or, a canton ermine.

Quarterly, 1 and 4, Argent, a lion rampant or ; 2 and 3, Vert *(blank)*.

SEE OF SALISBURY ; impaling, Argent, a chevron between three martlets sable [HENRY DEANE, BISHOP OF SALISBURY].

Per fess sable and argent, a pale counterchanged, three " greyhound's heads " erased.

Or, three lions passant in pale sable "old" [CAREW].

COURTENAY, with a label of three points azure.

Quarterly, 1 and 4, SCROPE ; 2 and 3, ARUNDEL.

Barry of six ermine and gules [HUSSEY].

4 window :

Gules, two keys indorsed in bend or, saltire-wise with a sword, point upwards, argent [? for the SEE OF EXETER].

Sable, a cross engrailed or between four "lillies" argent [ABBEY OF CERNE].

Arms of EDWARD THE CONFESSOR.

Vert, a cross flory argent [ABBEY OF GLASTONBURY].

Gules, on the dexter quarter a crosier or, over all a cross argent [ABBEY OF SHERBORNE].

Paly of eight or and gules [ABBEY OF BINDON].

Azure, a bugle-horn argent between three crowns or.

SEE OF EXETER.

ABBEY OF ABBOTSBURY.

Sable, three baskets argent, laden with loaves of bread or [ABBEY OF MILTON].

5 window :

SEE OF EXETER.

Gules, a pall argent, thereon three cross-crosslets fitchy and one in chief.

SEE OF CANTERBURY.

SEE OF EXETER.

Azure, three lures argent.

These are carved in stone and held by angels, north side quier :

On a bend three escallops.
A chevron between three garbs.
On a cross five roses [SEE OF St. DAVID'S].
SEE OF CANTERBURY; impaling, Quarterly ermine and argent, in second
    and third quarters a goat's head erased [ARCHBISHOP MORTON].
ABBEY OF SHERBORNE.
Three " baskets " [? ABBEY OF MILTON].
A wyvern, in chief the text letters 𝕲. [? 𝕮.] 𝕷.
A cross between four lilies [ABBEY OF CERNE].

North side of the crosse yle standes a monument arched, and the
statues of two knights in armor :

I. H.   E. H.
1546.   1564.

Quarterly, 1 and 4, three horse's heads [HORSEY]; 2, a chevron between
    three cross-crosslets fitchy within a bordure engrailed [TURGIS]; 3,
    three bars wavy, over all a saltire [MAWBANK].
HORSEY.
HORSEY, impaling MAWBANK.
The same, impaling TURGIS.
The same; impaling, on a chevron between three lozenges as many fleurs-
    de-lis [MAUDLIN].
The same ; impaling, a chevron between three roses [PHELIPS].

Upon the wall yet remaines divers yrons whereon pennons were.
Another old escocheon still remaynes :

A quarterly shield *blank*.

In the south yle of the church stands a faire arched monument, a
man and woman, sans inscription, called Fitz-James his yle :

Three battle-axes erect [LEWSTON].
The same ; impaling, a bend engrailed.
Quarterly, 1 and 4, FITZ-JAMES; 2, a cross-flory between fourteen
    billets ; 3, a cross engrailed [? sable], in the first quarter an eagle
    displayed.

For Leueson of Leueson, where Mrs. Fitz-James lives.
Another small one there :

Argent, a chevron between three chess-rooks ermine ; impaling, Per pale gules and azure, a lion rampant argent holding a tree eradicated vert, WINSTON.

Jane Walcott, late wife of John W. of Castletowne, com. Dorset, Esq. eldest daughter of Sir Henry Winston, of Standish, com. Gloucester, Knight, and one of the coheirs to her brother Hen. Winston, Esq.: ob. July 24, 1630.

In the south wall of this chappel lyes an ancient marble statue of a man.

Upon a frame:

Quarterly, 1 and 4, Azure, three horse's heads couped, bridled or, HORSEY; 2, Azure, a chevron between three cross-crosslets fitchy, within a bordure engrailed or, TURGIS; 3 [Barry wavy argent and gules], a saltire or [MALBANK]; impaling, quarterly, 1 [HOWARD OF BINDON]; 2 [BROTHERTON]; 3 [WARREN]; 4 [MOWBRAY]; 5, a lion rampant [MARNEY]; 6, a saltire [SERGEAUX]; 7, two bars.

A flat stone in the middle of the crosst yle:

These dead bones shall live.

No other inscription.

A pair of wings in lure, on a chief three martlets. [SEYMOUR of Hanford.]

Divers flat stones with inscriptions round about cutt in them; few or none of note; all new.

At the east end is an addicion of building, wheron, on the south wall, these following are carved in stone:

Quarterly, FRANCE and ENGLAND, the shield surmounted by a crown; Supporters, dexter a lion crowned, sinister a dragon.
Three horse's heads couped, bridled, "HORSEY," 1561.
Three battle-axes erect, "LEVESON," [sc. LEWSTON,] 1561.
A mill-rind between nine escallops, 1561.

Neare the east end of this church stands a schoole-howse built by King Edward 6th.

Behind this, large, on the north side stand the remnants of an antient abbey.

In Sherborne Lodge dyning roome this:

> Quarterly, 1, Sable, six martlets argent, ARUNDELL; 2, quarterly, 1 and 4,
> DINHAM; 2 and 3, ARCHES; 3, CHIDIOCK; 4, SCROPE.

This is carved in stone upon part of the building of the abbey:

> "ABBEY ARMS OF SHERBORNE."

Neare this stands the hall and part of the building of a priory also.
And when these were ruyned, the coates which adorned them
were removed into the church which stands there now, *ante.*

In the towne is a faire almeshowse of free stone, built (sayth the
old schoolmaster) by Morton, Bishop of Canterbury.

King Edward 4. gave the priory of Sherborne to Queen's College in Oxon. Vide Tab. Universitatis Oxon.

This coate is often in Sherborne Lodge, with many quarterings:

> Gules, a bend lozengy argent. Supporters, two "tigers" or [RALEIGH].

This also in the dyning roome windowes, Grenvil, Dawbney [a
mistake for Dinham], and divers others, coates of gentlemen of
this county, as Fitzjames, Horsey, Seymour:

> Gules, three rests or, GRENVIL.
> Erased, but quarterly, DINHAM, ARCHES, CHIDIOCK, and SCROPE.

Tuesday, 8th October. The King marched from Sherborne and lay
that night at Stawbridge [Stalbridge], the faire howse of the Earle
of Corke, formerly belonging to Awdley Lord Castlehaven. The
north yle of this church is full of old coates. Wee returned to our
quarters.

In the parish of Foake [Folke] an old seate belonging to the family
of Fantleroy; in the howse is many old matches in the windowes:

> Gules, three "children's heads" couped at the shoulders argent, crined or
> [FAUNTLEROY].
> The same; impaling, Barry of eight argent and gules, on a canton argent
> a bend lozengy gules [FROME].
> Gyronny of eight argent and gules, impaling FROME.
> Vair, a canton gules [FILLOLL or FILLIOL].
> The same; impaling, Gyronny of eight, &c.

FAUNTLEROY; with a double impalement, 1, Gules, a chevron between three roses argent [PHELIPS]; 2, Gules, three buck's heads caboshed or.

Wednesday, October 9. Foake Church is newly built; *stetit* 400*l.* no ant. [*sc.* antiquities] in it.

STOURTON CAUNDLE Church, com. Dorset.

A castle neare this church called Stourton Castle.

East window south yle, old:

Gules, three covered cups argent [ARGENTINE].
Quarterly per fess indented ermine and gules.

A monument of alablaster of a woman in the chancel, the body cutt out, old.

South window:

FAUNTLEROY; with in chief a "capp" sable.

North window, church:

Per fess embattled gules and argent, in chief two plates.
CHIDIOCK.

An old monument within the north wall of the chancel, arched; these two coates carved and painted at top:

" Gone."
Three covered cups [ARGENTINE].

From thence to Sturmister Newton, where on the south side of the river stands an old castle, called Sturmister [Stourminster] Newton Castle, the ancient seate of the family of Sturmy.[a]

Argent, three demi-lions rampant gules [STURMY or ESTURMY].
" Quartered by the Marquis of Hertford."

Stourton is not far distant, the seate of the Baron Stourton and the head of the river Stour, from whence the family beares six wells or fountaynes.

About a myle north-west of Sturmister Newton stands Marnehill [Marnhull], a faire place belonging formerly to the Lord Howard, Baron of Nott.[b]; now Williams, goldsmyth [of] London, owes it.

---

[a] This is an error.　　　[b] An error ; Viscount Howard of Bindon, co. Dorset.

This night the Prince Maurice's army lay at Sturmister Newton, the King's regiment of horse-guards at Dorison [Durweston].

His Majestie returned to Stawbridge, his old quarters.

Lord Generall broke his sholder. This day the King's horse-guard regiment lay at D. [Durweston].

Thursday, 10th October. This day the rendesvous was upon Dorison downe.

The court was at Mr. Rogers his howse in Braynston [Bryanstone].

BLANDFORD Church, com. Dorset.

Against the south wall of the chancel yle stands a small marble monument, altar and old arch, in which is the picture [a brass] of a woman; this inscription and these coates in brasse:

> Quarterly, 1 and 4, three buck's heads couped, DELALYNDE; 2 and 3, three herrings hauriant in fess [HERYNG].
>
> A kneeling figure of a woman habited in a long robe, the dexter sleeve emblazoned with the preceding shield, the sinister with that which follows.
>
> 1, A chevron between three annulets, GORING; 2, On a chief indented three mullets; 3, On a chief three roundles [CAMOYS]; 4, On a bend cotised three lions rampant [BROWNE]; 5, Barry of six, and on a canton [a leopard's face, RADMYLE]; impaling, 1 and 4, a chevron ermine between three martlets; 2, three pelicans; 3, fretty.
>
> Anne Delalynde, daughter to Sr William Goringe late of Burton in the County of Sussex, Kt. one of the privie chamber to King Edward the Sixte, and late wife to Sr George Delalynde late of Vointherbornboston [Winterborne Clenston] in the County of Dorsett, Knight, afterward wife to Mr. Francis Browne, Esq. brother to the right hoble Viscount Mountague: died the xxth of May 1563, and lyeth here intombed.[a]

This over her picture. This under her:

> This tombe was woollye finished at the private cost and charges of George Goring of Ovingdene in the county of Sussex, brother to the said Dame Ann Delalynde, the VI. day of October, 1564.

Betweene the pillars of the south yle of the chancel stands a playne altar tombe of marble; on the top is the picture of a man in armor

---

[a] Hutchins notices these inscriptions as having been copied by Symonds, but does not give the arms.

of our moderne fashion, and a woman ; picture of sixteen sons and four daughters.

This coate inlayed in brasse, west end:

> Quarterly, 1 and 4, [Argent, a mullet sable,] on a chief a fleur-de-lis, ROGERS ; 2 and 3, fretty, a chief; impaling, Quarterly, 1 and 4, Ermine, on a chief [vert] five bezants, WESTON ; 2 and 3, three camels.

> Here lyeth buried Sir John Rogers of Braynston, Knight, Steward of this towne of Blandford, who married Katrine, the daughter of Sir Richard Weston, Knight, and had by her sixteen sons and four daughters, which Sir John Rogers died the 22nd day of July at Beket in Berkshire,[a] at the howse of my lady Essex, and from thence brought to this towne of B. and buried under this T. 16 of Aug. 1565.

Both sides are hidden with seates.

Betweene the pillars of the chancel and the north yle stands another playne altar tombe, whereon is this inscription inlayed in brasse, and this coate only, west end :

> Argent, on a bend cotised sable three lozenges ermine, RYVES.

> Here lyeth the body of Robert Ryves, who departed this life the 11th day of February, anno 1551.

This coate is also in the north window.

A flat stone in the north yle, the pictures of a man and woman, four sons, nine daughters; this coate remayning, the inscription gone.

> RYVES.

This coate [i.e. the preceding] and this are both painted on the partition of the chamber :

> Barry nebuly of six argent and gules.

Aloft upon the south wall, south yle, chancel, is a faire monument of alablaster, well done, the statue of a man in armour kneeling, his head-piece and gauntlet lying by him, he praying.

> Gules, three covered cups argent. *Crest*, On a wreath a covered cup [ARGENTINE].

> The same ; impaling, a greyhound courant between three cornish choughs, the whole within a bordure gules, charged with twelve bezants [WILLIAMS].

---

[a] Misprinted by Hutchins " at Bed ... in Bedfordshire," vol. i. p. 135.

Here lyeth Lewes Argenton, Esq., who tooke to wife Mary the widow and sometyme wife of Robert Thornhull of Thornhull, Esq., daughter to Robert Williams of Heringston, Esq., sister to Sir John Williams of H., Knight, who died 27 June, 1611, etat. 72.

The south yle of the chancel is fairly windscotted about, and a doore in the middle into a valt. No seates in it. The windowes are lately adorned with the matches of Rogers, done in painted colours.

East window, 1629.

Quarterly, 1 and 4, ROGERS; 2 and 3, Argent, fretty sable, a chief gules; impaling STOURTON.

The same; impaling, COURTENAY, with a label of three points, each charged with three plates.

The same; impaling WESTON.

The same; impaling, Or, a bend sable between six martlets [LUTTRELL].

Quarterly, 1 and 4, quarterly, ROGERS, and Argent, fretty sable, &c.; 2, Gules, a bend between six cross-crosslets or; 3, Argent, fretty azure.

The Royal Arms with Scotland and Ireland.

1, SEYMOUR, the augmentation; 2, SEYMOUR; 3, BEAUCHAMP of Hatch; 4, Gone; 5, Argent, three demi-lions rampant gules [ESTURMY]; 6, Per bend, and three roses, also in bend, counter-changed [M'WILLIAMS]; 7, On a bend three leopard's faces [COKER]; 8, Gone, "within a garter and supporters."

Quarterly, ROGERS; and Argent, fretty sable, &c.; impaling, Ermine, two bars sable, each charged with three mullets or [HOPTON] and other coats not filled in.

The same; impaling, Argent, a fess indented counter-indented sable [WEST].

The same; impaling, Barry of six or and vert, a bend gules.

The same; impaling, Gules, a pair of wings in lure or [SEYMOUR].

The same; impaling, Argent, on a chevron sable, between three birds azure, as many escallops or [BROWNE].

The same; impaling, Ermine, on a bend sable three bezants [ST. AUBYN].

The same; impaling [STRANGWAYS].

Rogers hath a faire howse called Braynston, a parish neare the towne.

DURWESTON Church, a myle and halfe westward of Blandford.

This coate, old, in the south wall, chancel:

Within a flowering wreath or orle, Gules, three lions passant argent, debruised by a bend azure.

This quartering, old, west window, belfray:

Quarterly, 1 and 4, quarterly, 1 and 4, Or, a lion rampant azure [PERCY];
2 and 3, Gules, three fishes hauriant argent [LUCY]; 2, Quarterly, 1
and 4, Barry of six or and azure, a bend gules [POYNINGS]; 2 and 3,
Gules, three lions passant argent, debruised by a bend azure [FITZ-
PAYNE]; 3, Quarterly, 1 and 4, POYNINGS; 2 and 3, Or, three piles, the
points conjoined in base, azure [BRYAN. The whole very confused.]

North window this:

Barry of six argent and azure. [? for POYNINGS].

These are cutt in old text letters over the doore entring into the
church, south side:

Hic jacet sub tumulo Dowmō Will's humatus:
Rector erat ville Durweston, Okfordie natus.
Script' anno d'ni Mill'o cccclix.

Sir Richard Grenvil hanged the high constable and then asked
the Prince.

Sir Robert Cooke [Coke] of Ebsham owes this manor of Dorison,
and hath the guift of the parsonage.

Measure of the bushell in this county at Blandford is twenty-four
quarts to the bushell, six quarts the peck.

Friday, 11th of October. Sir Bernard Astley with 3000 foot went
to Portland against Weymouth, 18 myles from Blandford.

Also Sir Richard Grenvil with his 500 men retooke Saltash from
the Plymouthians, killed 200 of 500; they all refused quarter; the
rest (as he sent word to the King) he would hang.[a]

Two troopes came from Waller and told he was but 1,500, and
6 myles beyond Salisbury, toward Amesbury; were enterteyned by
Lord Bernard, and quartered, and the next night ran away agen.

Sunday, 13. His Majestie went to church at Blanford.

BRANSTON [Bryanston] Church, stands neare Mr. Rogers his howse;
few inhabitants besides the howsehold.

In the east window, chancel, these, pretty old:

Quarterly, ROGERS, and Argent, fretty sable, &c.; impaling STOURTON.
The same; impaling COURTENAY, with a label of three points.

---

[a] See Clarendon, who likewise admits the atrocities committed at divers times by this
man, especially in Ireland.

Against the north wall stands an altar arched monument of blew marble, nothing remaynes to tell what it was.

Against the south wall, church, the like, and under the arch in the walle is inlayed in brasse the picture of a woman; these coates; divers Latine verses, dated Martij, 1566.

> ROGERS; impaling, On a bend between six martlets a mullet for difference, " LUTTRELL."
>
> LUTTRELL.

Munday, October 14, 1644. This day his Majestie marched before the foot on foot.

Prince Maurice his army marched another way.

His Majestie left Brainston, and with his whole army marched that night over the downes to Cranborne, and lay in a faire stone howse of the Earle of Salisburies.

LA SAUCE POIGNANTE.

A ffrying pan over a quick fire ; putt into it mutton chopps or beefe, or, &c. Compound the liquor of old sharpe beere ; and some water, but more beere then water, a quantity of vinegar (wyne), a bunch tyed of parsley, tyme, rosemary, leman, orenge, 3 or 4 onyons, nutmeg, cloves, or other spice, store of salt.   Or in a pipkin.

CRANBORNE Church, com. Dorset.

Against the south wall is a large monument, the statues of a man and woman, no inscription, this coate:

> Or, on a fessazure, between three "hogs" passant, as many annulets of the first [HOOPER].

Against the north wall a larger monument, divers spaces for inscriptions, but blank; this impaled, besides divers quarterings:

> HOOPER; impaling, Argent, on a chevron between three "moores" heads proper two swords, conjoined in point, or [MORE].

For Edward Hooper's first wife, who was Serjeant More's daughter: he was the serjeant's clerke.   No gentleman.[a]

---

[a] The pedigree of this family with their arms, and going back three generations anterior to this individual, is in 1 C. 22, f. 34. Coll. Arm.—but *vide postea*.   He was a " rebel " !

This Edward Hooper, now living a rebel, no command, 7000*l.* per annum.

South window church, these four, old:

> Argent, three chevrons gules (old).
> Azure, six lioncels rampant, or, "LONGESPEE, EARL OF SARUM."
> Argent, three lozenges conjoined in fess gules, "MONTACUTE, EARL OF SARUM."
> Azure, three covered cups or.

This in the chancel east window:

> Argent, a chevron azure, between three bunches of "grapes, or mulberries," gules.

Nothing els worthy note, onely a monument of marble against the south wall [in] chancel for Hewes, Ar. [armiger], sans A. [arms.]

Lord Bernard lay this night at Knolton, at Mr. Hastings his howse called Woodlands, an antient seate with a large parke, brother to the old Earle of Huntingdon [uncle to the then Earl].

A myle from Cranborne is St. Giles parish, where Sir Anthony Astley (Ashley) Cooper baronet, that maried Lord Keeper Coventryes daughter, hath a faire brick howse. In this parish also a fair brick almshouse, built by Sir [Anthony] Astley. Ten almes men. This carved on the front: [viz. a cinquefoil ermine, the coat of ASTLEY].

Tuesday 15 October. The whole army marched to Salisbury, com. Wiltes. wett, cold, and wyndy.

SALISBURY CATHEDRALL.

Dedicated to the Virgin Mary.

The Lady chappel, being the east end beyond the quier, as at Exeter.

In the south window, not very old, supported by a greyhound, this in forme of a banner:

> A banner, the staff fixed in a mound of earth, at the foot a greyhound; Quarterly, 1 and 4, Argent, on a chief gules a bezant between two

buck's heads caboshed, attired or [POPHAM];[a] 2 and 3, Gules, a chevron argent between ten bezants [ZOUCHE].

His picture, with these on his coate, is in the next window.

Betweene the pillars of the north side of this chappel, upon an altar tombe, lyes the statue of a man in compleate chayned armour, a coat of blew painted with six golden lyons; his right hand lyes upon his right thigh, upon his left a large and long shield, the lyons embossing:

LONGESPEE.

Sir William Longspee, second son to Henry II. by Rosamond; Earl of Sarum.

Next behind him lyes the like altar tombe, upon the top the statue of a man in compleate armour like the Black Prince; upon his breast is painted:

Quarterly, 1 and 4, three lozenges conjoined in fess; 2 and 3, an eagle displayed [MONTACUTE AND MONTHERMER].

Under his head lyes a helme, and an eagle forth of it. These are carved and coloured on the north side:

MONTACUTE within a bordure sable; impaling MONTHERMER.
The same coats, quarterly.
The same coats, quarterly, but MONTACUTE within a bordure engrailed, " MONTAGUE, EARL OF SARUM."

In the middle of this chappel lyes a blew stone rising four ynches from the ground, the east end narrower than the west; this lately written: Anno M.XC.IX. For Bishop Osmond, first builder of this church.

Right over against the monuments of Longspee and Mountague stands an altar tombe of marble; on each side are three open holes in resemblance of six wells, for the Lord Stourton, who was executed (hanged) in this citty for killing the two Hurgalls, knights.[a] Sans inscription.

On the north side of this chappel is a faire chappel called Hun-

---

[a] Perhaps for Sir Stephen Popham, temp. Hen. VI.
[b] The two Hartgills, but not knights.

gerford; wherein stands a faire arched altar tombe of marble, the coate of Hungerford carved upon it; the inscription and brasse shield all stolne off.

Sable, two bars argent, in chief three plates [HUNGERFORD].

Three garbs, a chief [PEVERELL].

Upon the top lyes the statue of a man in compleate armour, a fashion different from, more antient, like a lobstar:

"Three sickles" interlaced.

The monument of the Lord Hungerford, beheaded in Queen Maries time.[a]

In the middle of the same chappel an altar tombe, the inscription and brasse shield gone. These are painted on the walls:

HUNGERFORD ; impaling, Argent, a griffin segreant gules [BOTREAUX].

HUSSEY ; impaling HUNGERFORD.

COURTENAY, impaling HUNGERFORD.

HUNGERFORD, the shield surmounted by a helmet; thereon for "creast a garbe or, two sickles argent encompassing," a "mantle gules, doubled ermine."

Under this atcheivement the picture of an angel holding this:

Consecratum erat altare istius capelle in honore dn'i n'ri Jhū Xpī, ac beatissime Virginis Marie . . . . . reverendum in Xpō patrem et dn'm [b] dn'm Will'm Sea . . . . , . dei grā istius ecclē Cathedralis Sar' Ep'm . . . . Margerie d'ne Hungerford et Botreaux q' istam capellam . . . . A.D. M.CCCCLX . . . mensis Octobr' die xiiij°.

These painted on the walls:

Argent, a griffin segreant gules [BOTREAUX]; impaling, Azure, semée of fleurs-de-lis, a lion rampant or [BEAUMONT].

Azure, three garbs argent, a chief or [PEVERELL]; impaling HUNGERFORD.

Argent, three toads erect sable [BOTREAUX][c]; impaling HUNGERFORD.

Over the door is painted the picture of a man in parliament robes; these two coates, on each side of him one:

HUNGERFORD.

Argent, a griffin segreant gules, armed azure, BOTREAUX.

[a] An error. Robert Lord Hungerford ob. 1459.

[b] The Bishop who consecrated was William Ascough, or Askew. Inf. Rev. J. E. Jackson, of Leigh Delamere, whose Hungerford Collections are most extensive and valuable.

[c] This and some of the preceding impalements with Hungerford are reversed.

Under him this writing :

Ye that understand the, &c.

And ye that purpose in this chappel to pray, call to the minde the sowle of the noble Knight Robert Lord Hungerford, which lived righteously, &c. and was servant to our blessed lady Moder to Xt Jhū, and to the noble church, which ordered this chappel to be founded perpetually. On whose soule J. have mercy. Ob. 18 May, MCCCC .. [He died 1459].

These are also painted on the walls :

HUNGERFORD, impaling PEVERELL.

Azure, a bend argent cotised or.

Gules, four lozenges conjoined in fess argent, each charged with an escallop sable [NEWMARCH].

Azure, semée of fleurs-de-lis, a lion rampant or [BEAUMONT] ; impaling, Argent, a griffin segreant gules, armed azure, BOTREAUX.

Divers other paintings on this wall still remaining, which were covered with windscott till of late; as two pictures of two sons of his, Death pictured a talking with them and telling them they must dye, &c.

On the wall also is painted St. Cristofer and the Lady Mother, very well done.

On the south side over against Hungerford's is Bishop Beauchamp's chappel.

These carved on the outside:

Three fishes naiant in pale [ROCHE].

A fess between six martlets [BEAUCHAMP].

Quarterly, 1 and 4, BEAUCHAMP; 2, two lions passant [DELAMERE] ; 3, ROCHE. The whole within a bordure charged with mitres, and surmounted by a mitre.

Over the doore this :

BEAUCHAMP within the garter, and surmounted by a mitre.

Under the first escocheon stands a monument of marble, the brasse inscription and shield all gone.

Another like monument of marble, these coates over it:

Seven mascles conjoined, 3, 3, and 1 [BRAYBROOKE].

Quarterly, 1 and 4, BEAUCHAMP ; 2 and 3, a fret, on a chief two roundles [ST. AMAND].

ST. AMAND.

In the middle of the chappel stands an altar tombe of marble, the inscription and shield gone.

Another, arched marble, the statue of a knight of the garter in compleate armor, the garter badge on his left sholder, upon a long robe.   Sir John Cheney.   [John, Lord Cheyney, ob. 1499.]

At the end of the quire without, a faire monument for Bishop John Blythe, Sarum episcopus, 1499.

On the north side of the crosse yle, above the quier, stands a playne white monument, but most curiously wrought.

Upon the north side this:

> A shield of six quarterings, viz. 1, lozengy, a chevron charged with a mullet [Gorges]; 2, on a chief three roundles [Russell]; 3, a gurges [Gorges]; 4, Newmarch; 5, a lion rampant [Oldhall]; 6, a chevron between three castles [? for Eglowese].[a]

> In hoc monumento sepultum jacet corpus Thomæ Gorges de Langford in hoc tractu Severiano, Equitis Aurati, quinti filii Edwardi Gorges de Wraxall in agro Somersetensi, Equitis Aurati, qui, post maximam vitæ partem servitio Reginæ Eliz. et Regis Jacobi beatæ memoriæ principum in sanctiore penetrali cum fidelitate impensam, resignavit animam in manus Redemptoris sui 30 die Martii, aº etat. 74. A.D. 1610.
>
> Edoardus Dominus Gorges Baro de Dundalk pientissimus filius hoc dormitorium Corporibus charissimorum parentum erexit, Aº Domini 1635.

Upon the south side this:

> The "first 6," impaling a coat of eight quarterings, very indistinct. [b]

> Hic sita sunt ossa Hellene Snachenberg, Swedanæ, quæ D'nam Ceciliam filiam Erici Regis Swethiæ in hoc regnum comitata propter venustatem pudicitiamque qua claruit grata Reginæ Elizabethæ per eam inter honorarias ministras sacræ suæ personæ intimo cubiculo attendentes ascita fuit et locata in matrimonio Gulielmo D'no Par de Kendal Marchioni Northamptoniæ, Quo sine prole mortuo nupsit Thomæ Gorges, Equiti Aurato, cui 4 filios et 3 filias peperit.   Cujus post obitum viduitate vitam egit per annos 25, quibus pie peractis excessit e vivis 1º die Apr. etat. 86, 1635.

> A shield prepared for twelve quarterings, but the first only given, viz. two bars within a bordure engrailed, "Parr;" impaling ten coats quarterly,

---

[a] See 2 C. 22, f. 364, Coll. Arm. Pedigree of Gorges.

[b] See Hoare's History of South Wiltshire, Cawden Hundred, p. 31, where are two folio engravings of this monument.

five of which only are given, viz. those mentioned in the impalement of the preceding shield. Surmounted by a coronet.

In the south side of the crosst yle above the quier stands a most stately monument as lofty as the roofe. The best worke I ever yet saw : two statues lying along, two sons kneeling.

M. S.

Edouardo Hertfordiæ Comiti, Baroni de Belcampo, &c.

Illustrissimi principis Edouardi Ducis Somersetensis Com. Hertfordiæ
    Procom. Belcampi, et Baronis de Sancto Mauro, Garteriani Ordinis
    Equestris celeberrimi Sodalis, Edouardi VI. Reg. Avunculi gubernatoris
    ejusque, Regnorum Dominiorum ac subditorum Protectoris dignissimi
    exercituumque Prefecti et locumtenentis generalis, Thesaurarii et Co-
    mitis Marescalli Angliæ, Gubernatoris et Capitanei Insularum de Garne-
    sey et Jersey, et ex Anna uxore splendidiss' orta natalibus et perantiquis
Filio et hæredi ;
Necnon conjugi suæ chariss' dilectiss :
Catharinæ

Henrici et Franciscæ Grai, D.D. Suffolc. filiæ et hæredi Caroli Brandon
    D. Suffolc. Ex Maria Hen. VIII. sorore et Galliar' Regin' dotaria
    pronepti et Hen. VII. abnepti,
Incomparabili Conjugum pari
Qui, &c.

Illa ob. 22 Jan. 1563.
Ille

Vir integerrimus, nobilitatis norma, morum ac disciplinæ priscæ conser-
    vator, &c.

Ut qui una cum Edoardo Princ. Reg. Henr. fil. in studiis adoleverat, &c.

Ad Archi. D.D. pro Jacobo Magnæ B. Reg. opt. Legatione functus, &c.

Plenus honoribus, plenus annis, octogesimum suum et tertium agens,
    anno 1621, 6° Apr. naturæ concessit.

Filios ex Heroina suscipit duos.

A shield surmounted by an Earl's coronet and prepared for thirteen quarterings, the first two only filled in ; viz. 1, SEYMOUR, the augmentation ; 2, SEYMOUR, impaling a coat prepared for eleven quarterings, the first only filled in, viz. Barry of six argent and azure, in chief three torteaux, over all a label of three points argent, each charged with three . . . . "GRAY."

ª Symonds's omissions may be found in the Description of Salisbury Cathedral, 4to. 1774, p. 70.

These matches upon two trees; the branches meete in Gray.

SEYMOUR, quarterly, impaling GREY; the shield surmounted by an earl's coronet.

SEYMOUR quarterly; impaling, quarterly, 1 and 4, Ermine; 2 and 3, Gules, [STANHOPE] the shield surmounted by an earl's coronet.

SEYMOUR; impaling, Sable, a chevron between three leopard's faces or [WENTWORTH].

The same ; impaling, Azure, a lion rampant or [DARELL].

The same; impaling, Argent, on a bend gules three leopard's faces or [COKER.]

The same; impaling, Per bend argent and gules, three "roses counterchanged" [MACWILLIAMS].

The same ; impaling, Argent, three demi-lions rampant gules [STURMY].

"GRAY," impaling, Barry of ten argent and gules, a lion rampant or, "BRANDON;" a coronet as before.

The same ; impaling, Argent, a cross pattee fitchy sable [WOTTON].

Neare this a monument for Bishop Young.[a]

North yle of the quier, a monument with a skeleton for Dr. Bennet.

Another adjoyning, an effigies cutt out lying on a matt; skeleton for Doctor Sydenham. These armes in the north window right against him :

Quarterly, 1 and 4, Argent, a bend lozengy sable [KITTISFORD] ; 2 and 3, STOURTON.

Quarterly, 1 and 4 KITTISFORD ; 2 and 3, Argent, three rams sable [SYDENHAM].

Under these this written :

Orate pro anima Magistri Georgii Sydenham, Eccl'iæ Sarum Archidiaconi, et Illustrissimi Henrici vii. et octavi Capellani.[b]

In another north window next, old :

Gules, a fess between four bars gemell argent.

Per pale indented sable and argent, a chevron gules "fretty" or.

In the north chappel a monument of marble, shield gone, the name not knowne.

South side, a chappel where Bishop Giles is buried.[c] In the south yle adjoyning to the quier wall, a monument for Bishop Capon.

---

[a] There was no bishop of the name of Young.

[b] He died 1523. His monument does not exist, nor is it given in the work before mentioned, published in 1774.

[c] Giles de Bridport, ob. 1262.

Another for Bishop Beuchamp, say they, who finished the church. These coates north side:

> "Our lady and the babe, armes of SEE OF SALISBURY."
> Honor Deo et gloria.
> Barry indented, " cutt in."
> Quarterly, FRANCE AND ENGLAND.
> EDWARD THE CONFESSOR.

A faire monument, onely thus inscribed, for Sir Richard Mompesson, Knight, and Dame Katherine his wife, on the wall of the quier south yle.

> Argent, a lion rampant sable [MOMPESSON], impaling (*blank*). " Many quarterings."

North side within the quier a faire monument for Bishop Awdley, like a chappel.

> SEE OF SALISBURY, impaling, Gules, fretty, or a fret, or [AUDLEY].

Divers shields alluding to the Passion.

> On a shield, the "seameless coat."

Upon the south pillar next the altar hanges the atcheivements of Herbert earle of Pembrooke, father to this man, buried in this quier; for the family are not buried at Wilton, where they live, but here.

Upon the south pillar next the lower steps of the altar hang the atchements, sword, and golden gauntlets of William earle of Pembroke, brother to Philip now living; buried here. None of them buried at Wilton, where this man[a] hath a faire seate.

In the middle of the quier lyes a very large flat stone, the picture of a castle very large, and a Bishop in the middle,[b] the picture of a soldier at bottome. Round about this inscription, inlayed in brasse. This shield four times:

> Quarterly, a cross between four mullets pierced [WYVILL].
> Hic jacet bone memorie Robertus Wyvill hujus eccl'e Salisburien' Ep'us qui eccl'am istam quadraginta quinque annis et amplius pacifice et laudabilit' rexit, disp'sa ejusdem eccl'ie prudenter congregavit, et congre-

---

[a] This expression, twice used, may be thus explained. He had sided with the Parliament!
[b] Engraved in Gough's Sepulchral Monuments and in Carter's Ancient Sculpture and Painting.

gata ut pastor vigilans conservavit. Int' enim alia beneficia sua innumera Castrum d'ce eccl'ie de Schirebo-rn per ducentos annos et amplius manu militari violenter occupatum eid'm eccl'ie ut pugil intrepidus recup'avit ac ip'i eccl'ie chaceam suam de la Bere restitui p'curavit. Qui quinto die Septembr' a° dn'i Mille'mo ccc^mo. lxxv^to et an'o consecr' sue 46 sicut Altissimo placuit in dc'o Castro debitum reddidit humane nature. Cujus an'e p'piciet' Ille in quo sp'avit et credidit, cuncta potens.

Another adjoyning, for bishop Juel, 1571. His picture and these coates, and divers Latine verses in one small peice of brasse:

On a chevron between three gillyflowers a maiden's head; on a chief a lure between two falcons [JEWELL].

"Our Lady." SEE OF SALISBURY.

Upon another flat stone:

Edmundus Geste Episcopus Sarum.

The SEE OF SALISBURY; impaling, a chevron between three "swan's" heads erased [BISHOP GUEST].

The picture of Goliah with a shield on his left arme. David with a sling by him.

Upon the seate coming into the quier, left hand:

Gules, "four bends or."

The cloister is on the south side of the Cathedrall, and within that goes a doore into the chapter-howse, just as at Worcester, —round.

These coates are very old and large, in one of the chapter-howse windowes:

Or, three chevrons gules [CLARE].

Or, a cross gules.

Azure, ten fleurs-de-lis, 4, 3, 2, and 1, or [? for FRANCE].

ENGLAND.

Or, an eagle displayed gules.

ENGLAND, with a label of five points azure.

Paly of eight or and gules.

Argent, a lion rampant gules within a bordure sable bezanty [? CORNWALL].

Betweene the pillars of the north side of the body of the Cathe-

drall is a place that is rayld in with yron barrs and faire woodworke
on the top; these following coates are painted in the worke.

These two goe round about on both sides *alternatim* :

> Per pale gules and vert, a sickle in bend proper, handle gules.
> HUNGERFORD, within the Garter.

South side these, on the outside:

> Or, three eagles displayed gules [RODNEY]; impaling HUNGERFORD.
>
> HUNGERFORD, with a mullet for difference; impaling, Gules, two lions passant argent [DELAMERE].
>
> HUNGERFORD; impaling, Or, a cross engrailed sable [MOHUN].
>
> HUNGERFORD, a crescent for difference; impaling [gone.]
>
> COURTENAY, with a label of three points argent; impaling HUNGERFORD.
>
> HUNGERFORD; impaling, Argent, a bend sable, a label of three points gules [St. Lo].
>
> HUNGERFORD, a label of three points; impaling, Argent, three escallops gules.
>
> HUNGERFORD; impaling, Argent, a griffin segreant gules, armed azure, BOTREAUX.
>
> HUNGERFORD; impaling, Argent, on a cross gules five escallops or [VILLIERS].
>
> HUNGERFORD; impaling, Barry of six or and gules, upon each three torteaux counterchanged, "COURTNEY."
>
> HUNGERFORD; impaling, Gules, on a chevron or three eagles displayed sable [COBHAM].
>
> HUNGERFORD; impaling, Argent, a fess or between six escallops gules.
>
> HUNGERFORD; impaling, Argent, two bars gules, in chief three torteaux [MOELS].
>
> HUNGERFORD; impaling, Or, three torteaux, over all a bend compony argent and azure [COURTENAY].
>
> HUNGERFORD; impaling, Azure, three garbs argent, a chief or, PEVERELL.
>
> HUNGERFORD; impaling, Barry of six ermine and gules, HUSSEY.
>
> HUNGERFORD; impaling, Per pale indented gules and vert, a chevron or [HEYTESBURY].

North side without:

> HUNGERFORD.
>
> Or, a bend between six martlets, sable.
>
> HUNGERFORD, a crescent for differenc .
>
> Argent, two bends wavy sable.

Quarterly, 1 and 4, SCROPE; 2 and 3, Argent, six eagles displayed, 3, 2 and 1, sable.

Or, on a chief azure three lions rampant or.

HUNGERFORD, a mullet for difference.

Argent, six roses, 3, 2 and 1, gules, seeded or.

Quarterly, 1 and 4, DELAMERE; 2 and 3, ST. JOHN.

STOURTON.

Quarterly, 1 and 4, Gules, eight lozenges in cross argent; 2 and 3, Azure, three bends argent.

Per fess gules and azure, two fleurs-de-lis in chief, and one in base, or.

Quarterly, 1 and 4, Sable, six lozenges in bend argent; 2 and 3, Argent, two bars gules, each charged with three cross-crosslets or.

Argent, three rams sable; impaling, Argent, six lozenges in bend sable.

Argent, a cross moline sable, charged with a [? mill-rind] of the field.

Ermine, on a chevron azure three buck's heads caboshed or.

Quarterly, 1 and 4, DARELL; 2 and 3, Argent, three bars gules, in chief two lions rampant of the last, CALSTON.

Azure, seven bezants, 3, 3 and 1.

These on the north side withinside:

PEVERELL.

Gules, five lozenges conjoined in fess argent, each charged with an escallop sable [CHENEY].

Or, fretty sable, on a chief of the last three bezants, ST. AMAND.

Gules, six escallops, 3, 2 and 1, argent [SCALES].

MOELS.

Quarterly, 1 and 4, MOELS; 2 and 3, Quarterly, 1 and 4, a maunche; 2 and 3 [? a hemp-break].

Quarterly, 1 and 4, Per bend argent and sable; 2 and 3, Gules, a fret or.

COURTENAY, a label of three points azure.

Gules, a cross flory vair.

Or, a lion rampant azure within a bordure azure [BURNELL].

Azure, a bend argent, cotised or, between six lioncels rampant of the last, BOHUN.

Or, a lion rampant within a bordure sable bezanty [CORNWALL].

These on the south side within:

Argent, a cross gules.

Quarterly, 1 and 4, Argent, two bars gules, each charged with three cross-crosslets or; 2 and 3, Checky or and azure, a chevron ermine [NEWBURGH].

Or, a chief indented azure.

Checky or and azure, a fess gules [CLIFFORD].

Or, a cross engrailed sable [MOHUN].

Gules, two lions passant argent, DELAMERE.

Argent, a lion rampant sable, a bordure azure, BURNELL.

Per pale indented gules and vert, a chevron or, HEYTESBURY.

Barry of six, ermine and gules, HUSSEY.

Barry of six or and gules, upon each three roundles " counterchanged."

Argent, a fess or between six escallops gules.

Argent, on a cross gules five escallops or.

Called Hungerford's chappel.[a]

Below the aforemencioned grates stands an altar tombe between the north pillars, shield and brasse all gone.

Not many flat stones now in all this cathedrall.   Some of Bishops [in the] Lady Chappell, but all the brasse gone.

The windowes in the body of the church are new glased at bottome, north side.   Written thus in most of the windowes:

Joh'is Jewell Ep'i. 1569.

South crosse yle, a monument for Robert, brother to James Earle of Carlisle, 1620.

Qui optimo Regi Jacobo Cubicularius intimus Domini gratia, &c. ad tubæ sonitum illinc resurget.

Argent, three escocheons gules [HAY] ;   *Crest*, on a wreath a falcon argent.

Sir Thomas Sadler's wife's monument, south wall, south side of the body of the cathedrall.

Checky or and sable [ST. BARBE.   She was Eleanor St. Barbe].

A small monument south crosse yle for Sir [Henry] Sandys his son :

A fess dancetty between three cross-crosslets fitchy [SANDYS].

In this faire cathedrall be as many chappels as moneths, doores as weekes, windowes as dayes, marble pillars as howres in the yeare.

---

[a] In some cases the above coats differ from those recorded by Gough in the Sepulchral Monuments.

Friday 18 October, 1644.   His Majestie, &c. left Sarum and marched toward Andevor, Waller's forces being then in Andevor. Generall Goring raysed a forlorne of horse, consisting of about 200 gentlemen that were spare commanders of horse, beate them out of Andevor, took Carr a Scot colonel, and another captain, a Scott, that died, who a little before his death rose from under the table, saying he would not dye like a dog under a table, but sate downe upon a chayre, and ymediatly dyed of his wounds.   Tooke about 80 prisoners, followed the chase of them two miles, who all ran in great confusion.   Had not night come so soone, it might have made an end of Waller's army, for our intention was to engage them, but they disapointed our hopes by their heeles.

This night the King lay at the White hart in Andevor; the whole army in the feild.

Satterday, as soone as light, the army marched after the enemy. The King lay at Whitchurch at Mr. Brookes his howse that night.

LONG PARISH Church.   Long-parish from its length.

In the middle yle a broad flat stone inlayd with brasse, and this shield with mantle, helme, and creast:

> Of your charity pray for the sowles of Richard Burley, Gent., and Agnes his wife, ob. 1541. She 1557, on whose s. I. h. m.
> Quarterly, 1 and 4, three boar's heads couped [BURLEY]; 2, a chevron engrailed [? wavy] between three cross-crosslets [BONHAM]; 3, three spears erect in fess. *Crest*, a demi-boar holding a thistle.

These Burleyes lived at the manor, and farmed it of the Lord Delaware, who lived at Horwell in this county of Hampshire.

Mr. Robert Wallop lives at Husborne Prior, a faire old howse and large parke with many ewe trees.   Sir Henry Wallop, father to Robert, bought it of Sir Robert Oxenbridge.

Regiment of horse guards lay at Long-parish Satterday night.

Sunday the whole army was marching, but they received orders to returne to their quarters.

Newes that 500 Scots were killed by the Irish in Scotland. The Scots sent five regiments from the seige of Newcastle. Crowland taken for the King. A party of the King's horse went and releived Donyngton Castle, neare Newbury.

The reason of the King's stay was for Generall Ruthin, who was behind, as also Earle of Cleveland, who was coming from the releife of Portland Castle, and a very wett forenoone.

WHIT-CHURCH Church.

Against the north wall chancel, a faire monument, the statue of a man in a barr-gowne, and a woman:

Thom. Brooke, Ar. etat. 52; ob. 13 Sep. 1612.

Susanna uxor ejus, filia natu max. Thomæ Forster Militis in parochia Hunsdon com. Hertf. [one of the Judges K.B. Mon. Insc. at Hunsdon].

Quarterly, 1 and 4, Checky, or and azure, on a bend gules a lion passant or [BROOKE]; 2 and 3, Argent, a fess embattled sable, in chief two estoils of the second [TWYNE]; impaling, Quarterly, 1 and 4, a chevron vert between three bugle-horns, sable [FORSTER]; 2, gone; 3, Argent, on a bend sable three martlets or. *Crest*, On a wreath azure and or, a demi-lion erased or.

Munday 21 October. His Majestie, &c. left Whitchurch, the generall rendesvouz upon the Downe neare Kingsmill's howse [at Sidmonton].

His Majestie lay at King's-Cleere, 7 myle from Basing; the troope at Newtowne; the head quarters of the horse at Newbery. This day the enemy, vizt. Essex, Manchester, Waller, were with all their forces, and made assault upon Basing. On Tuesday the generall rendesvouz was upon Red-heath, neare Newbery. His Majestie knighted Sir John Boys upon the hill, the Governor of Dennyngton Castle, that was so much battered, and so often sett upon by all their forces at severall times.

Sir John Boys is Leiftenant-Colonel to the Earle Rivers, who is the cheife governor.

The King lay at Mr. Duns [The Iter Carolinum says DUNCE, but ? DUNCH] his howse in Newbery; the troope at Welford, the manor belonging to Mr. Hinton *jure uxoris;* a faire habitacion, com. Berks.

Dennington or Demyston Castle, com. Berks., was the habitacion of Mr. Packer,[a] who bought it of Mr. Chamberlayne,[b] and antiently the seate of Geoffry Chaucer the poet. It was fairely adorned with tall trees, lately cut downe.

Wednesday 23 of October. This day was two yeare was Keynton fight. The armyes did not march this day.

These quarterings are often in the windowes of Dennyngton Castle :

> Quarterly, 1 and 4, Barry of ten argent and gules, over all a lion rampant or, crowned per pale gules and argent [BRANDON] ; 2 and 3, Quarterly ; 1 and 4, Azure, a cross moline or [BRUIN] ; 2 and 3, Lozengy, gules and ermine [ROKESLEY]. The whole within the garter, and surmounted by a coronet or [BRANDON, DUKE OF SUFFOLK].

As also this impaling :

> FRANCE ; impaling, quarterly FRANCE and ENGLAND ; the whole surmounted by a crown [LOUIS XII. AND MARY TUDOR].

Divers lyon's heads also, and this motto very often:

> LOIAVLTE OUBLIGE. [Crest and motto of BRANDON.]

During the often assaults and batteries of this castle, the governor lost but one man within the walls, and three that made a sallye, but killd many of the rebells. These also in the same windowes:

> A rose per pale gules and argent, crowned or, within the garter [BADGE OF HENRY VII.].
> Three bats displayed. " q. de colore."

The men within the castle were the Earle of Rivers his regiment, about 200, and 25 horse, 4 peice of cannon. The enemy made a great open battery with their hundreds of 36 pounds bullets, toto a 500 and odd bullets; most of them 36lb. some 6, some 12.

Thursday October 24. The horse army marched most part of Tuesday night, and met at the rendesvouz between Newbery and Dennyngton Castle, and about 10 of the clock all returned, both horse and foot, to their quarters. The reason was 'cause the enemy

---

[a] He was son of one of the clerks of the Privy Seal. See Vis. Berks C. 12, Coll. Arm.

[b] John Chamberlayne, married to Anne, daughter of . . . . Bushell, of Netherhaven, co. Wilts, was of Donnington Castle, 1623. *Vide* C. 18, Coll. Arm. f. 114.

had drawne into a body neare the head quarter, but retreated. The enemy moved their body toward Reading on Tuesday.

Dennington Castle hath three hundreds, out of which he [*sc.* the governor] weekely receives contribucion, viz. Kimbry [Kintbury] Eagle 20 parishes, Faire Crosse 14 parishes, and Compton hundreds 8 parishes; besides Newbery is in too. These found him beds, and weekely payment for the building the workes, which cost about 1000*l.* Faire Crosse hundred paid about 60*l.* a weeke.

KINGBURY [KINTBURY] Church, com. Berks.

In a small window, north side of the church, these four, very old, with this fashioned border [a quatrefoiled lozenge] about each:

> Argent, a bend dancetty, cotised gules, between six annulets, one within the other, three and three, of the second.
> Argent, a bend dancetty between two cotises gules.
> Purpure, a lion rampant per pale gules and or, facing the sinister side of the shield [LORTY, but reversed].
> Argent, three annulets, one within the other, gules [CHELREY].

North yle church hangs this helme and creast belonging to Sir John Darel's father, who lived at Denford, now the howse of Mr. Alexander Browne, in this parish, buried about 60 yeares since.

> Out of a ducal coronet or, a "man's head proper" affrontée [Crest OF DARELL].

Upon a flat stone, chancel, the pictures of a man and woman in brasse, these:

> Three dexter gauntlets, a crescent for difference [GUNTER.].
> Mr. John Gunter and Alice his wife, buried 2 Jan. 1624, aged 89.

He lived where Sir John Darel now lives.

Sir John Darel's estate 300*l.* per annum.

Friday 25. The rebells' whole army appeared upon the hills on the east side of Newbery, the place where the last yeares fight was.[a]

The King's army was drawne out upon the bottome between

---

[a] Query if not more south-east, viz. on Greenham Common, where, as well as on the Wash Common, the battle took place.

Newbury and Denington Castle.   Noe action all this day.   Toward night both sides fired upon one another from the hedges on their side of the river.   Wee at night retired to the passe and kept it all night; by that meanes there was shooting all night.

Satterday. They appeared more playne upon the hill and drew out some foot. Cannon on both sides played very much. They lay quiet all night, but

Sunday.   as soone as day they put over a tertia of foot over a bridge they made in the night, intending to surprize one of our guards. But that guard retreated to the next; and joyned, fell upon them, being nothing considerable in number, made their two bodyes retreat, killed some, tooke about 40 prisoners and a 100 armes: then they lay quiet till 3 afternoone, onely our cannon and theirs playd.

About 3 they approached with their mayne bodyes of foot and horse on the top of the hill towards Welford, from Newbury, where wee had a worke with 4 peice of cannon and 400 foot.   Gave hott fires, and, notwithstanding our cannon swept off many, they came on and tooke the worke [on] the hill, and some more of our cannon. This heate of fireing continued till 9 of the clock therabouts. At the same instant they made as hott an aproach on the other side upon Mr. Dolman's howse, which Colonel Lisle kept with a 1000 musqueteeres, but were beate off, with the losse of their cannon and ground, and (*blank*) prisoners.

About the same time, 4 of the clock, their bodyes of horse approached towards our field at the bottome of the hill neare the church called [Shaw], and one body came into our feild, [and] charged Sir John Campsfeld's regiment, which stood them most gallantly.   The King's regiment being neare, drove at them, which made them wheele off in confusion, and followed them in the chase, made all their bodyes of horse run in confusion, killed many, besides musqueteers that had lyned the hedges and playd upon us in the chase till wee cutt their throats.   Before these horse came up to us, while our regiment stood on the brinke of the hill, their musqueteers killed Mr. Jones, of the King's troope.

Sir John, now Colonel Campsfeild, Queen's regiment of horse, raysed in Lancashire. Leift.-Colonel Crofts. Major Sir John Campsfeild, now Colonel, knighted for Oney [Olney] buisnes, com. Northton., at [*illegible*] neare Newport Pannell.

1. Captain Jerves Clefton, (Lanc.) brought 60 men.

2. Captain George Markham, de com. Nott., raysed 70 men.

3. Captain Sherbo Franc, Queen's page, which was Captain Sir John Smyth's troope.

4. Captain Gotie Franc, 60 men.

Raysed when the Queene landed at Burlington Bay. Toto 500.

Crofts was Leift.-Colonel, Lord Jermin was Colonel, and Campsfeild Major.

Three of the Queenes troope and one of Sir Thomas Wilford's.

The Earle of Cleveland before our charge was taken prisoner, and most of his officers hurt and killed, his men beaten, being overpowered with horse and foot.

This night, after day spent an howre, his Majestie sent for his regiment and guard and went off the feild to Dennington Castle, stayd there halfe an howre, and saw the infinite shooting of musquets on both sides in all places. Not confident of the good success, marched with his regiment all that night towards Bath, and reacht it by 4 afternoone next day, made it 50 myles sans rest: being earnestly persuaded by the Generals to doe soe, notwithstanding his resolution he openly expressed to the lords that he would charge with his troope and dye with their lordships in the feild.

He was accompanied this sad night with Prince Charles, Duke of Richmond, Earls of Lindsey [and] Berkshire, Lord Capel, Earle of Newport, &c.

Tuesday, Generall Ruthyn, after he had safely brought off the army and sent them towards Wallingford, came to the King to Bath, but his lady was taken by the way.

Wednesday, 30 October, his Majestie, with Prince Rupert's horse, being about 3 or 400, 600 foot he had about Bath, and his owne regiment, marched from Bath that night to Sherston, and lay there, com. Wiltes.

Thursday to Cirencester, com. Gloucester.

Friday, 1 November, his Majestie, Prince Charles, and King's troope from Cirencester to Oxford that night, 32 myles. By the way, the King mett a messenger from Generall Gerard, that his forces consisting of above 3,000 were at hand. At this time our army was quartered at Woodstock, Witney, Burford, &c. The enemyes foot were besieging of Dennington Castle.

Satterday, 2° Novembris, the army lay still—till Tuesday.

Killed in the fight at Newbery on the King's side were Colonel Sir William Sellinger (St. Leger), Leift.-Colonel Leake, Captain Tophand of horse.

His Majesty, when he came to Oxford, knighted Colonel Gage for his good service of releiving Banbury and Basing, and Sir Peter Browne of his owne troop.

Munday night, in the presence at Christchurch, he knighted Leift.-Colonel Anthony Greene, Deputy Governor of Banbury Castle, and Captaine Charles Waldron (Walrond), both for their service in keeping that castle so long bravely against the rebells.

Tuesday, 5° Novembr. Bp. Arm. pr. ante R. at Christch. [*i. e.* Dr. Usher, bishop of Armagh, preached before the King at Christchurch].

Wednesday, a generall rendesvouz of all the King's armyes upon Shottover Greene.

This rendesvouz consisted of his Majesties owne army, Prince Maurice, Prince Rupert's, Generall Gerard's, and Colonel Sir [Henry] Gage, who commanded the Queenes regiment of foot out of Oxford, and Colonel Hawkins his regiment. Toto 15,000 horse and foot.

At his Majesties being at Oxford this time, Prince Rupert was made Leift.-Generall of all the King's armyes under Prince Charles, and the Lord Generall Ruthyn, Earl of Brainford [Brentford], was made Lord Chamberlayne to Prince Charles, Sir William Bronkard [Brounker] Vice-Chamberlayne.

His Majestie returned to Oxford on Wednesday night; the army marched on towards Wallingford. This night Lord Brainford lost most of his ledd-horses; taken by the enemy.

Thursday [Nov. 7] his Majestie marched out of Oxford and oretooke the army: all went that night to Wallingford, sans quarters.

Friday to Ilsley, com. Berks. This night also sans quarters in the feild, and sans provision this day. 15 taken there.

Satterday, before day, his Majestie marched and gott to Dennington Castle about one of the clock.

The enemy betimes in the morning drew off theire men betweene us and the Castle. About two of the clock all the King's army was drawne downe by the Castle over the river and pitcht in Batalia in the playne on the last ground wee had before, a body of horse and a body of foot rangd togeather. About 4 the enemy drew of Newbery two bodyes of horse and lyned a hedge with musqueteers, played upon our horse with their cannon as they marched up to them. And because the Queen's regiment of horse was drawne within danger of some musqueteers which they drew down below Mr. [Dolman's] howse, which Colonel Lisle last kept for us, and a body of the enemyes horse drew boldly out, the Prince Rupert commanded the Queen's regiment of horse and Prince Maurice his regiment of horse to charge them, who no sooner drew up to them but the rebells wheeled off behind their owne cannon and musqueteers, which galld that body of ours. Captain FitzMaurice killed of the Prince's regiment, and divers more killed and hurt. Their cannon playd on both sides and their musquets: little hurt on our side. A musquet bullet in volley shott the King's horse in the foot as he stood before his owne regiment in his armes.

It growing night, the whole army marched off in full bodies, drums beating and colors flying, trumpets pratling their marches, all in the face of the enemy, who followed not but with some piquering rogues. Our army drew up to the castle hill, and lay in the feild all night; the King lay in the castle.

Sunday morning, the King toke (*blank*) peices of his cannon which he left the last time in the castle. The wheeles of the cariages were then throwne downe without the pallizadoes.[a] Relieved this castle, and marched off with his whole army to Lamborne, com. [Berks], that night, 8 myles. Some of the enemy followed the reare, but Prince Rupert sett some horse in a barne and they fell behind them, the others chargd before them, killed 15, and tooke more.

King's troope quartered at Wanborough, 6 myles from Lamborne.

WANBOROUGH Church, com. Wiltes.

East window chancel these two and this inscription, old:

Per fess indented or and gules, over all a bend ermine.
Ermine, on a fess gules three martlets or, a crescent for difference.
     Orate pro dn'a . . . ia Fischere . . . .
     . . . . . ram fieri fecit, an'o d'ni M . . . .

This in the crosse north yle, old:

Argent, ten bezants, 4, 3, 2 and 1.

These two in the middle south window of the church, old:

Azure, a lion rampant or, crowned argent [DARELL].
A shield of six quarterings, viz. 1, Gules, on a bend between six cross-crosslets fitcheé argent an escutcheon charged with a demi-lion rampant or, within a tressure flory, HOWARD ; 2, [Gone, but BROTHERTON] ; 3, WARREN ; 4, MOWBRAY ; 5, Sable, a lion rampant argent, crowned or, [SEGRAVE] ; 6, Azure, a lion rampant or, within an orle of cross-crosslets fitchée [BRAOSE].

North window of the church, this old, small:

Or, a saltire argent, a label of three points sable.

This is in a peice of brasse in the wall of the steeple:

       Orate pro Thoma Polton et Editha ux'e ejus
       defunctis, Mag'ro Philippo Arch'no Gloucestrie,
       Agnete et xiiij aliis eor' lib'is, d'no Rob'to Everard
       Vicario et omnibus suis parochianis q[i] h° campa-
       nile iceperunt a° D'ni Mccccxxxv.

[a] At the side of a former page is this memorandum: " The cannon was throwne downe under Dennington castle, and the horses lost."

Upon a flat stone, south yle of the church, the two semy pictures of a man and woman, and these verses sans shields:

> Marmoreo lapide Thomas jacet hic et Editha,
>   Quem Polton vita quisque vocabat ita.
> Quos mors expulit hinc Milleno Virginis anno
> Quadringenteno deno quibus addimus octo,
> Undena luce Septembris hunc duodena;
> Hanc febrim gradiens fundas precamina plena.
> Octoque natorum natarum totque suarum
>   Collegium carum circumeundo Sarum.
> Ex obitu quorum Wanbergh curatus habebit
> Quatuor atque decem nummos quem rite tenebit,
> Post ortum matris d'ni d'nica die sequente
> Ellermis de et Halle plase Wanbergh retinente.

Neare unto Foxenbridge, in this parish, is the mote and some foundation of an ancient seate, belonging to the Lord Lovel. There close by stood the church called St. Margaret's: this church which now is called St. Andrewes, the chancel was a chappell and a steeple. The body is added since. So there are two steeples.

A playne monument of white stone. Divers verses in English.

On a bend cotised three martlets [HINTON].

Anthony Hinton, Esq. ob. 7 May, 1598, ætat. 66.

was grandfather to Mr. H. Privy Ch. to King Charles; lived in this towne.

Sir Humfrey Forster is now lord of this manor, who bought it of Sir John Darell, of Kingbury [Kintbury] by Hungerford, in whose name it was ever since Richard III.'s time, that Lovel ought it. 300*l.* per annum.

Colonel Sir Edmund Fortescue of com. Devon, neare Dartmouth, march in Sir Edward Caryes tertia of foot, Prince Maurice's army. Leift.Colonel John Valent. Bluett, com. Cornub. was first Major. So-

---

a The site of Hall Place, now the property of F. A. Carrington, Esq. may be identified by Ambrose field, where there is a tradition of a chapel attached to the mansion, said to have been dedicated to St. Ambrose.

mister was.　Major, (*blank*) Gawen, com. Wiltes.　1 Captain, William Hooper; 2 Captain, Nicholas Reynolds, Captain Leiftenant. Raysed in Devon by Sir Edmund Fortescue; at first 800, now 80. November 9.

Munday 11th of November.　The whole army rested, most part of it being in a rich countrey, the vale of White-horse, a deepe black soyle.

Tuesday, though a miserable wett windy day, the army moved over the playnes to Marlingsborough, where the King lay at the Lord Seymour's howse; the troopes to Fyfield, two myles distant, a place so full of a grey pibble stone of great bignes as is not usually seene; they breake them and build their howses of them and walls, laying mosse betweene, the inhabaitants calling them Saracens' stones, and in this parish, a myle and halfe in length, they lye so thick as you may goe upon them all the way.　They call that place the Grey-weathers, because a far off they looke like a flock of sheepe.

The difference of stones and quarries of stones in the West of England.

Dorsetshire stone is a white chalke, and quarries of the same; their churches are built of it, with low broad steeples generally; and divide the lands with it.

Somersetshire, about Martock, &c. a brave hard free stone of an umber colour; thereabouts and generally over all the countrey, the fairest churches in the West. About the northern parts a whiter free stone, very plenteous; all or most of the closes encompassed with them as a wall.

Devonshire.　The stones about Exeter are red, like the soyle; the churches in Exeter are built of it. The ordinary howses there are of the soyle mingled with straw, without posts.　Such stone and soyle as about Worcester.

Cornwall.　At Launceston, and so generally all over, a blew slate; and the doores, postes, and corneres of a hard shining stone, course, the grayne not much unlike grey marble.　About Liskerd quarries, the blew slate, very large.

FYFIELD CHURCH. Nul.

OVERTON CHURCH, a myle farther west of Fyfield. Nul. Earle of Pembroke is lord of it.

In a howse in Fifield these coates, sett up in Henry VIII.'s time:

> Quarterly, FRANCE and ENGLAND, within a wreath of roses, thereon the monogram HR, the whole surmounted by a crown.
>
> Or, a chevron azure between three roses gules.
>
> Or, on a fess azure, between three hares courant sable, three martlets argent.

Dymer sett them up and lived in this howse.

Friday, 15 November, two Welchmen of 140 were hangd at Marlingsborough for running away.

Satterday a commanded party of horse and foot marched towards (*blank*).

Friday, Prince Rupert, because the King would not give him command over the guards, did give the King his command, and asked leave to leave the kingdom. The King consented; he required a passe, and the King denyed, because he would be not seene to consent to his going. It was all quiett that day, but his highnes yeilded to the King's resolucion.

Thursday before Lord Wentworth gave up his commission of Major-Generall of the horse.

Newes that the Scotts were beaten by the Irish in Scotland.

Sunday, 17° Novembris, left Marlingsborough, and that night the King lay at Hungerford, com. Berks, seven myles, five myles short of Newbery, where the head-quarters of the enemy was. The King's troope at Chilton, a myle from Hungerford. Mr. Packer, who owes Denyngton, and was Secretary to the Duke of Buckingham, owes a pretty faire howse. A little on the left hand this dayes march, wee left Ramsbury, the faire seate of the Earle of Pembrooke. Wee marched thorough a forest belonging to the Marques of Hertford.

CHILTON FOLIOTT Church.

Upon the ground in the chancel lyes the statue of a knight in mayle armour, neck, armes, and legs, the body covered with a loose coate. Upon his left arme a shield, his right hand drawing his sword, and his right leg over the left; under his head a pillow, at his feet a lyon.

> The recumbent figure of a Knight Templar in chain mail, his feet resting upon a lion.

The traditionary relation of the inhabitants call him Foliott, called Chilton Foliott from him ante Conq. Sir Henry Foliot.[a]

The body of the church newly built, no shield or any other monuments. Popham owes the manor of Chilton.

Popham, descended of Judge Popham, owes a faire large seate, halfe a myle distant from this, the manor of Littlecott, with a parke.

RAMSBURY Church.

In the chancel lyes a flat stone, in the midst the demy picture of a preist, two shields, and the inscription is circumscribed in old French letters; darke at night, could not reade them.[b]

Another adjoining, the picture of a man in armour inlayed in brasse, two shields and the inscription circumscribed, but all the brasse is stolne.

Another, arched, of marble, and altar tombe with pictures, shields, and inscription, which were in the side inlayed, but all the brasse gone.

No shields in the windowes.

The manor is the Earle of Pembroke's, a faire square stone howse, a brave seate, though not comparable to Wilton, and a fine parke, two myles from Chilton, com. Wiltes.

Munday the army mett at a rendesvouz, and returned to their old quarters. The enemy on Munday left Newbery, and marched neare Basing.

Tuesday, 19 November, the army marched. His Majestie lay at Great Shefford in the old manor howse of Mr. Browne, Esq. com.

---

[a] Probably Sir Sampson Foliot, living temp. H. 3 and Edw. I.; see Hundred Rolls, vol. i. p. 13, &c.

[b] Symonds, from the same reason no doubt, failed to notice the chapel, now known as the Darell aisle, containing vestiges of very interesting brasses of that family, though then perhaps, like the rest, "gone."

Berks; a parke belonging to it. This day in the march a soldjer hangd for plunder, but the rope broke.

Lord B. and troope at Little Fawley, the neate and faire habitacion of the Lady Moore, wife to Sir Henry.[a] This day Colonel Gage was sent towards Basing to releive it, with 1,000 horse.

Colonel Lunsford we heard went out of Oxford with 500 horse, and drew towards Middlesex, to fetch in, &c.

Painted over the porch at Lady Moore's howse:

> Argent, a moor-cock sable [MOORE]. Motto, Regi et legi.
> The same; impaling, Argent, a saltire engrailed gules, a chief azure, "TWITTYE." Suum cuique pulchrum.

Champion all this part of Berks.

He that built this howse was Serjeant Moore, temp. D. Egerton Canc.: Sir Henry was his son, Nothing but Moore's coate in the church of Fawley.

Wednesday the King marched to Wantage, 5 myles.

Thursday to Faringdon: the King lay at Sir Robert Pye's howse neare the church. The troope lay Wednesday night at Kingston Lisle, 4 myles from Wantage. Hyde is lord of it, a faire howse.

Ego absens.

FARINGDON Church, com. Berks.

West window church:

> Quarterly, FRANCE and ENGLAND.
> Gules, on a quarter indented per pale or a rose gules.
> Sable, three bells argent.

Middle yle of the church, upon a brasse, and the picture of a man and woman :

> Hic jacet Mr. Davit Eoys, qui ob. 25 die Apr. 1408, et Alicia ux' ejus : quorum a. p. d. a.

Two stones for Vicars, chancel. [Ashmole gives one only, viz. RICHARD LENTON].

East window, north yle, chancel:

> . . . . . Draper . . . . fenestram fieri fecit, a. d. M. i. h. i. h. (1515 ?)

[a] A great portion of this mansion, not mentioned by Lysons, still exists, and is occupied as a farm-house. The arms over the porch have disappeared, as also those which were in the church.

A flat stone in the said chappel :

A bend between two Cornish choughs, a chief checky [Pleydell].

Hic jacent Tobias Playdel Ar. et Elianora vx' ejus : ob. 18 Oct. 1587.

Their pictures and escocheon cutt upon the stone, embossing, a blew stone.

A north chappel, north side of the church, is adorned with four monuments :

1. An altar tombe adjoyning to the wall; the south side hath these shields following, coloured and carved.

Upon the top lyes the statues of a man and a woman, she on the right side, he in compleate armour, the fashion of the Lord Hungerford in Sarisbury Cathedral. Upon his breast his quarterings are carved; under his head lyes this creast upon a helme :

On a wreath a "dog's head couped sable, his fore-legs erected."

Round about the verge of this all alablaster monument this inscription cutt in old text; the letters embosse out :

Here lyeth Sir Thomas Unton, Knight, and Dame Elizabeth his wife, the wych Sir Thomas departed the iiij day of August, in the yeare of our Lord God Mcccccxxxiii.: whose sowles God pardon. Amen. Nolite plangere mortem meam quia solum corpus obijt.

These 8 shields adorn the sides of this faire monument, guilt and coloured. West end these two :

Quarterly, 1 and 4, Azure, on a fess engrailed or, between three spearheads argent, a greyhound courant sable [Unton]; 2 and 3, Gules, two chevrons or [Fetyplace]; impaling, Per fess or and azure, three griffins segreant, counterchanged [? the field azure, and the charges argent.]

Quarterly, Unton and Fetyplace.

These four south side :

The last two shields alternately repeated.

These two, east end :

Quarterly, 1 and 4, Unton; 2, Fetyplace; 3, Gules [Azure], three griffins segreant or [argent]; over all a label of three points argent.

The preceding coats; impaling, Quarterly, 1 and 4; Quarterly, 1 and 4, Argent, a cross engrailed gules between four water bougets sable,

"Bourchier;" 2 and 3, Gules, a fess between thirteen billets, seven in chief and six in base, Louvaine; 2 and 3, Quarterly or and vert.

Against the same north wall stands an altar arched monument of blew marble; the side is inlayed with brasse, and fairely painted, the picture of a knight, and seven sons behind him, between two women, and four escocheons; the inscription in text:

> Here under lyeth Sir Alexander Unton, Knight, Mary[a] and Lady Cecyll his wifes, whiche Alex. decessed the xvj day of Decemb. Anno M.v^cxlvij in the first yeare of our soveraigne Lord King Edward the VI. On whose soules and all christene [soules] I. h. m. a.
>
> The kneeling figure of a man in plate armour, the hands raised in the attitude of prayer. The sleeves and body of his surcoat, are embroidered, quarterly, Unton and Fetyplace, the latter charged with a martlet in chief, and an ermine spot upon the upper chevron.
>
> The kneeling figures of two ladies, each wearing a long mantle embroidered with arms, viz. upon the right side of each, quarterly, Unton and Fetyplace, and upon the left, by the first lady, quarterly, Bourchier and Louvaine; by the other, quarterly; 1 and 4, Sable, a stag's head caboshed argent, attired or, between the horns a cross patty-fitchy of the third, through the nostrils an arrow [Bulstrode]; 2, Quarterly, i. Paly of six argent and azure, on a chief sable two knives in saltire argent [Knyfts]; ii. and iii. Ermine, a horse's barnacle gules [Wyott]; iv. Argent, five cinquefoils gules, on a canton sable an etoile within a crescent argent [Palton or Freisell]; 3, Argent, a chevron gules between three squirrels sable [Chobington].
>
> " 3 daughters behind this woman" [viz. the second; but she had issue a son also].

Over this monument hangs this fashioned sheild [a Tudor shield], an old helme, and a demy dog for a creast:

> Quarterly, Unton and Fetyplace.

These two coates behind the woman on the left hand:

> Unton and Fetyplace, impaling, quarterly, 1 and 4, "Bourchier and Louvaine, quarterly;" 2 and 3, Quarterly or and vert.
>
> Quarterly, Unton and Fetyplace.

<hr>

[a] She was the daughter and coheir of John Lord Berners.

These two behind the other woman:

Quarterly, UNTON and FETYPLACE, impaling, quarterly, BULSTRODE, &c.

Quarterly, "BOLSTRODE," &c. as before, with an inescocheon on the quarterings of KNYFFS bearing Argent, a fess dancetty gules, in chief three leopard's heads sable [PULTENAY].

Quarterly, UNTON and FETYPLACE.[a]

Upon the east wall of this chappel stands a faire and neate monument, the statues cutt in alablaster:

Here lyeth Sir Edward Unton, Knt. of the noble order of the Bathe, who married Ann Countesse of Warwick, daughter to Edward Seymer, Duke of Somerset and Protector of England, by which he had five sons, whereof three dyed younge in the life of their father; two, namely Edward and Henry, onely survived, and succeeded him, the one after the other, in their father's inheritance; and two daughters, Ann, married to Sir Valentine Knightley, Kt. and Cecyll married to John Wentworth, Esq. He died in the (*blank*) yeare of the raighne of Qu. El. Sir Henry Unton, Knight, second son, erected this monument.[b]

These sheilds upon this monument; over his head these:

UNTON impaling BULSTRODE.

A shield of six quarterings, viz. 1 and 4, UNTON; 2, FETYPLACE charged with a martlet; 3, three griffins segreant [YONGE]; 5, Gules, on a bend argent three martlets sable [DAVERS]; 6, Gules, a fess between three sinister hands, couped and erect [QUATERMAINE].

The "last 6;" impaling, 1, SEYMOUR, the augmentation; 2, SEYMOUR; 3, BEAUCHAMP; 4, ESTURMY; 5, MACWILLIAMS; 6, COKER.

Over her head these:

A shield prepared for twelve quarterings; two only are filled in: viz. 1, Or, a lion rampant azure, "DUDLEY;" and 5, HUNGERFORD; impaling SEYMOUR with the five quarterings, the whole surmounted by a ducal crown.

SEYMOUR, with its quarterings, in a lozenge-shaped shield, and surmounted by an earl's coronet.

The same; impaling, quarterly 1, Quarterly ermine and gules, STANHOPE; 2, Vert, three "dogs" [wolves] passant in pale or; 3, Sable, a bend between six cross-crosslets or; 4, Argent, three saltires sable, a crescent for difference; the shield surmounted by an earl's coronet.

[a] There is some discrepancy between these arms as given by Symonds and those drawn by Ashmole, C. 12, f. 114. Coll. Arm. See also the Unton Inventories, edited by Mr. John Gough Nichols, 1841, 4to.

[b] Sir Edward Unton's will was proved 1582.

Upon the west wall of the same chappell a very large and faire monument, two statues:

> Virtuti et honori sacrum. Henrico Untono Equiti Aurato, Edouardi Untoni Equitis Aurati filio, ex Anna Comitissa Warwici filia Edouardi de Sancto Mauro Ducis Somersetti et Angliæ Protectoris, qui optimarum artium studijs a prima etate in Academia Oxon. enutritus magnam orbis Christiani partem perlustravit ; ob virtutem bellicam in Zutpheniæ obsidione dignitate equestro donatus, propter singularem prudentiam, spectatam fidem et multiplicem rerum usum, iterum legatus a serenissima Angliæ Regina ad Christianissimum Regem missus in Galliam, e qua ad celestem patriam emigravit 23 Martij, Aº. Salutis 1596. Dorothea uxor charissima, filia clarissimi viri Thomæ Wroughton ex equestri ordine, quæ maximo cum luctu corpus huc transferendam curavit, in mutui amoris et conjugalis fidei testimonium hoc Monumentum mœstissima posuit 1606.[a]

> *Blank* for Quarterly UNTON and FETYPLACE ; impaling, quarterly, 1, a chevron between three boar's heads couped [WROUGHTON] ; 2, Argent, a chevron engrailed between three raven's heads erased sable [RAVENSCROFT] ; 3, Bendy of six or and azure, a bordure gules [MOUNTFORD] ; 4, a chevron engrailed between three unicorn's heads erased.

> " His creast," on a wreath a griffin passant sable.

> UNTON, impaling WROUGHTON.

This is painted on a frame:

> UNTON, with two impalements, 1, WROUGHTON ; 2, Paly of six or and azure, a canton ermine, an inescocheon of Ulster [SHIRLEY. She remarried Sir George Shirley, Bart.]

In all his coates besides this frame the fesse is engrayled.

Over this tombe hangs a sheild, mantle, helme, and creast.

A flat stone in this yle inlayed with brasse, the picture of a man in armor and two women. This in brasse in text (four shields, all gone):

> Orate pro animabus Thomæ Faryndone Armigeri, quondam domini de Farnham et de Lustehull, qui obiit 2do die Feb. Aº. D. M.ccclxxxxvjº. Margarie uxoris ejus, que obijt 9 die Maii, A.D. 1402, et Katherine

---

[a] The present stone (Vide Ashmole's Berks) is not the same, but restored in 1658 ; " the former," he says, " was pulled down in the Civill Wars about 1643." But it was in 1646 that the church received material injury, during the siege of the adjoining manor-house.

Pynchepole filie et heredis predictorum Thome et Margarie, que obiit xj. Dec. 1443.　Quorum animabus propicietur Deus.

> We pray you in yͤ worchip of yͤ Trinite
> For our soulys sei Pater and Ave.

In the south crosse yle two flat stones inlayed in brasse for the Parkers, covered most of them with seates:

> Jo. Parker mercator ville Calis. ob. 1480 ;

and his wyfe under another stone.

Sir Robert Pye lived in the manor howse called the Place, neare the church, a faire habitacion.

CLANFEILD Church, com. Oxon.

An altar tombe covered with marble, a brasse inlayed, sans shield, north yle chancel:

> Here lyeth buried Leonard Wilmot, Gent. who dyed at his howse in Clan-feild, 25 June, 1608, ætat. 59.

A flat stone adjoyning:

> Here lyeth the body of James Hyde, Gent., ob. 24 March, 1610.

In the chancel a flat stone:

> John Rogers of Clanfeild, ob. 20 May, 1635.

Friday his Majestie rested at Faringdon.

Satterday, Novembris 23.　His Majestie left the army in their severall quarters about Faringdon, and with his regiment of horse went that day to Oxon.　Prince Rupert with a commanded party of the King's troope, and as many out of each of the other two, and a party commanded by Sir Marmaduke Langdale, gave a strong alarme to Abingdon, then under the government of Browne the ffaggot-monger.　Skirmishing on both sides; little hurt.　They came out in four bodyes, neare 200 horse.

When the King's army was in Cornwall, the infantry was divided into three tertias, and every tertia should consist of three brigades, and thus they continued the march backe againe.

First tertia was commanded by Colonel Blague, governor of Wallingford Castle; his regiment was there at Wallingford.

Colonels:
    King's Life Guard.
    Lord Generall Ruthin's.
    Sir Jacob Astley, Major Generall.
    Colonel Sir Henry Bard.
    Duke of Yorkes.
    Sir James Penniman's.   Eldest Regiment of the army.
    Lord Percies.
    Sir Lewis Dives.

    Second tertia was commanded by Colonel George Lisle.

Colonels:
    Colonel Cha. Lloyd, Quartermaster Generall and
      Enginere Generall. (Ebor.)
    Colonel George Lisle's, which was Colonel Bolles.
    Colonel Thelwel's, Wales.
        Owen, raysd in Wales.
        Ewre, vulg. Euers.
        Blackwall, Nott.
        Gilby, raysd Ebor.
        Stradling, Wales.
        Vaughan's, Wales.

    Third tertia commanded by Sir Bernard Asteley, son to Sir Jacob.

Colonels:
Lord Hopton's Regiment.
    Colonel Apisley.
      Talbot.
      Cooke.
      Courtney, &c.

                       (Sir Ja. Penniman told me.)
    Prince Maurice his army marched by it selfe.
    Colonel Sir James Penniman's regiment of ffoot, whiche was
his cousin's Sir William P., first Lt.-Colonel to Sir William (*sic*).

George Symons, Leift.-Colonel now, was Major at first. Ebor.
Major Will. Wyvell, Ebor.

1 Captain, Richard Page, now Leift.-Colonel, Nov. 1644.

2 Captain, Fr. Lawson, Lincoln.

3 Captain, William Bridges, a scrivener in Chancery Lane, knighted at Leicester.

4 Captain, Fr. Bateson, Ebor.

5 Captain, Jo. Jackson, Ebor.

6 Captain, Anthony Norton, Ebor.

7 Captain, George Etherington, Ebor.

8 Captain, Robert Carington, Ebor.

All raysd in Yorkshire: and came with the King from Yorke.

(Told me by Sir Ja. himselfe, 29 November, 1644.)

Sunday, 8 December, 1644, Sir Charles Lloyd, Quartermaster-generall of the King's army, was knighted at Christchurch.

Tuesday, 17 December, night, at Christchurch, the King knighted Sir William Rollock, Scotus, for bringing the newes of the [Lord] Montros his victory over the Scotts in Scotland; was Leift.-Colonel to the Lord Mountros, and a minister that had received orders and officiated.

Knights Batchelors made by King Charles since October 1644.

*Sir John Boys, governor of Denington Castle, knighted upon Redd heath, neare Newbery, 22 October, 1644.

Sir Henry Gage, 1 or 2 of November, at Oxford.

Sir Peter Browne, of com. Oxon. knighted then.

*Sir Anthony Greene [a] and Captain Sir Charles Waldron, both knighted in the Privy Chamber, Oxon. 3 November.

Sir Charles Lloyd, Quartermaster-generall, knighted December 8, at Christchurch, Oxon. [Governor of Devises.]

*Sir William Rollock, (Scotus, and in orders,) 17 December, 1644, knighted for bringing the newes of the Scotts.

[a] A coat of " Greene " is here sketched : viz. Argent, on a chevron sable between three acorns slipped proper, a " granado " or.

*Sir Lewis Lewkner, Colonel.

*Sir James Croft, the pentioner.

Sir Henry Chichley, knighted 24 or 25 January, second brother to Mr. Thomas Chichley of [Wimpole], in com. Cantabr.

Sir George Bonkley [Bunckly], Leift.-Governour of Oxford, knighted in Christ Church, Oxon. Thursday, 30 January, 1644.

Sir Stephen Hawkins, whome the Earle of Dover procured to be made Leift.-Colonel of the garrison of Oxford, in roome of Sir George Bonkley, and gott knighted 31 January, 1644.

Sir Edward Walker, Garter Principal King of Armes, knighted on Sunday 9 February, 1644. (Q. if not the 2?)

28 February. Colonel Sir Thomas Dabridcourt [Dabridgecourt], sometime Leift.-governor of Marlinsbury, knighted.

Sir Charles Cottrell, Master of the Ceremonies, knighted in Christ church, Oxon., 6 March, 1644.

Sir Thomas Rives, Doctor of Law, and the King's Advocate, knighted Sunday, 16 March, 1644. (Q. if not Wed. foll.?)

1645. Upon the King's coronacion day, 27 March, 1645, Sir Richard Mauleverey [Mauleverer] was knighted in Christ church, Oxon.

Sir Robert Peake, sometime picture-seller [a] at Holborne Bridge, and Leift.-Colonel to the Marquis of Winchester, was then knighted. [Deputy-Governor of Basing House.]

Sir (*blank*) Leift. Governor of Wallingford.

*Sir William Mason.

Those Knights marked * are not recorded in the Lists of Knights, M. 5 and M. 15, Coll. Arm.

[a] The print-seller whose name is attached to many portraits and other engravings, now rare.

The Marches, Moovings, and Actions of the Royall Army, his Majesty being personally present, from his coming out of his Winter Quarter at Oxford, May 7, 1645, till the end of August following.

Thursday, April 24, 1645. Cromwell's horse and dragoons ruined some of our horse that quartered about Islip, of the Lord of Northampton's command. 21 buried in Islip. 18 men buried in (*blank*) over against Kidlington; and this day they demanded the delivery up of Bletchingdon, a howse belonging to Sir Thomas Coghill, wherin Colonel Windibanke had 200 foot, sans workes, and provision onely for two or three days. This afternoone, one [of] the Oxford troopes kept the bridge of Gossard [? Gosford]. At night came some commanded foot out of Oxford, thither; also Colonel Palmer's regiment of horse.

About two or three of the clock, Friday morning, the colonel valiantly gave up the howse and all his armes, &c., besides 50 horse that came in thither for shelter; and this without a shott.

Friday, in the afternoone, he was condemned by a councell of warr to dye; and those that were his councellors and advisers, viz., Leift.-Colonel Hutchinson, Major Earnley, Mr. Eedes, were disabled for ever bearing armes any more.

Satterday morning. Wallingford troope came to Oxford to releife the Lord of Northampton, &c. Some horse and foot came from Farringdon from Colonel Lisle's garrison, and all the horse in Oxford were to be drawne out (and many horses were this day plundered upon that pretence).

When we had drawn out and marched, newes came that the enemy was gone. We returned to our severall quarters. At seven of the clock the Queenes troope of Life Guard was beate up, and 60 horses taken, but [only] 6 men.

On Sunday the enemy pursued Lisle's men, and took and killed neare 200 of them.

This afternoone also many foot and horse were drawne out of Oxford.

Satterday 3d of May. Colonel Winnibanke was shotte to death, after he was reprived from Wednesday before.

This Satterday Cromwell's forces removed from before Farringdon, els if they had stayd Prince Rupert and Generall Goring had falne upon them; they were twice repulsed by Farringdon men, with great losse to them.

Sunday morning, May 4. Prince Rupert and Prince Maurice came to Oxford. Generall Goring came on Munday.

Wednesday May 7. His Majestie left Oxford, attended with Prince Rupert, Prince Maurice, Earl of Lindsey, Duke of Richmond, and Earl of Northampton. His troope and the Queenes lay that night at Woodstock.

Woodstock Church.

In the west window of the church four pictures kneeling, large, with the armes of France and England quarterly.

In scrolls over their heades:

1. Joh'es f. . . . . .
2. . . . Thome frat' ejus, Dux . . . . . Clarenscie.
3. Rex[a] . . .
4. Humfray frater ejus . . . .

This has a border argent about it. The rebells have lately broke the window.

> A male figure kneeling, clad in armour, and wearing a surcoat with the arms of France and England quarterly.

In the lowest window south side this coate:

> Azure, semée of fleurs-de-lis or [FRANCE].

In the middle of the chancel, upon a flat stone inlayed in brasse, an armed knight and a lady, the inscription circumscribed:

---

[a] Henry the Fifth and his three brothers, but carelessly copied.

. . . . buried the bodyes of Sir Edw. Chamberlen, Kt. that
was made Leift. of . . . . memory King Henry
the 7th, and Dame Cyceley his wife, the which . . . . . .

Four coats, and impaling several.

A shield prepared for six coats, two only of which are given : viz. 1, nine
mullets, 3, 3, and 3 [TANKERVILLE]; 2, a chevron between three escallops,
[CHAMBERLEYNE], with a blank impalement.   [See these coats, C. 29,
f. 34, Coll. Arm.]

Thursday, May 8.   This morning at one of the clock an alarme
waked us, and at daybreake the King marched with his 4 peices of
cannon, 8 boates in cariages, &c.: vizt. all manner of amunition, his
troopes of life guard and foot regiment, the Earle of Northampton's
regiment of horse, Sir Thomas Dalyson's regiment of horse, and
part of the regiment of Lifeguard in the van; amunition, &c. next,
then his Majestie, &c.   Earl of Northampton in the reare.

Neare Stow on the Would, wee joyned Prince Rupert's army of
horse and foot, eighteen myles.   The King quartered at Stow on the
Would.   This morning Generall Goring tooke forty of Cromwell's
horse prisoners, and two colonels, neare Burford, which newes
saluted us in Woodstocke Parke.   Newes that Sir Thomas Fairfax
was marched with his body to releive Taunton.   Troop at Maw-
guresbury [Mangersbury].

Mr. Chamberlayne lives here, under his grandfather Sir William Chamberlayne.   SERVIENDO GOVIERNO.

Colonel Sir Marmaduke Roydon is come to Farringdon with his
foot to be governor there.

Friday, May 9.   His Majestie marched to Evesham, where he
joyned with the Lord Asteleyes foot, consisting of 3300; in the
primeir place was Prince Rupert's regiment of foot, consisting of
500, and ten of these colours:

Pily bendy argent and sable, in dexter chief point an annulet of the last.
[A banner.]

Colonel John Russell commanding this regiment.   Major,—
Mitchell.

"Piley bendy argent and sable," in bend three annulets.

It was Colonel Lundsford's regiment (500), raysed in Somerset-shire. [This refers to the second banner.]

This day, Generall Goring marched into the West with 3,000 horse. 300 foot taken out of our garrison of Camden; the howse (which was so faire) burnt.[a]

The King's troope garrisoned at CHILD'S WICKHAM in Glouc., three myles from Evesham. In the church this onely in the east window:

Gules, a fess between six cross-crosslets or [BEAUCHAMP].

Horse. Langdale's, which wee mett at Stow, 2,500; lifeguards 800.

Foot. This day wee marched in foot; King's lifeguard 200, Colonel Lisle's foot 500, Bard's regiment 300, Prince Rupert's, which wee mett at Stow, 1,000, Lord Astleyes 3,300. Toto 5,300.

Satterday, May 10. The King quartered at Inckburrough Magna, com. Wigorn. 9 myles from Worcester.

INCKB. [INKBARROW] Church.

In the south window church, these two, old, in small:

Argent, within a bordure sable, charged with thirteen estoiles or, a saltire gules [HODINGTON].

The same; impaling, Argent, on a bend engrailed between two bendlets sable three estoiles argent [THURGRYN].

In the south yle a monument for [John] Savage, Esq. who lived in this parish [at Egeoke]: ob. 1631.

Argent, six lions rampant sable, 3, 2, and 1 [SAVAGE].

This night an out-howse, where Sir Henry Bard quartered, was burnt, and fifteen horses of his, &c.

Sunday, May 11. The King marched to the rendesvouz of the whole army of foot, &c. His Majestie, with his owne regiment of foot and horse guards onely, marched to Salt Wiche [Droitwich], com. Wigorn.

The head-quarters of the army this night is at Bromsgrove.

---

[a] Clarendon confirms the wanton burning of this house.

Garrisons in com. Wigorn. 1645.

Pro Rege: Worcester, Colonel Samuel Sandys, governor post mortem Colonel Gerard.

       Evesholme, Major Robert Legge, governor, Major of horse to Prince Maurice his regiment.

       Wiche [Droitwich], five myles from Worcester.

Pro Reb. Strensham Howse, belonging to Sir William Russell.

       Hawkesley Howse, two myles from Bromsgrove, four myles from Edgbaston.

King: Hartlebury Castle, Bishop of Worcester's howse, four myles from Wich, Sir . . Sandys, governor, but his kinsman was under him governor.

His Majestie stayed at Droitwiche till Wednesday. In this time his highnes Prince Rupert sate downe before Hawkesley howse; one Mr. Middlemore owes it; Lord Astleyes Tertia of foot made the approaches (which were left for us with a great deale of advantage to us), vizt. bankes, and a lane and trees.

Captain Backster, troop of horse, was killed here, and some foot-soldjers and pioneeres.

On Wednesday about two of the clock in the afternoone the King left Wiche and went with his guards to the leaguer before Hawkesley, and just as his Majestie appeared in view it was delivered unto the mercy of the King and the officers, and that they might be free from the insolence of the common soldjers.

In this howse was a moneth's provision and ammunition, but the soldjers would not fight when they perceived it was the King's army.

Gouge, the son to Dr. Gouge, was the captain of foote and governor, and Whichcott commanded the horse. 60 foot, and above 40 horse.

After Lord Astley had the pillage of the howse and the soldjers prisoners, the howse was sett on fyre.

This night the King lay at Cofton-hall, two myle off.

Thursday at fowre in the morning, the King and the army mett neare this howse, the workes slighting.

These colonels and governours were this night with his Majestie:

Colonel Scudamore, governour of Hereford.

Colonel Leveson, governour of Dudley Castle, com. Stafford.

Colonel Michael Woodhowse, governour of Ludlow.

Colonel Leveson's regiment of horse had these three cornetts, belonging to Dudley Castle:

> Sable, an ostrich or, holding in its mouth a sword proper, and standing on a scroll with the motto Hoc NUTRIOR.
>
> Vert, with a charge somewhat like a sun in splendor.
>
> A scroll with the letters SA.—SA.

Earl of Shrewsburyes howse, called Grafton, is within a myle of Bromsgrove, com. Wigorn.

The troopes of life-guard quartered this night at (*blank*).

Wee marched from four in the morning till six, sans rest.

This night the King lay at Homley [Himley] hall, com. Stafford, where now the Lord Ward lives, who is son to Ward sometyme goldsmyth [in] London, which son married the Lady Dudley; an old howse moted.

In the church of Hombley [HIMLEY], this is circumscribed on a flat stone, with the pictures of two women:

> Hic jacet Willelmus Suttonn et Constantia soror ejusdem filia p'nobilissimi Domini Edwardi Sutoon Militis, Domini Dudley et Powes, qui quidem Wilhelmus obijt 22° Dec. 1504. Constancia v°. 15 Marcii, 1501. Quorum A.

This coate:

> Quarterly, 1 and 4, quarterly 1 and 4, two lions passant [SOMERY] ; 2 and 3, a cross flory, SUTTON ; 2 and 3, quarterly 1 and 4, a lion rampant [? gules, for SUTTON] ; 2 and 3, a saltire engrailed.

Friday May 16, 1645. The rendesvouz was neare the King's quarters, began after four of the clock in the morning here; one soldjer was hangd for mutiny.

The Prince his head-quarter was at Wulverhampton, a handsome towne, one fayre church in it.

The King lay at Bisbury [Bushbury], a private sweete village, where Squire Gravenor (as they call him) lives ; which name hath continued here 120 yeares: before him lived Bisbury of Bisbury.

In Bisbury church, com. Stafford, in the south yle or chappel of the church belonging to the manor-howse, these, old, in glasse:

> Argent, on a fess cotised sable three escallops of the field [Bushbury].

These two pictures and subscription are in the east window of this chappel:

> Two kneeling figures of an armed knight and his wife ; the surcoat of the knight, which is marked argent, is embroidered with the arms just described. The armour is gilt, the ornaments of the "girdle" around the waist are marked azure. The robe of the lady has also the same arms embroidered upon it.

> Under him, HENRY DE BUSCHEBURY ; under her, [AMY]CE SA FEMME.[a]

Some flat stones in this chancel of a course free stone; the inscriptions are circumscribed in black pitch letters, and the statue of the partie scratcht in black.

This coate is in glasse in the parlor of this Grosvenor's howse, old:

> An ill-arranged shield, bearing in the upper part, as if in chief, the coat of BUSHBURY, and below, quarterly, 1, Azure, a garb or between three bezants [GROSVENOR] ; 2, Argent, a lion rampant sable; 3, Argent, a chevron between three leopard's faces sable; 4, Azure, a bend or, in sinister chief a buck's head caboshed or.

This in a paper for a funeral there:

> 1, GROSVENOR; 2, BUSHBURY; 3, Argent, a bend between three mullets gules [CLAYTON] ; impaling, Argent, a bend between three pellets [COTTON].

Satterday, May 17, 1645.

His Majestie marched by Tong, com. Salop, a faire church, the windows much broken, and yet divers ancient coates of armes remayne.[b] A fayre old castle neare this church called Tong Castle, belonging

---

[a] There is a drawing of this glass in C. 36, f. 31, Coll. Arm. Three shields of arms are also given, viz. 1, Or, two lions passant azure ; 2, England ; 3, Bushbury.

[b] Vide for these, C. 35, f. 18, 39, &c. Coll. Arm.

to Peirpount this 18 yeares; it was the ancient seate of Stanley, who came to it by marrying Vernon of the Peake at Haddon.[a]

Thence thorough Newport.

NEWPORT Church, com. Salop.

North window, north yle, these two, old:

Azure, a chevron between three mullets or.
Argent, a chevron gules between three leopard's faces sable [NEWPORT].

East window, *ibidem*.

Quarterly, FRANCE and ENGLAND.
Quarterly, FRANCE and ENGLAND within a bordure argent.

East window, same yle:

Quarterly, 1, Or, three roses gules [YOUNGE]; 2, Argent, seven lozenges conjoined sable, 3, 3, and 1; 3, Or, a pale nebuly sable; 4, Or, a fess gules between three lions rampant.

Younges coate of Keynton, within 2 myle off. Reb.

An altar monument of alablaster, two statues of a man and woman.

An escocheon within an orle of martlets; impaling, Barry nebuly, on a chief a lion rampant.

For Judge Salter, 1492.

Divers flat stones of common people.

His Majesty lay at Mr. Pigott's, at Chatwynd, one myle beyond Newport.

The two troopes at Edgmonde.

In EDGMOND Church, com. Salop.

South window, chancel, very old:

Gules, a lion rampant or.
Or, fretty gules.

North window, *ibidem*:

Azure, a·stag's head caboshed argent.
Checky or and azure [WARREN].
MORTIMER.

---

[a] Sir Thomas Stanley married Margaret the daughter and coheir of Sir George Vernon of Haddon, co. Derby, called "King of the Peake." Vincent's Derby, f. 11, Coll. Arm.

In north window, north yle church, and yle belonging to Mr.
Young, of Keynton, in this parishe:

> Quarterly, shield defaced, third quarter apparently, Gules, two bars ermine ;
> impaling, Argent, a chevron between three martlets sable.
>
> Quarterly, 1, "Gone" [YOUNGE]; 2, Seven lozenges conjoined; 3, Ar-
> gent, a pale nebuly sable ; 4, Or, a fess between three lions rampant
> gules.

In the upper south window of the church, these two coates and
inscription at bottome of the window:

> Azure, a chevron between three roses or.
>
> Quarterly, 1 and 4, Sable, six martlets argent, 3, 2, and 1, ARUNDEL; 2,
> SCROPE; 3, Checky or and sable, a chief argent gutty de sang.
>
> Orate pro statu Joh'is Pigot de Chatwyn Ar. qui hanc fenestram . . . . .
> an'o D'ni 1501.

This second coate is in the second and third south window church,
with this miter.   As also in the east window of the church.

> The same quarterly coats, surmounted by a mitre.[a]

Upon a large flat stone in the middle yle of the church, the
statues of a man and woman inlayed in brasse, two shields, and this
inscription:

> Quarterly, 1, YOUNGE; 2, seven lozenges conjoined, 3, 3, and 1; 3,
> a pale nebuly; 4, a fess between three lions rampant; impaling, Quar-
> terly, 1 and 4, a fret [EYTON] ; 2 and 3, two bars ermine.
>
> Quarterly, 1 and 4, a lion rampant, debruised by a bend; 2 and 3, ten
> roundles 4, 3, 2 and 1 ; impaling, 1 and 4, two bars; 2 and 3, checky.
>
> Of your charite ye shall pray for the sowle of Francis Young, sometyme of
> Caynton, Esq., son and heire of Sir William Young, Knight, and dame
> Margaret his wife, daughter of Nich. Eyton, of Eyton, Esq.: ob. 1533,
> &c.

Mr. Corbett is lord of this manor, 300*l*. per annum.

At Longford, the parish adjoyning, and neare Newport, the Earle
of Shrewsbury has a large brick howse and seate, spoyld and abusd.
A garrison of the rebells 1644, delivered up to Prince Rupert.

---

[a] John Arundel, Bishop of Lichfield 1496, translated to Exeter.

Colonel Bagott's regiment of horse, three blew cornetts without any manner of badge, motto, or distinction.

Bagott's foot colors:

Azure, a mullet or, on a canton a cross.

Colonel Bagott, the Governour of Lichfield, joyned with the King's army, 300 foote and 200 horse.

Garrisons in com. Salop.

K. Tong Castle. First the King had it; then the rebells gott it; then Prince Rupert tooke it and putt in a garrison, who afterward burnt it when he drew them out to the battaile of York.

K. Longford Howse, the Earle of Shrewsbury. First the rebells made a garrison 1644, and held it till Prince Rupert tooke it at the same time he did Tong Castle. Colonel Young is Governour.

Young's estate 300*l*. per annum, his wife a clothier's daughter.

K. Lindsill, three myle from Newport, a howse of Sir Richard Leveson's. (Lindsill Abbey.) Sir Richard L. made it himself aboute hallowmas 1644, and still remaynes so *pro Rege*, 160 men in it. (He lives in the lodge.) Bostock Governour obijt.

K. High Arcall [Ercall], a howse belonging to the Lord Newport, made a garrison about the same time that the former was, made a garrison by my lord himselfe. 200 men in it. Captain Nicholas Armer is Governour.

R. Wemme, a towne pro Parl.; King, a Chandler in Chancery lane, is Governour.

K. (*Blank*) Castle, Sir Henry Fred. Thinne owes it.

R. Morton Corbet Castle. Sir Vincent Corbett owes it. Pro Rebells. 4 myles from Shrewsbury.

R. Shrewsbury, betrayed to the rebells in winter 1644.

K. Bridgnorth Castle, Sir Lewis Kirke Governour: 300 foot.

K. Ludlowe towne and castle, Sir Michael Woodhowse.

K. Stoake Castle, Captain Danet commands it under Woodhowse. (Lost in June following.)

K. Shraydon [Shrawardine] Castle. An Irishman under Sir William Ball commands it.

K. Chirke Castle, Leift.-Colonel Watts, Governour.

R. A howse within three myles of Bridgnorth.

Garrisons in Staffordshire.

R. Eggleshall Castle, 1644, 6 myles from Newport in Salop.

K. Lichfield. Colonel Bagott, Governour.

R. Stafford. Lewis Chadwicke, Governour.

R. Russell Hall; a taylor, Governour.

R. Mr. Gifford's howse at Chilleton [Chillington], three myles from Wolverhampton, now slighted by themselves.

K. Dudley Castle. Colonel Leveson, whose estate and habitation is at Wolverhampton, is Governour.

R. Tamworth Castle, four myles from Lichfield.

R. Alveton, or Alton Castle, in the parish of A., about 40 or 50, in the Moorelands.

R. Peynsley Howse, neare Cheddle [Cheadle], in Lee parish. Mr. Draycott, p. Reg. owes it. About 50 men in it.

R. Caverswall Howse. Mr. Cradock, pro Rege, owes it. About 50 men in it. Captain Ashenhurst is Governour, whose father was a justice of the peace in Derbyshire.

Garrisons in Cheshire.

K. Chester. Lord Byron, Governour.

R. Nantwiche.

K. Holt Castle.

K. Harding Castle.

K. Beeston Castle. Captain Vallet Governour, lord Byron's Captain.

These garrisons shutt up by the rebells: Houghton Howse, Mr. Stanleyes, three myles distant from Chester; Puddington, Sir William Masseyes howse, three myles distant from Chester. . . . . towne. These three are in the hundred of Worrall, com. Cestr.

CHATWYN [Chetwynd] Church, com. Salop.

East window chancel, this, very old:

A male figure, having apparently wings depending from the shoulders, holding in the right hand a sword, and bearing on the left arm a shield, charged with Argent, a cross flory sable [PESHALL].
Sable, a chevron between three crosses flory argent, " old" [CHETWYND].
Azure, a chevron between three mullets or, " newer."

Upon the ground in the chancel, against the north wall, lies a knight crosse-legged, with a shield on his left arme. They call it the monument of.... Chetwyn, ante Conq.

In the middle of the chancel a flat stone, thus:

An ancient cross, with floreated staff, resting on a lion, on the right side of the cross is a circular shield bearing the coat of CHETWYND.

This flowery crosse is wrought handsomely and embosses out.

Against the south wall of the chancel two monuments, statues lying in armour, about Hen. 5 or 6 time. Alablaster, very curiously wrought. Under their heads upon a helme, forth of a wreath, a fox head. He next the east end oldest, and a chayne about his neck. The other in a different fashiond armor, and a chayne of collar of S. and a rose at the end hanging about his neck. Two angells support at west end these two shields:

Quarterly, 1, Ermine, three fusils conjoined in fess sable [PIGOTT]; 2, Azure, a chevron or between three mullets or [CHETWYND]; 3, Argent, a cross flory sable, on a canton gules a lion's head erased argent [PESHALL]; 4, Vert, two lions rampant or.

Quarterly, but arranged perpendicularly, 1, PIGOTT; 2, CHETWYND; 3, PESHALL; 4, Vert, two lions rampant in fess or; with two impalements, 1, Argent, a lion rampant gules within a bordure engrailed sable, bezanty [? CORNWALL]; 2, Barry nebuly or and sable [BLOUNT].

In the parlour windowes of this pretty howse of Mr. Pigott's:

A blank shield quarterly, above which is written "former quarterings."
PIGOTT; impaling, Azure, a fess nebuly per fess argent and sable, between three laurel leaves slipped or [LEVESON].
Or, a raven sable [CORBET]; impaling, PIGOTT. " And many more."

Tuesday, May 20, 1645. His Majesty with his army removed from Chatwyn thorough Drayton, com. Salop, and lay a myle farther. Earl of Lichfield, &c., at Norton, at a howse sometimes the habitation of Grosvenor, now Cotton's.

The King lay at Church his howse in Drayton parish.

This Grosvenor built it [*i. e.* the house at Norton] temp. Qu. Mary.

> Azure, a garb or, a crescent for difference [GROSVENOR]. "This garb is impaled often in this howse, lately."

The elder howse of Grosvenor in this county is Bellaport in the parish of Norton, com. Salop.

These are painted in a chamber window of this howse:

> A large crucifix, before which kneel the effigies of a male and female. The male is habited in armour, but without the helmet, and wears a surcoat embroidered with his arms, viz. Argent, a cross flory sable. In the upper part of the surcoat there is a slight difference in the charge, being per saltire and a cross flory, counterchanged. Over his head is a talbot's head erased or, for crest. Upon the lady's mantle is this coat, Azure, three water-bougets or.

𝕮𝖍𝖔𝖒𝖆𝖘 𝕲𝖗𝖆𝖘𝖚𝖊𝖓𝖆𝖗, 𝕰𝖘𝖖. 𝖆𝖓𝖉 𝕸𝖆𝖗𝖌𝖊𝖗𝖞 𝖍𝖎𝖘 𝖜𝖎𝖋𝖊, 𝖉𝖆: 𝖔𝖋 𝕵𝖔𝖍𝖓 𝕮𝖔𝖙𝖙𝖊𝖘 𝖔𝖋 𝖂𝖔𝖔𝖉𝖈𝖔𝖙𝖙, 𝕰𝖘𝖖.[a]

Wednesday the army rested, because Sir Marmaduke Langdale, the Major-Generall, was sent the night before with a party of horse and foot to surprise Wemme, which then had but 150 men in it; but, coming too late, fayled.

Thursday, May 22. Wee marched from Drayton to Stone in com. Stafford; his Majestie lay at Mr. Crompton's howse, a sweet place in a fyne parke; he a rebel.

Friday the army rested.

Satterday the 24. Wee marched to Uttoxater. His Majestie lay at Sir Thomas Milward's howse at Eaton, in com. Derb. Wee marched this day thorough a parke belonging to the Lord Cromwell;

---

[a] This must be an error. The male is a Peshall, and the female coat is not that of Cotes. Thomas Grosvenor of Bellaport married Isabella, daughter and coheir of Richard Peshall.

then by a house of Sir Harvey Bagott's, in the Moorelands in Staffordshire, a woody enclosed country all the way, except the moores on the top of the hills; a black earth where they digg and cutt a heathy turfe; a rebellious place.

Earl of Lichfield, &c., quartered this night at Marston, near Cubley, in com. Derby.

> Ermine, on a fess gules three plates, "MILWARD."
>
> Same; impaling, Or, two bars gules, charged with two trefoils slipped argent, in chief a greyhound courant sable, "PALMER."

This day a foot soldjer was tyed (with his sholders and breast naked) to a tree, and every carter of the trayne and carriages was to have a lash; for ravishing two women. *Secundum usum Hispaniarum.*

Garrisons in Derbyshire.

R. Derbye. Sir John Gell is Governour. Five churches in it.

R. Barton Howse. Mr. Merry owes it. Captain Barton, a clergyman, sometime chaplain to Sir Thomas Burdett, and Captain Grenewood, a skynner at Ashbourne in this county, are Governors. 700 horse.

R. Bolsover Castle, the seate of the Marquis of Newcastle.

R. Wingfield Manour.

R. Welbeck Howse, belonging to the Marquis of Newcastle.

Whitsunday, May 25, 1645. The army marched to Burton upon Trent, the head quarters. His Majestie lay at Tedbury Castle, under the command of Lord Loughborough; Sir Andrew Kniveton, Governor. Wee lay at Roulston in Staffordsh.

ROULSTON [Rolleston] Church. C.

North window chancel, old:

> Sable, an inescocheon vair or and gules, between six martlets argent.

East window, south yle, church:

> ENGLAND, with a label of three points azure, charged with three fleurs-de-lis of the second.
> ENGLAND.
> Azure, semée of quatre-foils, a lion rampant guardant argent.
> BOHUN.

This is also in north window church, old:

> Argent, a cinque-foil azure, on a chief gules a lion passant guardant or, " ROLSTON."

In the south yle church is a low altar tombe, upon the top a white stone circumscribed in old text black letters; the pictures of a knight in armes and a woman scratcht in black lynes, the fashion of this country.

This shield at bottome betweene them:

> Hic jacet Joh'es Rolleston ar', filius et heres
> Alveredi R. ar' et Margarete ux' ejus, una filiarum
> Joh'is Agard de Folston, quiquid. Joh'es ob. 28 July
> 1485, et d'c'a Marg. ob.: die . . . aº D . . . .
> Quor' a'i'abus misericors sit Trinitas S'c'a.

> ROLLESTON, impaling a chevron between three boar's heads couped. [AGARD.]

Another flatter adjoyning, of the same fashion and coate, Laur R. Esq. [Grandson of John and Margaret.]

These Rollestons lived here (till of late) time out of mind. Rolston had 400*l.* per ann.

Sir Edward Moseley bought it of Rolston of Rolston.

Against the south wall chancel, the statue of a lawyer, is a faire monument:

> Sable, a chevron between three pickaxes argent [MOSELEY]; impaling, a fess between three eagles displayed sable. "The same also quarterly."

> Sacrum Memoriæ Ed'i Mosley Milit' Cælib. Atturnat-General Ducat' Lancast' et hujus ecclesiæ patroni, filii Nicholai Mosley militis, famaliæ Lancast.

Here was no need of law lattine.

Munday 26, the army rested; some of Derby (Rebel) horse gave Colonel Caryes quarters an alarm.

Tuesday his Majestie marched to Ashby-de-la-Zouche, com. Leicester, the head quarters of the Lord Loughborough in com. Leic. Earl of Lichfield to Packington.

In this march this day wee marched neare Shelford manor, com. Nottingh. a faire seate of the Earl of Chesterfield.

Church at Packington com. Leicester, this coate, old, north window church:

Three garbs or [colour of field not given].

Garrisons in com. Leicestr.

R. Leicester, the committee of Reb. governes; Theoph. Gray, third brother to the Earl of Kent, writes Governour: 600 men.

K. Ashby-de-la-Zouch, Henry Hastings, Baron of Loughborough, Gov. the ancient seate of Hastings Earl of Huntingdon. 600 men.

R. Cole Overton, a house of the Lord Beaumont's, one myle from Ashby. Temple, Governour. 50 men.

R. Bagworth House, or a lodge in a parke, the Lady Manors [Manners'] howse; five myle from Ashby. 50 men.

R. Kirkby Belhows [Belars], a howse belonging to Sir Erasmus Delafountayne. The men ran away at the newes of Sir Marm. Langdale, but came in again. 50 men.

To all these garrisons above mentioned the yearly contribucion amounted to fourscore and seaventeene thousand pounds, within this county of Leicester onely. Of late Belvoir Castle has one hundred allotted to it out of this shire. And the whole number of men were not above 1,500 in all these garrisons.

Wednesday, May 28, 1645. His Majestie marched with his army neare Cole Orton, garrison of the enemyes; then by the Abbey of

Gracedieu, where Sir Thomas Beaumont lives.   There remaynes an
entire church, with cloisters, hall, &c.   These coates painted lately
in one of the chambers:

> Azure, semée of cinquefoils, a lion rampant guardant argent, "BEAU-
> MONT;" impaling, Argent, a cinquefoil azure, "MOHUN."[a]
> "BEAUMONT;" impaling, Argent, semée of cinquefoils gules, a lion ram-
> pant sable, "PIERPOINT."
> BEAUMONT; impaling, Argent, a maunche sable, "HASTINGS."

and many more.

The head quarters was this night at Loughborough, com. Leicestr.

His Majestie lay this night at Sir Henry Skipwith's house, called
Cotes, in the parish of [Prestwould], com. Leicester.

This day Sir Richard Willys (and Colonel Villiers), the Governor
of Newarke, came from thence with 1,200 horse.

Newes this day that Evesholme was lost.—*Ajourduy avec T. T.*

Thursday his Majestie marched and pitcht downe before Leicester
citty, a garrison of the rebells, and commanded by Theoph. Grey,
third brother to the Earle of Kent.

Friday, May 30.   His highnes Prince Rupert sent a trumpet (after
he had shott two great peices at the towne) to summon it for
his Majestie, offering the burgesses and corporacion pardon, &c.
They deteyne his trumpet, and about one of the clock afternoone, in
this interim, the Prince rayses a battery for six great peices upon a
hill, where sometymes of old had byn such another.   About two of
the clock one of the Leicester trumpets was sent to desire time to
consider of it till the morrow morning, and to tell him that they
wondered he would rayse any worke, &c. during this summons.
His Highnes told the trumpet if he came agen with such another
errand, he'de lay him by the heels.   About half an houre after he
comes agen with this note directed thus: " To the Commander
in Cheife;" desiring time to consider till the morrow morning.

The Prince commits the trumpet to his Marshall.   Still the first
trumpet they keepe.   Then the Prince about three of the clock

---

b Not the coat of Mohun, nor was there any match of Beaumont and Mohun.

sent them an answer in lowder termes; six great peices from the fort on the south side of the towne playing on a stone wall unlyned, and made ere six of the clock a breach of great space. Musketts and cannon continually putting us in mind of some thing done.

The towne of Leicester was cheifely governed by a committee, vizt. Mr. Huett of Dunton; Mr. Haslerigg; Ludlom, a chandler there; Mr. Payne of Medburne; Newton of Houghton, a receiver, sometime high constable; Read of Thirlby; Mr. Lewyn; . . . . . Stanley, a mercer there by the West gate.

Sir Robert Pye of Farringdon came two or three dayes [before] into the towne, and was a great meanes of resisting the Prince.

After the breach was made in the wall by our cannon, by six of the clock, they in the towne had gotten up a handsome retrench-ment with three flankers, (a great Spanish peice,) within four or five yards of the wall.

All the evening was a generall preparation to assaulte the towne, and a little before 12 of the clock in the night this violent storme began, and continued till after one. Colonel George Lisle's tertia fell on upon the breach; once beate off, and the King sent his foot regiment of lifeguards to assist, but they gott fully in before.

Colonel Bard's tertia fell on with scaling ladders, some neare a flanker, and others scaled the horne worke before the drawbridge on the east side.

Sir Bernard Asteleyes tertia fell on, on the north side, which is the river side, and a draw[bridge] next the abbey.

Colonel John Russell, with the Prince's regiment of blew cotes, and also the Prince's fferelockes, assaulted.

They sett the Prince's black colours on the great battery within. Earl of Northampton's horse about one of the clock were lett in at the ports, and they scowred the lyne and towne. In the meane time the foot gott in and fell to plunder, so that ere day fully open scarse a cottage unplundered. There were many Scotts in this towne, and no quarter was given to any in the heat.

More dead bodyes lay just within the lyne farre then without or in the graffe.

I told 30 and more at the breach, as many within as without. Every street had some. I believe 200 on both sides were not killed.

Wee lost Colonel St. George. Major Bunnington, gentleman pensioner, shott in the eye just as he was on the top of the ladder. 28 or 30 officers. Major of the Prince Rupert's firelocks.

The army of horse faced in bodyes all night in severall places. About day, about 10 of the enemy gott out and escaped by the river side; were followed.

The King's Army of Horse was in this order this yeare 1645 before Leicester. May.

The King's lifeguards, consisting of two troopes, King's and Queenes.

His Highnes Prince Rupert's lifeguards of horse. One troope commanded by Sir Richard Crane.

His Highnes Prince Maurice's lifeguard. One troope consisting of above 100 gentlemen, &c. and reformados, commanded by the Lord Molineux.

Prince Rupert's regiment of horse, consisting of 400, 8 troopes, commanded by Sir Thomas Dalyson. Leift.-Colonel William Legge, now Governour of Oxford.

Lord Loughborough's regiment, blew colours, 3 troopes, 100.

Colonel Horatio Caryes regiment, not 200, independent.

The bodye of horse was devided into 4 brigades; 2 Southerne, 2 Northerne horse.

James Earle of Northampton's [brigade], consisting of these four regiments:—

Queenes regiment, commanded by Sir John Campsfeild, 150.

Prince Maurice's regiment, commanded by Leift.-Colonel Guy Moulsworth, 150. Major Robert Legg.

Each of Northampton's owne regiment, 250.

Sir William Vaughan's regiment; 'twas Sir Thomas Lucas' regiment in Ireland, consisting of 7 troopes, 400 in all.

150, 250, 150, 400——Total 850 [950].

Colonel Thomas Howard's brigade, consisting of these 7 regiments:

Colonel Samuel Sandys, of Worcestershire, Governour of Worcester, consisting of 150.

Colonel Thomas Howard, 80.

Colonel Leveson, Governour of Dudley Castle, 150.

Colonel Bagott, Governour of Lichfield, 200.

Colonel Sir Robert Byron, 100.

Colonel Sir Henry Bard, Governour of Campden Howse, 100, commanded [by] . . . . . Barker.

Colonel Worthen, were Colonel Marrowes horse, 100. Toto of this brigade 880.

Major-General Sir Marmaduke Langdale's brigade, divided into 3 divisions.

Sir William Blakeston's brigade, and so is the Northerne horse divided into 2 brigades. Toto 1,500.

Sir Richard Wyllis his horse from Newarke, 1,200.

Suma totalis of the whole army of horse.

King and Queenes troopes . .	130	Colonel Howard's brigade . .	880
Prince Rupert's	140	Sir Marmaduke Langdale's and	
Prince Maurice	120	Sir William Blackston's bri-	
Prince Rupert's regiment of		gades	1,500
horse	400	Sir Richard Willys	1,200
Lord Loughborough	100		
Colonel Carye	200		5,520
Earl of Northampton's brigade.	850		

LEICESTERSH.

The names and places of the dwellings of the cheife famelyes.

K. Earl of Huntingdon, lives at Ashby.

K. Sir Henry Hastings, of Branston, neare Leicester.

Lord Beaumont, of Cole Overton [Sapcote 2nd Viscount].

Sir Henry Hastings, Bart. of Humberston, lives private.

K. Henry Hastings, Baron of Loughborough.

R. Sir Henry Beaumont, of Stoughton [cousin of Lord Beaumont].

K. Sir Thomas Beaumont, of Gracedieu.

K. John Skevington, of Sk. [Skeffington].

Sir Richard Hawford [Halford], of Wistowe.   At London.

K. Sir John Bale, of Carlton, with the Lord Loughborough.

R. Sir Arthur Haslerig, of Nosely, Knight of the shire.

R. Henry Gray, Earl of Stamford, of Bradgate, 3 myle from Leicester.

K. Mr. Henry Nevill, of Holt, neare Halaton.   2 sons with Lord Loughborough.

K. Sir John Pate, neare Melton.

K. Sir Henry Skipwith of Cotes.

R. Sir William Herrick, she. R.ᵃ

R. Mr. Purfrey [Purefoy], of [? Caldecote].

R. Mr. Cotton, of Laughton, great with the Earl of Stamford.

R. Mr. Bent, of Enderby.

R. [Thomas Ford], Grey of Groby, [son of the Earl of Stamford].

R. Mr. Sharpe of Rolleston, neare Hallaton, cœlebs.

K. Sir Geo. Villers, of [Brokesby].

R. . . . . . Palmer, high Sheriffe the first year the Parliament began, whome the Lord Loughborough succeeded.

Sir Wolstan Dixie, one of the chiefe in this county, of Market Bosworth.

Sir Richard Roberts of Thorpe Langton.

At the taking of Leicester by his Majestie, these garrisons of the rebels were slighted by themselves:

Burley Howse, the onely garrison of Rotel' [Rutland].

Cole Overton. The King commanded Lord L. to burne it, but they gott into it agen.

Bagworth Howse.

ᵃ It is difficult to interpret this, unless the writer meant to stigmatize the wife also as a Rebel.   That Sir William was plundered by the Royalists, and that his wife was a most exemplary and religious woman, may be seen by reference to Nichols's Leicestershire, vol. iii. p. 155, &c.

Barton Howse (neare Tedbury) in Derbysh.

His Majestie quartered this Friday night at Leicester Abbey, the Countesse of Devon's howse.

ASHBY-DE-LA-ZOUCH Church.

East window, chancel.

> Quarterly, 1 and 4, gone; 2, quarterly, 1 and 4, a lion rampant [FITZ-ALAN]; 2 and 3, checky or and azure [WARREN].

In the south chappel is a stately altar monument of alablaster, the two statues of a man and woman lying on the surface; he very old, with a long beard; in armes, and the robe and badge of the garter on the left shoulder; under his head this creast, vizt. a bull's head sable. Round about the verge of the monument is an English inscription in old text:

> Here lyeth, &c., Francis Earl of Huntingdon, Lord, &c. Knight of the Garter: ob. 1561.[a] Many escocheons with large quarterings.

> A shield, with divisions for seven coats, and an impalement, but containing only the following: viz. 1, HASTINGS; 2, (*blank*); 3, BOTREAUX; the rest blank. The only coat in the impalement is, 1, Quarterly FRANCE and ENGLAND, a label of three points argent.

Two or three new monuments of other families lately sett in the walls, small.

In the old hall windowes of Ashby this cote often sett up, new:

> HASTINGS.

> The same; impaling, quarterly, 1 and 4, quarterly 1 and 4, Argent, three fusils conjoined in fess gules; 2 and 3, Party per pale, a saltire; 2 and 3, Argent, a saltire gules [NEVILLE].

His Majestie rested at Leicester Abbey, the army of foot in Leicester, the horse round about in dorpes and villages. The whole county was summoned in to Leicester to list themselves under the Lord Loughborough; Colonel George Lisle was made Leiftenant General of this shire under the Lord Loughborough, and Colonell Apleyard is made Governour.

[a] Francis the second Earl, and his wife Catherine Pole.

Munday, June 2nd, his Majestie knighted Colonel Sir Mathew Apleyard, Colonel Sir Richard Page, and Major Bridges, Major to Page.

Because Oxford was beseiged, his Majestie turnd his course thitherward.

Wednesday, June 4th, his Majestie marched to the rendesvouz at Newton Harcourt neare Great Glyn [Glen], the way to Harborough; the King quartered at Wistowe, Sir Richard Hawford [Halford] lives there. His horse-guards at Kilby and Foston. Another Hawford lives at Kilby. *H. W. et moy avec Col. Sm.* by NOSELEY, Sir Arthur Haselrigs parish, not above two cottages besides his, a sweet place.

A neate church, the windowes very old and many old coates in the windowes, and old words in yellow under every coate.

Second window south chancel:

ENGLAND.
ENGLAND, with a label of five points azure, " sur each five fleurs-de-lys or."
Gules, a fess between twelve cross-crosslets fitchy.

First window, divers shields more, very old.

Against the north wall in the chancel is a monument with two statues for . . . . Haselrigg.

A blank shield divided fess-wise, or having a chief. Another shield bearing a chevron between three laurel leaves [HASELRIGGE.]

GLYN [GLEN] MAGNA Church.

East window, north yle church, old:

Gules, seven mascles conjoined, 3, 3, and 1, or [QUINCY].
Gules, a lion rampant, double-queued, argent [MONTFORT].
Gules, three hammers or.

A flat stone neare the window circumscribed in old letters; nothing els.

Here you may see twelve or thirteen churches at once, they stand so thick, and very small parishes.

STRETTON MAGNA and PARVA Church, nil; ROLSTON, nil; GODEBY Church, nil.

Sir Richard Willys went back to Newarke with four hundred horse; the rest march with the King.

The county of Leicester is generally champaine pastures and erable, little or no wast, and small wood; some quick hedges, and the parishes stand less then one myle distant.

Wednesday. The Northerne horse left his Majesties army, and notwithstanding his promise to them on the word of a King he would go into Yorkshire after Oxford was releived; but upon persuasion returned and marched with us.

Thursday June 5. His Majestie marched to the rendesvouz neare Haverburgh [Market Harborough], com. Northampton, which was the head-quarters this night.

Colonel S[andys?] to Desborough, com. North'ton.

DESBOROUGH Church.

East window, chancel, old and very large:

Azure, six lions rampant or.
Gules, six mascles or [QUINCY].

Upon a flat stone inlayed with brasse, chancel:

A fess between three mullets [PULTON]; impaling a fess wavy and in chief three piles, also wavy, points meeting in fesse, argent [ISHAM].
Here lyeth Elizabeth the daughter of John Isham of Langport in this county of North'ton, Esq. and wife to George Pulton, lord of this towne of D. Esq. she dyed May 12, 1584.

This knot carved upon the stayre east up to the rood-loft. Painted also in the church. [A drawing of the Stafford knot.]

Mr. Pulton is now lord of this towne.

West window, belfry:

Argent, a chevron gules between three mascles azure, each having within it a fleur-de-lis or, a bordure gules.

Garrisons in Northamptonshire.

R. Northampton.

R. Rockingham Castle. Sir John Norwich is governour, Lewis Lord Watson, Baron of R. owes it.

Garrisons in co. Buckinghamsh:

R. Newport Paganell, also a garrison of the rebells.

RUSHTON Churches, com. Northampt.

There are two churches in this small village, a myle from
Desborough; one called St Peter's, which is next the faire stone
howse of the Lord Cockaines, the other, St. Andrewes.

In St. Peter's Church. An altar tombe, and upon it the statue
of a man, long beard, short haire; in armes, and a long loose
gowne or coate over it, and a sword and belt over all; his helme
and creast under his head.

Monument of Tresham, last master or lord of St. John's, London;
they call him Lorde of St. Joanes, Ordinis Militiæ Templi.

Sir Thomas Tresham built part of this faire howse, and also the
pretty Warren howse.

Sir Thomas was father to him, in the 5 Nov. plott.

> Per saltire or and azure, in chief four trefoils slipped of the first, the
> same in base, " TRESHAM."

This coate is carved on the house for Tresham, and this also for
Cockaine:

> [Azure] three cocks [gules].

RUSHTON ST. ANDREW Church.

East window, chancel, very old:

> Azure, semée of fleurs-de-lis or [FRANCE].

East window, north yle chancel, this very old:

> Sable, a bend between six martlets or. Below the shield are two eagles
> as supporters, argent.

In the middle of this chappel or yle is an altar tombe, playne, two
foot high, and thereon a faire and large statue cutt in grey marble,
in chayn armor, crosse-legged, a loose coate and a belt and sword
over all, he drawing it. On his left arme a large shield three foot
in length. The parson told me it was for one Goldingham, some-

tyme lord of this place; and that this was a large towne, but
decayed since inclosures began there.

Satterday, June 7, 1645. His Majestie marched to Daventree,
co. North'ton p'd. The army of foot lay in the feild. His horse
guards went to quarters at Staverton, one myle distant. *Ajourduy
R. S. readm.* [*sic orig.* perhaps " readmitted," but to what does not
appear.]

Newes that the enemy had raised the seige from before Oxford,
and had received a blow on their reare by Bostoll, Wallingford,
Oxon, and some of Goring's horse.

DEDFORD [DODFORD] Church, com. North'ton.

Two myles from Daventree towne, Northton.

South window in the church, in this position [*i. e.* the shields disposed three in first row, one in the second, and three in the third]:

> Gules, ten bezants, a canton ermine [ZOUCHE OF HARYNGWORTH].]
> Vair argent and azure, two bars gules [KEYNES].
> Gules, three piles or, a canton ermine.
> KEYNES ; impaling, Vair azure and argent.
> KEYNES ; impaling " gone."
> KEYNES.
> Gules, a cross flory or.

East window chancel:

> Quarterly, FRANCE and ENGLAND.

Upon a very broad altar tombe of grey marble, betweene the
pillars of the north yle church, lyes the statue of a knight in mayle
chayne armour, a loose coate and sword over all; his left leg over his
right; his right hand drawing his crosse-barrd sword, and upon his
left arme a shield with barry of six peices vaire and . . . . . carved
upon it very deepe; under his head a pillow. The vaire and
escocheon of this forme. They call him lord of Kaine in Normandy.

> The recumbent figure of a Knight Templar, bearing an oval shield, with
> the arms of KEYNES. [Sir William Keynes, ob. 1344.]

Under an arch in the north yle of the church lyes upon a low altar tombe the statues of two women, very old.

In the same north yle stands a faire altar tombe; on the top lyes the statue of a knight in the fashiond armor of the Black Prince, a collar of S about his neck; his head bare, his haire cutt round like a dish, and lying upon his helmet, with a mantle.

Creast: a cap turned up ermine, on the top a demy man holding a sheild of ovall forme in his left hand.

Rude drawings of this crest, &c.

The inscription is circumscribed, and the letters cutt in and black, in text.

> Hic jacet Joh'es Cressy miles d'nus istius
> Ville, quondam capitaneus de Lyucux [Lisieux]
> Orbef et Pontleusque in Norma'dia ac
> Consiliarius d'ni Regis in Fran—, qui obiit
> Aput Toue [Toul] in Lorenia iij die Marcij an'o
> D'ni M·cccc·xliiij. c. a. p. d. a.

This escocheon above on the west end, for the east end joynes to the wall:

Quarterly, 1 and 4, A lion rampant double-queued [CRESSY]; 2 and 3, MORTIMER; an escocheon of pretence [KEYNES.]

These four shields on the north side:

Quarterly gules and argent, in centre point a mullet [? for VERE].
MORTIMER.
KEYNES.
CRESSY.

In the south side:

CRESSY.
KEYNES.
MORTIMER.
A fess wavy between three " buckets bard."

Upon a flat stone the two statues of a man and woman inlayed in brasse, he in armes; two shields, both gone.

Hic jacet Joh'es Cressy armiger et Cristina ux' ejus, quiquid' J. obiit 1° Oct. 1414.

Another like one shield, gone:

Hic jacet Will's Wylde ar. et Cecilia mater Christine Cressy, quiquidem Will's ob. 23 Nov. 1422, c. a. p. d. a.

The manor of Dedford was the Staffords, next to Cressy, then the Wyrleyes, who now owe it, and have had this six descents.[a]

Newes that Fairfax the enemies Generall and Browne the woodmonger fell out at the seige of Oxford and cudgelld one another, and that those forces stormed Bostall [Borstall] Howse, and weare beate off with the losse of 400 at least, and that night they raysd the seige, Browne to London to complaine; his men to Abingdon; Fairfax towards Bedfordsh. In this seige Oxford horse made a sally and tooke their whole guard at Hedyngton.

Certayne intelligence that Lord Goring near Taunton had met with Lord Roberts' forces, killed and taken 2,000, and had pennd up Skippon in a parke thereabouts.

Tuesday, June 10. A trumpett came from Fairfax for exchange of prisoners from Newport Paganell.

Garrisons in Warwickshire.

R. Warwick.

R. Coventree Citty. Barker Governour, a draper in the towne. Flower commands a troope there. A Committee governes.

R. Killingworth [Kenelworth] Castle.

R. Edgburston [Edgbaston] Howse, Mr. Middlemore's howse; the rogue Fox[b] pulld downe the church to make the workes.

R. Compton Howse, Purfrey son to Gam. Purfrey is Governour.

---

[a] The celebrated Colley Cibber is deduced from the Wyrleyes and Keynes. See pedigree, Baker's Northamptonshire, vol. i. p. 356.

[b] In a former page of the MS. (fol. 8 b), where the "Garrisons in Warwickshire" were commenced but erased, this man is described as "Tinkar Fox governour, sometime tinkar, and livd in Woodstock."

R. Nutman's End, Mr. Chamblaines howse, of the Court of Wards.
R. Rushin Hall.   Fox, G.

2,556*l*. 13*s*. 1*d*. ob. this was halfe of the part of fower hundred thousand pounds this county was taxed at by them at London, toto 5,113*l*. 6*s*. 3*d*.

Every fortnight this sume is paid in contribucion to those garrisons out of this shire.

The hundred of Knightloe in com. Warwicksh. paies every fortnight in contribucion 177*l*. 10*s*. 11*d*.; to the garrisons of Warwick, Coventree, and Banbury; to Warwick halfe.

The King's guards to Willoughby, com. Warwick.

In WILLOUGHBY church, this onely, east window north yle:
ENGLAND.

Church is small.
This also carved, old, on the chest:
A cross engrailed.

Magdalen Coll. Oxon. is Lord of this village.

Gentlemen of Warwickshire.

K. Earl of Northampton livd at Compton in the Hole.   James Lord Compton, Knight of the shire, now Earle of N.

K. Earl of Chichester,[a] Dunsmore; at King's Newnham 3,000*l*. p. a. in this county, 4,000*l*. more at Abscourt, and other places.

K. Thomas Lord Lee at Stonley within a myle of Killingworth.

R. Lord [Monmouth] owes and lived at Killingworth Castle.

K. Sir Simon Clarke at Broome.
Sir Edward Underhill.

K. Sir Rich. Shuckborough of S., now prisoner in Killingworth Castle, Knight of the shire, 200*l*. p. ann.

K. Sir William Bowden [Boughton], Knight and Baronet at Little Lawford, lives now at home, 1800*l*. p. ann.

---

[a] Sir Francis Leigh, created Baron Dunsmore and Earl of Chichester.

K. Sir Clement Fisher [of Packington] beyond Coventree.

R. Sir Thomas Holt [of Aston].

R. Captain Comer [? Colemore], is made Sheriffe this yeare by the Rebells. One of no note.

R. Thomas Bowden, active.

R. John Purfrey [Purefoy], a Colonel of horse seated at Westow neare Tamworth, 300l.

R. Gam. Purfrey of Coventry, 200l. per ann., made justice of peace and quorum by the R. Captain of a foot company in Coventry.

R. Justice Combes, of Stratford-upon-Avon, sitts at home.

K. Sir Francis Nethersall [Nethersole], (now prisoner in Killingworth Castle,) near Tamworth, 400l. per. ann.

K. Mr. Bowden [Boughton] of Cawson, not in armes, 400l. per ann.

Mr. D[evereux] at Shistock [Shustock], 100l. per ann.

K. Mr. Chamberlaine of the Court of Wards, of Nutman's End, 1,000l. per ann.

BRANSTON [BRAUNSTON] Church, com. North'ton.

North window, chancel, old:

> Gules, three water-bougets argent [Ros]; impaling, Argent, a fess between four barrulets gules [BADLESMERE].

A playne course altar monument which has beene inlayed with brass, four shields, two pictures, all gone, in the chancel.

South window, south yle church, old:

> Quarterly, 1, Sable, "2 lyons" passant argent, crowned or; 2 and 3, Fretty, a chief; 4, Argent [the charges unintelligible].

A flat stone for one Moseley, ob. 1500 and od, sans armes.

                                                    buck
Thursday the King was hunting a deare: when two myle of Daventree there came a strong alarme, so that the whole army was drawne on the Beacon Hill, and lay there that night.

Friday, June 13. Early in the morning (the convoy being

returned from Oxford, that being the cause of this unhappy stay here so long,) the whole army marched just back agen to Haverburgh [Market Harborough].

His Majestie lay at (*blank*).

King's troope at Tedingworth [Theddingworth] in com. Leic.

Certayne intelligence that Sir Thomas Fairfax was with all his forces neare Northampton, following of the King.

Satterday wee marched out of our quarters about two of the clock in the morning, and intelligence was that the enemy was very neare, and had beate up some quarters, at least given an alarme.

A generall rendesvouz of all his Majesties army this morning at Haverburgh at seven of the clock; wee marched in battalia back towards the enemy, who was then very neare ; marching up the hills, wee discovered some of the enemyes horse, in parties.

About twelve of the clock the battailes joynd; they kept their grownd on the top of the hill, and wee marched up to them through a bottome full off furse bushes; they shott two peices of cannon, wee one: one of theirs was at the King's body of horse, where he was before. No question they had certayne intelligence where he was, for one that came in to the King's troope ran over to them, and they left all others to charge up to his body.

The King was accompanied this day with these peeres: the Duke of Richmond. Earl of Lindsay. George Lord Digby. Lord Bellasis. Earl of Kernwath [Carnwath] Scotus. Lord Astley.

The horse escaped to Leicester this afternoone, and were persued by a body of the enemyes horse and loose scowters, to Great Glyn, and there the Earle of Lichfield charged their loose men with halfe a score horse and beate them back.

Killed this battaile of Navesburge, Naseby, Navelsburgh, in the Navel of the Kingdome.

Sir Thomas Dalyson, Colonel of the Prince Rupert's regiment of horse (taken prisoner, and dyed).

Sir Richard Cave.

Sir Peter Browne of the King's troope, shott, taken prisoner and dyed.

The battaile consisted of three tertias of foot.

Colonel Sir Bernard Astley's consisted of these regiments: [not given].

Colonel George Lisle's tertia consisted of these regiments :

Colonel George Lisle.

Littleton, Leift.-Colonel, and was Major of this tertia, was killed here.

Major Fowler.

Colonel Gilby.

Colonel Owen, absent.

Leift.-Colonel Roger Burges.

Colonel Sir Henry Bard's tertia of foot consisted of these regiments: [not given].

The King's regiment of life-guards, commanded by the Earle of Lindsey their Generall.

Colonel, Layton; Major, Markham.

" Six ensignes, silver."

1, Argent, the cross of St. George gules; impaling, Gules, a lion passant or, in chief the motto DIEU ET MON DROIT.

2, The same; impaling, Gules, a rose or, seeded of the field, and surmounted by a regal crown of the second.

3, The same ; impaling two roses in pale, each surmounted by a crown.

4, The same; impaling, Gules, a griffin rampant or.

5, The same ; impaling (*blank*).

6, The same; impaling (*blank*).

Towards night this dismall Satterday, his Majestie, after the wounded were taken care for in Leicester, and that the two Princes were come safe to him, and had taken order with that garrison, and left two regiments of horse there, viz. the Queenes and Colonel Caryes, he marched that night (for now wee had left running), to Ashby-de-la-Zouch.

Sunday, June 15, 1645, his Majestie about ten of the clock in the morning left Ashby, and went to Lichfield that night. He lay in the close that night. The horse were quartered in villages round about, some in the citty.

Here the King left Colonel Bagott's regiment of horse; the stout governour left here, wounded in his right arme.

Munday, his Majestie marched to Wolverhampton. Tuesday to Bewdley. Earl of Lichfield to Neather Arley; Mr. Mucklo [a] lives there. Wednesday wee rested.

Thursday, 18 June, to Bramyard, com. Hereford, and to Hereford that night, twenty-six myle; this march was very bad way, hilly and woddy. Very poore churches and thin in this part of Worcestershire and Herefordshire. King's troope to Brinsop; afterwards to Pembridge.

Colonel Barnabas Scudamore, brother to the Lord S., is governour of Hereford citty.

Mr. Coningsby was governour of Hereford first,[b] and when Sir William Waller came against it and shott a peice of cannon and killed one man 'twas rendred upon conditions. 2,500 soldjers in it.

Waller stayd about a month in it and left it.

Then Colonel Wynne was governour, and was killd at Red Marley in Gloucestershire by Masseyes men.

Then Prince Rupert putt in Colonel Scudamore.

Gentlemen of Herefordshire.

K. John Scudamore, Viscount Slego in Ireland, lives at Hom Lacy, three myle from Hereford, now prisoner in London. 4,000*l.* per annum.

R. [Henry] Coningsby of Hampton Court, (for every manor-house is called a court here,) Governour of Hereford. 4,000*l.* per annum.

R. Sir Robert Harlow [Harley], of Brampton Bryan Castle: he kept it pro Parl., (and 1644, the King's forces under the command of Woodhowse won it, and pulled it downe). 1,500*l.* per annum.

K. Sir Walter Pye of Meene [Mynde] in Dowchurch parish; his father was master [Attorney General] (25,000*l.* per annum), of the Court of Wards: owes Kilpeck Castle in this shire near Hereford, the last decayed, a parke about it now.

---

[a] William Mucklow.—See Ped. C. 30, f. 89, Coll. Arm.

[b] A line is afterwards inserted : " Sir W[m]. Vavasour first Governor of Heref."

K. Sir William Croft of Croft, killd neare Ludlowe at Stoke Castle, a garrison of Parliament; since his howse beate down by us least the Parliament should garrison in it. 2,000*l*. per annum.

K. Sir Giles Bridges, Bart. at Wilton.

N. Sir Richard Hopton, two sons with the King, two with them at [Canon] Frome neare Ledbury, Usurrer.

Sir John Kerle [Kyrle] of Marckle.

K. Mr. Wallop Brabazon, at Eaton by Lemster, his father an Irish Baron. 1,000*l*. per annum.

K. Sir Robert Whitney, of Whitney. 1,000*l*. per annum.

K. Sir Humfrey Baskervile, of Earsley [Erdesley] Castle, travailer. 300*l*. per annum; was 3000.

K. Mr. Tompkins, of Manington [Monington], Burges for Webley. 1,200*l*. per annum.

K. Mr. Roger Dansey [Daunsey], of Brinsop Court. 800*l*. per annum.

[Walter] Baskervile of Canon Peawne [Pion], small estate, [*jure ux.*] first for the Parliament, then for the King, then theirs, then taken prisoner by us, and [with] much adoe gott his pardon, and now *pro Rege*, God wott.

BRINSOP Church, com. Heref.

East window, chancel, fairely painted, the borders with semy of fleurs-de-lis and lyons; these coates as old and large:

> Or, a lion rampant, double-queued, gules.
> Gules, a lion rampant, a bordure engrailed, or [TALBOT].
> Quarterly, 1 and 4, Per pale or and argent, over all three bars wavy gules, "DANSEY"; 2 and 3, a fess, a label of four points.
> A knight standing in complete armour, the breast of his surcoat charged with the cross of St. George, in his hand he holds a pennon, and on his left arm is a shield, both charged with the same cross.
> A lady kneeling. On her robe these arms, viz. Argent, a chevron gules between three hurts.

Divers old-fashioned flat stones in the chancel with flowry crosse wrought on them.

HEREFORD Minster, dedicated to St. Ethelbert.

South yle windows of the quire these coates :

Upper window:

> Or, five chevronels azure [DEANERY OF HEREFORD].
> Gules, a fess or, in chief three bezants.
> Argent, a cross gules.

Second window:

> Vair ermine and gules, two bars azure.
> Ermine, on a chief gules two mullets pierced or.
> Gules, a cross or.

South window, crosse yle, not so old:

> Quarterly, FRANCE and ENGLAND, within a bordure argent.
> Gules, three leopard's faces inverted jessant-de-lis or [CANTALUPE, SEE OF HEREFORD].
> MORTIMER.
> Quarterly, 1 and 4, Gules, a maunche or [HASTINGS] , 2 and 3, Argent, three bars azure, each charged with two martlets sable.
> Gules, a fess or between six cross-crosslets, a crescent for difference [BEAUCHAMP].
> Azure, three crowns or.
> Or, five chevronels azure [DEANERY OF HEREFORD].
> Or, three lion's heads erased gules, a bordure engrailed azure.
> Ermine, a bend lozengy gules.
> Paly of six argent and azure, on a bend gules three eagles displayed or [GRANDISON].
> Argent, on a bend sable three mullets or, a crescent for difference.

East window, north end of the quire:

> SEE OF HEREFORD.
> MORTIMER.
> ENGLAND.
> Vair ermine and gules, two bars azure.

North window, same crosse yle, east end:

> DEANERY OF HEREFORD.
> Or, three chevronels gules [CLARE].
> Gules, an eagle displayed argent.
> Paly of six or and gules.

North window, north yle, quire:

DEANERY OF HEREFORD.
Gules, an eagle displayed argent.
Vair ermine and gules, two bars azure.
Gules, a cross or.
The figure of a knight, in chain mail, holding in his right hand a spear, and bearing upon his left arm a shield or, charged with a cross pattee gules. The belt by which it is suspended is marked azure, the armour argent, and the surcoat or.[a]

South yle windows of the body of the church. Three shields in each window, one above large, the other two small:

ENGLAND.
Or, two bars gules, a bend azure [PEMBRUGGE].
Gules, a fess lozengy or [NEWMARCH].

Second window:

SEE OF HEREFORD.
Gules, fretty or [AUDLEY].
Checky or and azure, within a bordure gules a canton ermine [DREUX DUKE OF BRITTANY].

Third window:

Or, four barrulets gules, in chief a lion passant of the last [TREGOZE].
Azure, semée of fleurs-de-lis or [FEANCE].
Checky or and azure, a chevron ermine [WARWICK].

Fourth window:

DEANERY OF HEREFORD.
Or, a lion rampant sable.
Gules, a fess argent, on a chief gules two roses of the last.

Fifth window:

CLARE.
Bendy of six or and azure, a bordure gules.
Sable, a lion rampant or.

---

[a] There is a drawing of this figure, C. 25, f. 3, Coll. Arm. where also many of the coats here recorded, are given.

Sixth window:

Or, a lion rampant gules.
Bendy of ten or and azure, a canton ermine.
Argent, three roses gules.

Seventh window:

Per pale or and vert, a lion rampant gules [MARSHALL].
Per pale azure and gules, a fess between two chevrons ermine.
Paly of six or and azure [GOURNEY].

Eighth window:

" Gone."
Paly of six argent and azure, on a bend gules three eagles displayed or [GRANDISON].
Paly of six or and gules [GOURNEY].

North windowes, body of the quire.
This in the two uppermost window next the east:

Gules, three fleurs-de-lis or [? for the SEE OF HEREFORD].

Window below the north dore:

ENGLAND.
MARSHALL.
CLARE.

Second window:

ENGLAND, with a label of three points azure, each charged with three bezants; impaling, Azure, a bend argent cotised or " imperfect."
Argent, a maunche gules [TONY].
Or, a maunche gules [HASTINGS].

Third window:

A lion rampant gules, a bordure sable bezanty [CORNWALL].
MORTIMER.
MORTIMER, debruised by a bendlet gules.

Fourth window:

BOHUN.

Azure, three cinquefoils or.

Azure, two bars or, on a chief argent a demi-lion rampant gules.

Lowest window:

Azure, " gone."

Azure, a fess between six cross-crosslets or.

Bendy of ten or and azure [MOUNTFORD].

Under arches, south yle quire, the statues, larger then ordinary, of four bishops, with mitres and crosiers cutt in stone.

1. Verus, 1199 [WILLIAM DE VERE, son of AUBREY EARL OF OXFORD].
2. Robert Foliot, 1186.
3. Robert de Melun, 1167.
4. Robert de Betun, ob. 1148.

Three such like, north yle quire.

One very faire statue betweene north yle and quire, of a bishop in alablaster:

Two chevrons engrailed, between two mullets in chief and one in base.

Another for bishop Bennet.

The SEE OF HEREFORD; impaling, quarterly, 1 and 4, a cross or between four demi-lions rampant gules [BENNETT]; 2 and 3, Paly of six or and vert. " *Motto*, Ben' et melius."

Another statue between the north yle and the crosse yle north side. A north chappel, with this coate often in it:

Argent, two chevrons engrailed sable between two mullets in chief and one in base.

Against the wall, in the south yle, east end, a statue of a bishop.

Ludovicus Charlton, ob. 1369.

These two shields are also upon a crosse out of Hereford, as we ride to Wales:

A lion rampant between six cross-crosslets fitchy.

A lion rampant.

A new statue gainst the south wall, same yle.

> Ludovicus [? Augustinus] Lindsel Ep'us Heref. [ob. 1634].

A chevron between three leopard's faces.

Under the wall of the quier, south side, an old statue of a bishop holdinge a church in his left arme:

> D' Robertus Losinga, Ep'us Heref. consecratus 1072, qui eccl'iam a fundamentis excitavit, et p'fecit. Sedes episcopalis Heref. primū constitut' est.

A handsome alablaster monument against the wall, south crosse yle:

> Two bars gules, in chief three cinquefoils sable.

Another bishop there:

> Three lion's heads erased, a bordure engrailed.

Between the two pillars in the south side of the body of the church, upon an altar tombe, lyes the statue of a knight in alablaster, in armes, fashion of the Black Prince, a garter about his left legge, buckled. **Honi soit.** This coat carved about his tombe:

> Barry of six, over all a bend [PEMBRUGGE].

Upon his breast the same carved. Under his head a large helmet and forth of a [wreath] vert:

> A "helmet" and "mantle" surmounted by a crest, viz., a plume of feathers issuing from a wreath of "roses."

Upon the pillar hangs this shield, painted and fairely guilt.

> Barry or and azure, a bend gules [PEMBRUGGE].

A helme guilt hangs upon the other pillar, the creast, &c. gone. They call him Pembridge. [Sir Richard Pembrugge ob. 1375.]

Within the north wall, body of the church, the statue of a mitered bishop, written

Carolus Booth Ep'us Heref. ob. 1535.

This coate is often spild [*sic orig.*] upon the hall of the pallace:

Argent, a rose gules between three boar's heads erect and erased sable.

In the east end of all the cathedral, upon a large flat stone, the picture of a man in armes, in brasse, inlayed:

Joh'es Delamare Ar. ob. 1400 and od. [RICHARD DE LA MARE].

Three bars dancetty [DE LA MARE].

Divers flat stones in the body of the church for churchmen, some in the quire for bishops.

PEMBRUGE [PEMBRIDGE] Ch. com. Hereford.

East window chancel:

Quarterly, 1 and 4, The Cross of St. George; 2 and 3, MORTIMER.
Quarterly FRANCE and ENGLAND.
The same, with a label of three points argent.
MORTIMER.
Argent, three barnacles extended in pale or, on a chief of the first a demi-lion rampant gules, "PEMBRUGE" [an error,—GENESNELL].
MORTIMER.

North window crosse yle, very old, this coate three times, faire:

GRANDISON.

South window, chancel:

Vair azure and ermine, two bars gules.

Under this window, upon two low altar tombes of playne stone, lye the four bodyes of men and their wives, *ad hanc formam*, old:

Recumbent figures of a man and his wife, probably of the time of Henry VI. The man is attired in a tightly fitting jupon, closely buttoned in front, and has a sword depending from the left side ; over his shoulders is an open robe or cloak fastened with a fibula on the right shoulder.   The figure of the female is rudely defined ; the sleeves are open and the head-dress is of the time of Henry VI.   The hands of both are joined upon the breast in the attitude of prayer.

This is observable, for never afore have I seene a thing of that age (unles a churchman) without armor.

The other is of another fashioned habitt, not so observable, in a kind of a long robe, without any thing on his head.

The inhabitants say they were in memory of the Gowres of Worcestershire.

About five myle from Pembruge is Wigmore, an antient seate of the Mortimers of Wigmore; now Sir Robert Harlow [Harley] the Reb. owes it.[a]

Steppleton Castle, in this shire, another ancient seate of the Mortimers Earl of the Marches; now Sir Gilbert Cornwall owes it.

> Argent, a lion rampant gules, within a bordure engrailed sable, bezanty,
> " CORNWALL."

The antient seate of Cornwall is at Burford, neare Tenbury, which also Sir Gilbert owes.

Steppleton Castle was strong, but because there was no water neare, it was pulld downe by Ludlowes governour, least the enemy might make use of it.   Defaced.

Croft howse defaced by Ludlowe['s] men.

Mr. William Littleton's howse defaced, least the enemy should make use of them.

Here in Herefordsh. a quarter of mutton 14d. rye 12d. a bushel: rye is the best grayne growes generally in the county, and oates and pease: little timber in the shire.

The day before we came to Hereford his Majestie had intelligence that Fairfax had appeared before Leicester, and that the Lord Loughborough had yeilded it upon conditions.

To march away the soldjers, sans armes, officers with swords.

a Grandfather of Robert Earl of Oxford.

Two regiments of horse, vizt. Queenes and Caryes; the men marched, but horses and armes the enemy had.

1,500 foot marched out of Leicester withe those gentlemen and wounded men that came in I suppose.

At Hereford, Wednesday, 25 June, the King knighted Sir Dudley Wyatt and sent him to France.

Munday, 30 June, the King's horse-guards removed to Gresmond, com. Monmouth.

There is the walls of an old castle on the north side of the towne, moted, but in part dry; upon the quarry of stone.

No armes nor monuments with inscriptions worth noting in Gresmond church.

GRESMOND [Grosmont], com. Monmouth.

In the east end of the church in the yard lyes a flat stone, whereon is cutt the statue of a preist called John of Kent, and the picture of the divell.

> A rude representation of the slab in question. The priest and Satan, who is represented with long ears, a beak-shaped nose, and cloven feet, face each other, and each has his hand familiarly placed on the other's shoulder.

John of Kent's patron Scudamore was sued a very sudden day of appearance about ten of the clock at night to be there next morning at London. John gott a black horse and carried his patron to London at that time. At last John[a] cosend the divell.

Here and in other parishes of this shire they dresse the graves with herbs every Sunday or holy-day.

Garrisons in com. Monmouth.

K. Monmouth. Sir Thomas Lundsford is Governour; Herb. Lunsford, Governour.

K. Ragland Castle, the habitation of the Marq. of Worcester. His fourth son Charles Lord Somerset is Governour. 300 foot. No contribution, and constantly paid.

[a] See the account of this (somewhat) apocryphal personage, in Coxe's Monmouthshire, with the references to Leland, &c.

K. Abergaveny. Colonel James Prodgers is Governour; Charles Prodgers, Leift.-G.

K. Chepstowe. Sir John Winter is Governour. The county payes for 500. 300 men now in it.

K. Newport. Colonel Herbert, first son to the Lord Cherbury. 50 men; contribution for 500.

Cheife Inhabitants of Monmouthshire.

K. H. Herbert, Marquesse of Worcester, lives at Ragland Castle, his whole estate *ubique* was esteemed 24 thowsand pounds per annum. Writes thus:—H. Worcester. Lord Herbert is his eldest son.

K. Sir William Morgan, lives at Tredegar.

K. Mr. Thomas Morgan, son to Sir William of Marghen [Machen].

K. Sir Philip Jones of Treowen, Knight, two sons in armes pro R.

K. Sir William Herbert of Colbrooke.

K. Sir George Probert at Pantlace.

Sir Trevor Williams, Baronet, of Llangubby.

Mr. Davie Lewis, of Llantheney, Esq.

Mr. William Baker at Abergaveny.

Mr. Henry Baker.

Tuesday, 1° of July, his Majestie left Hereford and marched to Abergaveny, com. Monmouth. He marched onely with these horse: King's troope, Queenes troope, Prince Rupert's troope of life-guard, Prince Rupert's regiment of horse.

The Governor of Hereford with the gentlemen of the shire attended the King to Mr. Pritchard's howse neare Gresmond, where the King dyned.

There his Majestie knighted Sir Henry Linghan [Lingen] of Herefordshire. [Knighted July 6, 1645.]

King's troope quartered this night at Treargaire [Tregare], Broingwine [Bryngwin], Bettus, and Clethey [Clytha], com. Monmouth, neare Ragland Castle.

Castles in com. Monmouth.

Chepstow; now habitable; Lord Marquis of Worcester owes it.

Ragland ; idem; Marquis of W. lives in it.

Monmouth; idem owes it; habitable.

Uske; Philip Earle of Pembrooke owes it; habitable.

Carlien [Caerleon]; idem; ruined.

Newport; idem; ruined.

Abergaveny; Nevill, Baron thereof, owes it; ruined.

Arnold; Lord Abergaveny owes it; ruined.

Casgwyn, or white castle; Marquis of Worcester owes it; ruined.

Gresmond; idem owes it; ruined.

Skenfrith [Skenfreth] ; idem owes it; ruined.

These three last were belonging to the Dutchy of Lancaster.

Langebby [Langibby]; Sir Trevor Williams in it; strong and inhabited and fortified; sixty men in it.

Cast-roggy ; Marquis of Worcester; ruined.

Pencoad [Pencoed]; Sir Edward Morgan lives in it; very faire, now high sheriffe.

Pen Howe [Penhow]; Sir Edmund Morgan lives in it; very faire.

Beeston (Beetson neare Seaverne) [Bishton]; Bishop of Landaffe owes it, and habitable.   Bishopstowne.

Callicot [Caldicot].

Trewilliam.

Grenefeild Castle, no ruines left.

Thursday, July 3, his Majestie went to Ragland Castle and lay there.

Upon the pictures of the family of the Earles of Worcester in the gallery at Ragland Castle is upon the two antientest the armes and his name written: vizt.

Quarterly, FRANCE and ENGLAND, within a bordure gobony argent and azure, debruised by a bend sinister or ; the shield is surmounted by an earl's coronet, the whole encircled by the garter.

CAROLUS COMES WIGORNII, " father, and first Earle."

Quarterly, 1 and 4, Or, on a fess the arms of SOMERSET ; 2, Per pale and three lions rampant [HERBERT] ; 3, Argent, a fess and canton gules [WIDVILLE], surmounted by an earl's coronet, the whole within the garter.

HENRICUS COMES WIGORNII, " son, and second Earle."

RAGLAND Church, com. Monmouth.

Against the north wall in a chappel a faire monument, the statue of one man in armour, and parliament robes, and knight of the garter :

Perpetuæ Posteritati Monumentum, Gulielmo Somerset, Vigorniæ Comiti, D' de Cheapstow Ragland et Gower, præclarissimi ordinis Garterij Equiti Aurat', Edwardus modo Comes, solus filius et hæres p'd'i Gulielmi, erexit.   Obijt 21 March, ætat. 61, 1589.

Uxor Cristiana filia D'ni Edw. North, Baronis.

Quarterly, 1 and 4, Or, on a fess FRANCE and ENGLAND quarterly within a bordure gobony argent and azure ; 2, HERBERT ; 3, Or, a fess and canton conjoined gules [WIDVILLE].   The whole within a garter. Supporters, dexter a " tiger chayned sable " ; sinister, a " goat sable."

The same ; impaling, Azure, a lion passant between three fleurs-de-lis or [NORTH].

Another faire one, two statues of a man and woman, under an arch betweene the chancel and this chappell.   He in parliament robes, garter, badge, *sans glorie*, an earles crowne, and the Privy Seale purse.   Edward Somerset, died about 16 years since.·   Same quarterings; supporters, the black goat chayned or, greene dragon chayned or.   Leopard upon a chapeu crest; Motto, " Mutare vel timere sperno."

SOMERSET ; impaling, HASTINGS, the whole within a garter.   Supporters; dexter, a "leopard chayned and spotted of several colours ;" sinister, a " bull or ;"   Motto, " Mutare vel timere sperno."
" Somerset's supporter   " Hastings' supporter
          one side."   this side."

This is an old proverbe in this shire:

Pyn ddel y brenin i Raglan, yna bytt duedd y Cymre.
Woe be to the Welchmen when the King comes to Ragland.

These are old in the hall windowes of this strong and princely castle:

Argent, a lion rampant sable within a garter [THOMAS LORD MORLEY, ob. 1416].
HERBERT, within a garter.

This is carved, old, on the wall on the outside:

Three lions rampant; impaling, a fess, in chief three martlets.

Herbert was the antient owner of this castle.

His Majestie stayd at Ragland till Wednesday, July 16, 1645.

About the 8 of July the two troopes were going to Black Rock, and the King intended to goe over, had not Goring's newes stopt.

Within a myle of Margham, where Sir Edward Seabright lives, in com. Glamorgan, upon the crosse in the street of this village, thus:

Sketch of a stone cross, upon which is sculptured a crucifix occupying nearly the entire length of the stone, the upper part of which is supported by a male figure crowned with a tiara, seated, which, with the addition of a dove upon the arm of the cross, is intended to represent the Trinity.

Almost in every parish the crosse or sometime two or three crosses perfect in Brecknockshire, Glamorganshire, &c.

H. W. and R. S.   Friday, 4 July, to Brecknock, where Colonel General Herbert Prise lives, and is Governour.   Colonel Turbervil Morgan is Governour under him.

BRECKNOCK Church, without the towne.

In a window, north yle church, old:

Or, a chevron gules [STAFFORD]; impaling, Quarterly, FRANCE and ENGLAND, within a bordure argent.

In the crosse yle, south side, is a large playne altar tombe of course stone, arched, and under the arch two statues; he in armes chayned; the shields about the sides are painted, and almost gone.

Quarterly, 1, Gules, a saltire argent [NEVILLE]; 2, a lion rampant; 3 and 4, (blank).

It looks old as Black Prince; under his head a helme and a garbe upon it.

Another there, the body of a man cutt in wood crosse-legged, a shield on his left arm, very old and decayed.

In the chancel is a monument of three storyes one above another; each hath the statues of a man and woman; this coate:

A chevron between three spear heads.
Crest, on a wreath a wyvern gules.

Prise his ancestors.

In the body of the church a multitude of flat stones, the west end broader then the east, and a crosse flowry carved on them; the inscription is circumscribed, commonly in Latine, and in many the armes of his family.

Sketch of the stones described.

And some has a Welch rhyme to ornifie them.

[July] 5. To Golden Grove, the sweet and plentiful seate of Vaughan, Earl of Carbery in Ireland.

Quarterly, 1 and 4, Per fess sable and argent, a lion rampant counter-changed, VAUGHAN; 2 and 3, Argent, a chevron gules between three pheons sable.
The same, "with many quarterings," impaling, Per pale azure and sable, three fleurs-de-lis or.

Golden Grove church, nil; but Sir John Vaughan built it, and his armes ut supra.

Wednesday, July 16. His Majestie, attended with the Duke of Richmond, Earles of Lindsey, Lichfield, Kernwagh [Carnwath], Lords Digby and Bellasis, his two troopes, went to Sir William

Morgan's howse com. Monmouth, and dyned, and that night to Cardiffe; the castle is the ancient possession and barony of the Earle of Pembrooke.

To meet the commissioners to rayse men, and settle the towne.

Thursday night his Majestie lay at Sir William Morgan's.

Friday to Ragland.

About Thursday, July 10, Sir Thomas Fairfax and Lord Goring had a touch about Ilchester com. Somerset; lost two great guns and not 200 men. Goring putt his ordnance into Bridgwater, and his cariages, and (*blank*) hundred foot; himselfe and the rest retreated to Teverton com. Devon.

An army of Scotts at this time at Droit Wiche com. Wigorn. Parl. shipps tooke many of Swansey boates, and some from Cardiffe.

About the 16 of July, Prince Rupert beate Sir Robert Pye's quarters at Wells, with some horse out of Bristol.

Bridgwater beseiged by Fairfax from about the 11 of July.

July 17. Came a gent. to Cardiffe with newes to the King that Lord Montrose had beate the Scotts neare Endenburgh, killd Bayly their Leiftenant-Generall, rowted the rest. Montrose was about 8,000 foot, two troopes of horse.

Tuesday, July 22. His Majestie went to Creeke, Mr. Moore's howse, attended with the Duke of Richmond, Earls of Lindsey and Lichfield, Lord Digby and Astley, his servants, and other gentlemen, and met Prince Rupert from Bristoll. The resolution was to send over the horse as soone as may be, and putt all the new raysed foot in that principality into garrisons. His Majestie returned that night to Ragland, his highnes the Prince to Bristoll.

Thursday, 24 July, came intelligence to Bristoll that Sir Thomas Fairfax had taken Bridgwater the day before. Propositions were sent into the towne, that the inhabitants and townesmen should have quarter. The townesmen sett it on fyre in divers places. In the meane time they stormed it and got it. Most of the towne was burnt, except some howses neare the castle.

The Scotts at this time, about Wednesday, 23 July, stormed a

howse called Cannon Froome, a garrison of the King's in Herefordshire; Colonel Barnard, Govcrnour: all were putt to the sword.

Thursday, 24 July, the King came to Black Rock, intending to
gett over towards Bristoll; the gentlemen of Wales earnestly persuaded his stay, and ymediately raysed the hoop hoop.

The newes of Bridgwater's unexpected losse rather stayed him.

Colonel Taylor's regiment of foot in Bristoll, townesmen; six
colours:

Drawings of two standards bearing,

  1. Argent, in fess point a heart gules in bend, on a canton a cross. Motto,
     " Pro Deo et Rege."
  2. The same, with the addition of another heart in bend.

The rebells are making a garrison of a howse three myle from
Bathe, Bromham More.

In the Colledge Church, upon the Greene in BRISTOLL.

Divers windowes; amongst other coates, cheifly and most frequent
this of Berkley:

Gules, a chevron between ten crosses pattee argent [BERKELEY].

Under an arch south side of the quire, old, the cheveron and
crosses embosse out:

Sketch of the recumbent effigy of a Knight Templar, in chain mail.
The right hand grasps the hilt of the sword, and from the left arm
hangs a shield charged with the coat of Berkeley.

A little below lyes another like the former, the charge as aforesaid, embossing and cutt upon the sheild; the cheveron stands
in cheife:

Sketch of a similar effigy.

Under an arch neare the north yle, body of the church, two
statues of a man and woman upon an altar-tombe. The chevron and
ten crosses carved upon his breast.

Upon the portall or gatehowse of the monastery, two statues, one of a king, the other of a churchman. Under each these coates:

Three lions passant guardant [ENGLAND].
BERKELEY.

Carved over the gate in old text:

Rex Henricus S'c'dus et d'nus . . . fil'.—Herdyngi filij Regis Daci. primi huius Monasterij fundatores extiterunt.

St. MARKES Church; upon the Greene, ibidem, commonly called the Gaunts.

Against the north wall, chancel, the statue of a bishop, called Bishop Berkley; no mention of him by shield or inscription.

Upon an altar-tombe in the chancel two statues fairely cutt in alablaster, he and she.

Sketch of a knight templar, as above, but without a shield, the hands being folded on the breast. On the surcoat the arms of BERKELEY.

Sunday, July 27, 1645.   His Majestie lay at Ruperrie [Ruperra], a faire seate of Mr. Morgan, com. Monmouth.   The Castle of Abergeney burnt, viz. the habitable part.   The garrison drawne out and quitted.

About this time the garrison of Kilpeck Castle, in Herefordshire, slighted.

Tuesday, July 29.   His Majestie, attended by the Duke of Richmond ; Earl of Lindsey, High Chamberlain; Earl of Lichfield; Lord Kernwagh; and his regiment of guards, went from Ruperrie to Cardiffe, there dyned, and in the afternoone went to a rendesvouz of the country men and inhabitants of Glamorganshire: there he mett the gentlemen of the county in a body on horsebak, and the rest drawne up in a battaile, winged with horse and a reserve.   His Majestie returned that night to Cardiffe.

LANDAFFE Cathedral, com. Glamorgan.

North window of the Ladies Chappel. Very old, twise, and very large.

Or, three chevrons gules [CLARE], "fifteen ynches."

A chappel where they have Welch prayers onely.

Under an arch, north side of this chappel, upon an altar tombe two statues in alablaster: he in armour and collar of S fairely guilt, his helme and creast under his head. About the verge this :—

𝕺rate p' a'i'abus Xpoferi Mathew Armigeri et Elizabethae ux' sue, que quidem Eliz. obiit penultimo die Januarii, aᵒ. d'ni M . . . . . . (About 1500.)

Sable, a lion rampant argent, armed gules; impaling, Argent, a griffin segreant sable.

Another upon an altar tombe against the north wall in a chappel, mantle, helme, and creast under his head. Dove his creast.

For great David Mathew, standard bearer to K.

A lion rampant.

In the east window of that chappel:

Quarterly, 1 and 4, BEAUCHAMP; 2 and 3, WARWICK.

In the north yle of the quire a statue of a bishop. A naked body, with a miter on his head, going out of his mouth, and layd hold on by an angel, for his soule.

This coate, large, carved on the wall:

A shield upon which are sculptured the instruments of our Lord's Passion

In the quire three statues of bishops lying on the ground cutt into the stone.

Six monuments of bishops in all in this church. Whereof [one] is a flat stone inlayed in brasse, the brasse gone.

The oldest is cutt into a stone in blew marble lying on the ground; upon the steps of the altar.

In a chappel, east end of the south yle of the quire:

Barry of six or and vert, semée of fleurs-de-lis counterchanged.

Against the wall the statue of woman, old, for Cristian Maudlem, the first beginner of the family of Mathew.

East window aloft; over the altar, large and old:

ENGLAND.
Gules, a lion rampant guardant or.
Gules, ten bezants, 4, 3, 2 and 1 [ZOUCHE].
CLARE.

Painted upon the bishop's seate the Virgin Mary carryed up by angels; the picture of a bishop praying neare, with a miter and crosier.

Virgo scandens sis Marshall celica pandens.

Betweene two pillars in the north side of the quire, upon a faire altar-tombe, two statues in alablaster, fairely carved and gilt collar of S, and this [viz. a cross pattée] hanging on it. His helme and creast under his head. About the verge this:

Orate p' a'i'abus Will'mi Mathew Militis, qui obiit decimo die Marcii A° D. 1528, et etiam Jenete ux'is ejus, que Deo reddidit . . . . die mensis . . . . A° d'ni 1500 q. a. p. d. a.

About the sides, angels hold the shields, painted:

Sable, a lion rampant argent; impaling, CLARE.
Quarterly, 1, A lion rampant; 2, Per pale, i. Gules, a lion rampant argent; ii. Argent, on a cross sable five crescents or; 3, Gules, three chevronels argent; 4, Argent, a chevron or, in chief a lion passant gules.
Intended to be quarterly: 1, Gules, a lion rampant argent; 2, Per pale azure and argent, on a cross sable five crescents or; 3, Ermine, a chevron or, in chief a lion passant gules.

A dove the creast, upon a wreath.

St. Faggin's Church, com. Glamorgan, two myle from Landaffe.

East window of the church this, twice:

Or, three chevronels gules.　[Clare.]

Neare the church stands a faire howse within the old walls of a castle, called St. Faggin's, the heire of Mr. Edward Lewis, Esq. owes it.　Lewis his coate:

Quarterly, 1, A lion rampant; 2, a chevron between three fleurs-de-lis (?); 3, Three chevronels; 4, A chevron between three broken spears (?)

In the orchard of this howse, under an old ewe tree, is a spring or well within the rock called Saint Faggin's Well: many resort from all parts to drinke it for the falling sicknes, and cures them at all seasons.　Many come a yeare after they have dranke of [it,] and relate there health ever since.

At this rendesvouz, in com. Glamorgan, some articles or propositions were tendered to his Majestie, which if he would please to grant, they would march and continue in a body for the defence of his Majestie and their countrey.

Propositions were [one only is given] :— ·

That the garrison of Cardiffe might be governed by a countrey gentleman of their owne.

Wednesday, 30 July.　This body of the inhabitants of Glamorganshire had their rendesvouz within four myles of Cardiffe.

They lay in the field this night, and provision brought unto them.

Thursday, this body chose their officers of their owne countrey. Every hundred chose their owne captains, &c.　Their rendesvouz was at Kevenon, four myles from Cardiffe, the same place as the day afore.　This day the King and they agreed upon their propositions.　Friday the rendesvouz was Llantrissent.　They first called themselves the Peaceable Army.

Cheife Inhabitants of Glamorgansh.

David Evans, Esq. commissioner of aray, of Neath towards Caermarthenshire. 1,000*l*. per annum.

Bushie Maunsell, Esq. of Burton [Britton] Ferrie. 1,100*l*. per annum.

Sir . . . Maunsell, Baronet of Margham. 4,000*l*. per annum. Infra etat. Sir Edward Seabright married his mother.

. . Llougher, Esq. of [? . . . Esq. of Lloughor.] 400*l*. per annum.

Sir Edward Stradling, Bart. of St. Donat's Castle. 4,000*l*. per annum if out of lease.

. . . . Turbervill, Esq. of the Skerr. Descended from one of the twelve knights that came in with Fitzhamond at the Conquest. 600*l*. per annum.

Edward Kerne [Carne], Esq. of Wenney[Ewenny]. 1,000*l*. per annum. Fine seate, a priory.

. . . . Winne of Llansannor, Esq. 600*l*. per annum.

Sir Edward Thomas, Baronet, of Bettus. 1,600*l*. per annum.

Sir Richard Basset, of the Beaupare [Beaupré], Knight. 1,000*l*. per annum.

John Van, Esq. of Marcrosse. 500*l*. per annum.

Sir John Aubrey, Baronet, of Llantrithid. 1,000*l*. per annum.

William Powell, barister-at-law, of Bonvilstowne. 300*l*. per annum.

David Jenkins, of Hensoll, judge of three counties, Caermarthenshire, Cardigan, and Pembroke. 2,000*l*. was paid, 1,200*l*. per annum, raysd *a nihilo*.

Miles Button, Esq. of Cottrel, 400*l*. per annum, ancient in this place. Buttons of Wiltshire descended hence.

Robert Button, Esq. of Worlton. 400*l*. per annum.

Sir Thomas Lewis, Knight, of Penmarke. 800*l*. per annum.

Nicholas Lewis, Esq. his elder brother, of Carne Lloyd. 400*l*. per annum.

William Thomas, Esq. of Wenvoe. 2,500*l*. per annum.

William Herbert, of Coggan Peele [Cogan Pill], Esq.; his father slayne at Edghill. 1,000*l*. per annum, near the sea.

Edward Lewis, Esq. de Van and St. Faggin's [St. Fagan's], 5,000*l*. p. a. all improvable.

Humfrey Mathew, Esq. Colonel of the county, had his command from the King; of Castle Mennich [Mynach], or Monkes Castle. 800*l*. per annum.

...... Mathew, Esq. of Aberaman. 800*l*. per annum.

Edw. Prichard, Esq. of Llancayach. 800*l*. per annum.

Sir William Lewis, Kt. of Killachuargod. 400*l*. per annum.

Thomas Lewis, Esq. of Llanissent (? Llantrisaint). 500*l*. per annum.

William Herbert, Esq. of the Fryars, in Caerdiffe. 1,000*l*. per annum.

David Mathew, Esq. of Landaffe. 600*l*. per annum.

Marmaduke Mathewes of Landaffe, Esq. a lease.

Sir Nicholas Kemys, Baronet, of Kaven Mabley [Cefn Mabley], a fine seate. 1800*l*. per annum.

.... Morgan, Esq. of Ruperrie, a faire seate. 1000*l*. per annum.

George Lewis, Esq. of Llistalyfron. 400*l*. per annum.

Walter Thomas, Esq. of Swansey, was governour. 600*l*. per annum. His son high sheriffe.

Jenkin Morgan, Esq. 300*l*. per annum. Serjeant-at-arms to the King. Towards the mountaynes westward.

William Basset, Esq. of Bromisken. 600*l*. per annum, 20,000*l*. in (*blank*) p.

All aforesaid, and so generally against any that are against the King.

Men from 40*l*. per annum to 200*l*., above 100 men more in this county.

Garrisons in Glamorganshire.

K. Cardiffe; Sir T. Tyrell made governour by Generall Gerard.

Sir Anthony Mauncell was first governour; killed at Newbery: William Mathew of St. Faggin's [St. Fagan's].

Sir Nich. Kemys was governour when Gerard came, and putt out himselfe, and then Tyrel putt in.

K. Swansey; Walter Thomas first governour; putt in by the King before Gerard came. Then Colonel Richard Donnel was made by (*blank*).

This county never dealt with the militia. Never admitted.

Thursday, July 31, in the Castle of Cardiffe the King knighted his cornet, Sir John Walpoole.

CARDIFFE Church, com. Glamorgan.

In the lower north window of the north yle, this very old and large, the lower part of the bodyes and the glasse is gone, *ut hic*:

> A heater-shaped shield bearing ENGLAND, debruised by a bendlet azure [HENRY EARL OF LANCASTER]; impaling, Barry argent and gules [CHAWORTH].
>
> Beneath are the figures of a knight in armour and his wife facing each other, with their hands raised in the attitude of prayer. The knight's surcoat is embroidered with the charge on the dexter side of the shield, the lady's robe with that on the sinister.

In the north yle of the chancel is a large monument for one of the family of Herbert, Knight, not long since erected, and that is all worth observation there.

Some matches of the family of Herbert in the windowes of Cardiffe Castle, not old.

In the church of Aburgaveny, com. Monmouth, are antient monuments, statues of this family of Herbert.

Munday, 4 Aug. King's guards marched toward Brecknock.

Tuesday 5. His Majestie left Cardiffe, and went that night over the mountaynes to Brecknock.

Wednesday to Radnor; by the way dyned at Sir [Henry] Williams, Baronet's, howse, and faire seate in Brecknock shire [Gwernyet].

Thursday to Ludlowe. In this march he was accompanied with these horse:

General Gerard's.	Sir Marmaduke Langdale's.
His life guards 300.	Sir William Vaughan's.

Sir Thomas Glemham's foot, that came from Carlisle to Cardiffe, marched as the King's life-guard.

His horse in all 300.

Friday 8, to Bridgnorth, a pretty towne, one church beside that in the castle. Sir Lewis Kirke is governour.

In the hall windowes of Ludlow Castle:

> Quarterly, FRANCE and ENGLAND, a label of three points argent; impaling, Gules, a saltire argent [NEVILLE].
>
> Argent, a fess between four barrulets gules [BADLESMERE].
> Or, a fess gules.
> (*Blank*).
> [Azure], three barnacles extended in pale or, on a chief or a demi-lion rampant gules "PEMBRIDGE" [an error—GENESNELL].

Satterday rested. Sunday to Lichfeild, 24 myles.

Munday rested. Tuesday to Tedbury.

Wednesday to Ashborne, com. Derb.

Three garrisons of the enemies lately erected in com. Salop. since Shrewsbury was lost:—

R. Stoke Castle.

R. Broncroft, the howse of Mr. John Lutley in Dilbury parish.

R. Benthall.

ASHBORNE Church, com. Derb.:

East window, chancel.

> Quarterly, FRANCE and ENGLAND, a label of three points ermine.
> ENGLAND, a label of three points azure.
> Gules, ten bezants, a canton argent [ermine, ZOUCHE].
> Gules, three water-bougets argent [Ros].
> Argent, a pile gules charged with a martlet argent.
> Argent, an eagle displayed azure, legged gules.
> Paly of six or and gules, a bendlet argent [? BURGHILL].
> Vair or and gules.
> Paly of six argent and azure, a bendlet gules [? BURGHILL].
> Argent, on a bend gules three mullets or [BRADBURNE].
> Argent, two bars and a canton azure, the latter charged with a martlet or.
> Per pale indented sable and ermine, a chevron gules fretty argent; impal-

ing, Gules, a fess between four barrulets argent [? for BADLESMERE, colours misplaced].

Ermine, two bendlets gules.

Argent, a chevron engrailed between three crosses pattée fitchy sable.

Argent, two bars and a canton sable, the latter charged with a cinquefoil argent.

Argent, a chevron gules between three crescents, an annulet for difference or.

Quarterly, 1 and 4, Or, a castle azure [AYALA]; 2 and 3, Barry nebuly or and sable [BLOUNT].

Argent, a chevron per pale azure and gules, between three eagles displayed gules.

Argent, a buck's head caboshed gules, between the horns a fleur-de-lis.

Ermine, on a chief gules three bezants.

Gules, six fleurs-de-lis, 3, 2 and 1, argent.

Sable, fretty or, a canton ermine.

Gules, on a chevron or two " bars nebuly " sable [Vair or and sable].

South window, crosse yle, old:

Paly of six or and gules, a bendlet [? BURGHILL].

Ermine, on a chief dancetty gules three crowns or.

Quarterly, 1 and 4, Argent, three cocks gules, COCKAYNE: 2 and 3, Argent, two bars vert [HARTHULL].

Argent, a buck's head caboshed, attired gules, between the horns a fleur-de-lis.

Argent, on a bend gules three mullets or.

North window crosse yle, coming in, old:

Quarterly, FRANCE and ENGLAND [a bordure argent].

Sable, a bend or, between six escallops.

Gules, a chevron vair argent and sable, in dexter chief a key argent.

The same, with a martlet for a difference.

Ermine, two bendlets gules.

In the south crosse yle, upon an altar tombe, two statues, he in armour; this and divers coates painted on the side, old:

Argent, on a bend gules three mullets or [BRADBURNE]; impaling, Argent, fretty sable, " SACHEVEREL " [an error—VERNON].

Another large one with divers coates[a] and quarterings on the sides:

> Sir Humfrey Bradburne, Knight, ob. 1581.
> Argent, on a saltire azure five water-bougets or [SACHEVERELL].
> The same; impaling, Argent, on a bend gules three mullets or [BRADBURNE].

In the east window of the north crosse, yle, aloft:

> Quarterly, 1 and 4, Argent, three cocks gules, "COKAINE"; 2, HARTHULL; 3, (*blank*) impaling, 1, a fess between "three maiden heds"; 2, Gules, a chevron between three cross-crosslets or, "like Rich his coate."
> Or, three piles gules, a canton argent charged with a griffin segreant sable; impaling, Quarterly, 1 and 4, COCKAYNE; 2 and 3, HARTHULL.

A faire altar-tombe, two statues, under his head forth of a wreath a cock's head.

Another there, north yle, two statues of men, he on the right hand in armes of the fashion of Black Prince. Three cocks carved on his breast. One of the statues was serjeant-at-law, the other a soldjer. See the fashion of the serjeant's habit.

> Sketch of a male figure habited in a tightly fitting jupon with embroidered belt; the right arm is bare, the left nearly hidden by cloak or robe.

Another for Cockayne, with divers quarterings. Rather for one that married a Cockayne, this coate:

> A chevron between three crescents; impaling, COCKAYNE.

Two more, one whereof late, for Cockaine.[b]
Now Mrs. Cockaine lives in a faire brick howse in this towne.

---

[a] These coates are given in C. 34, f. 95, Coll. Arm., as also the preceding coats in glass, though with some variations. See also the pedigrees of Bradburne and Sacheverell, Vincent 146.

[b] All these tombs are described in C. 34, Coll. Arm. See also the pedigree of Cockayne, same MS., and in Vincent 146.

LICHFEILD Cathedral, com. Staff.

In the body of the church and yles few or no coates of armes.
Some of the royall family in the west window, and some in the
north window, crosse yle.

Four or five matches of this family in the south window, south
yle of the quire:

> Or, two lions passant azure [CAMVILLE]; impaling (*blank*).

At the east end, in the crosse yle, beyond the altar, upon an
altar-tombe, the statue of a knight in chayned armour, not unlike
the fashion of the Black Prince, and a lady by him; many shields on
the sides painted, much defaced and abused when the rebells were
there:

> Three piles gules, a canton. " They call it BASSET's monument." [a]

In the middle of the crosse yle was a faire and lofty monument,
not long since erected for the memory of the family of Paget, but
now pulld a pieces and the statues throwne about.

> A cross engrailed between four eagles displayed, " PAGET's coate."

Three or four monuments, statues for bishops, and two or three for
deanes, is all worth observing besides in this pretty cathedrall.

Without the wall on the south side are two statues for deanes of
this church.

Wednesday, August 13, in this march a body of 500 of the
enemies horse fell upon our reare, neare Barton garrison, by Tedbury; were well received by us, twenty of ours hurt, three or four

---

[a] Ralph Lord Bassett of Drayton, K.G. ob. 1390. See a drawing of this monument,
C. 36, f. 58, Coll. Arm.

on both sides kill'd; wee toke twelve prisoners and lost some, and a captain. Generall Gerard's reere.

The Scotts beate up Prince Maurice's troope of Reformadoes, commanded by Lord Molineux, at their quarters at Bewdley; tooke them almost all.

When the King came from Lichfield he drew out thence— Foot 100, which march now with him.

Sir Thomas Glemham's foot were made dragoons in Brecknockshire, and march too with us.

Thursday, August 14. His Majestie marched over the Peake to Chatsworth, com. Derb., a very faire howse of stone amongst the barren hills belonging to the Countesse of Devon.

[CHATSWORTH.]

In the gallery of this howse is a pedigree of the family of Cavendish written on the wall, and the coate depicted underneath on the wainescot. 1575 gallery.

A saltire engrailed azure, on a chief three roses [HARDWICKE].

This coate is often about the howse.
The howse was built 1° Queen Mary.

In the gallery.

Sir William Cavendish, Treasurer of his Majesties chamber, second son to Thomas Cavendish, of Cavendish, in ye county of Suff. Esq.

Blank shield.

Sir Thomas Cavendish, knight of the Rodes, slayne in Hungaria against the Turkes.

Sable, three buck's heads caboshed argent, attired or, a crescent for a difference, on a chief gules a cross or.

Sir William Cavendish, Treasurer of the King's Majesties chamber, married Elizabeth, daughter of John Hardwick, of Hardw., Esq.

CAVENDISH, with a crescent for a difference; impaling HARDWICK.

Friday to Wellbeck, a garrison, the howse of the Marquis of Newcastle, where Colonel Fretesvil [Fretchville] is Governor.

King's guards at Warsop [Worksop], com. Notting.

Welbeck was surprised by Newarke horse under the command of Sir Richard Willys, about three weekes since. In a wood neare the port stood his horse in ambush, and when the trevall was beate, and [they] lett downe their bridge for their scouts, our horse under the command of Major Jarnot, a Frenchman, rid hard, and, though they pulld up the bridge a foot high, yet they gott in and tooke it. They disputed every yard, and our men alighted, and with their pistolls scalld and gott in.

Satterday rested, 17 August.

Warsop Manor, com. Derb.: is a faire stone howse belonging to the Earle of Arundell.

Here are three large noble howses, very neare, within (*blank*) myles of each:—

Warsop Manor.

Welbeck, the Marquis of Newcastle.

[Thoresby] the howse of Marquis Dorchester.

Scotts removed their seige of Hereford, and are advaunced towards Chester.

Fairfax is before Sherborne Castle, where Sir Lewis Dyve is Governour.

Sunday, after sermon at Welbeck, the King went into Yorkesshire, and lay at (*blank*).

General Gerard lay at Tickhill, com. Ebor.: where the enemy has a castle comanded by a high constable.

The King's guards to Doncaster, com. Ebor.

Munday morning the King came to Doncaster.

The foot which were at Pontfract Castle when it was yeilded were putt into Welbeck howse under Colonel Fretesvill's command, and when his Majestie marched to Doncaster he drew them out, vizt. 250, four blew colours and one red:

> A standard azure, on a canton a cross, issuant therefrom a pennon wavy argent.

Munday, August 19, 1645.

His Majesties army consisted of these :—

His lifeguard of horse commanded by Lord Bernard Stuart, Earl of Lichfield, consisted of the King's troope, Queenes troope, Lord Lichfield's troope, Sir Thomas Glemham's horse commanded by Sir Henry Stradling. Toto effectually 300
Generall Gerard (Lord Brandon) [a] 800
Sir Marmaduke Langdale's brigade 700
Sir William Vaughan's brigade, with Prince Maurice's regiment 400

Effectually fighting Horse toto 2,200

Foot.

Welbeck 250
Lichfield, drawne out when the King came thence . 150

400

Some ammunition carried upon horses, three or four carts full of pikes, which the King had from Tedbury, which were Colonel Nevill's of Holt.

A medicine for the Botts in horse.

Two spoonfull of honey in a good quantity of milke, given in a horne. This is sweet, and drawes the wormes out of the mawe, and fill their bellies, and drawes them on a heape.

Then a while after give him the like quantity of sweet ale or beere, and in it a handfull of salt, and that will kill them all.

[a] Not so created until Oct. 8, in that year.

For a blow in a horse's eye.

Burne salt, and blow it in.

Pro eod.—Ground ivy, salindane, goose dung, of equall proportion, the juice spouted into the eye, and a quarter of an howre
after burnt salt.

The following notes are at the beginning of the book :

Brackley, in Northamptonshire, bordering upon Buckingham,
divers knights templars buried.

Stotterne [Stathern], in Leicestershire, two myles from Belvoyr
Castle, where Dr. Dereham[a] lived, that received one Horner to be a
schoole-mr. to some youthe in his howse. This Horner maintained
many atheisticall opinions, dyed suddenly, and his grave is still to
be seene in that churchyard bare and suncke, without any grasse
ever that grew there since. D[r] F.

Here follow some "Harbingers' papers" relative to the billeting of the
troops, but which are too indistinct and uninteresting to admit of being
printed. On another leaf is a drawing of a banner with the following regimental colours, viz. Per bend or and azure, on a bend the motto UT REX SIT
REX.

---

[a] Robert Derham was Fellow of Peter House, Cambridge, and incumbent of Stathern.

A Continuation of the Marchings and Actions of the Royall Army. His Majestie being personally present. From the 17 of August 1645.

Sunday, August 17, 1645.

His Majestie, after sermon at Welbeck, marched that night to . . . . . Guards to Doncaster. Drew out Pontfract and Scarborough foot from Welbeck.

Monday, Tuesday, rested at Doncaster.

DONCASTER Church, com. Ebor.

North window, north yle, chancel:

> A standard, bearing quarterly FRANCE and ENGLAND.

East window, north yle:

> Quarterly, Gules and argent, on second and third quarters a martlet sable; impaling (*blank*).

Aloft, north windowes, middle yle, church: divers matches with both these:

> Argent, a cross moline sable, "COPLEY;" impaling (*blank*).
> Argent, three "magpies" [PICKBURNE]; impaling (*blank*).

In the south yle of the chancel, an altar monument for Booth:

> Three "bore heads" erect and erased [BOOTH].

Wednesday, August 20, to Retford, the King's quarter, com. Nottingham.

Thursday 21, the King and court went to Newarke. The King's regiment of horseguards to Suthwell. This is a faire cathedral church, peculiar to the Bishop of Yorke.

Friday, to Belvoir Castle, where one Lucas, sometime horsekeeper to the Earle of Roteland, is Governour.

Carved in stone over the dore of Belvoir Castle:

> A shield charged with a bend and surmounted by a helmet, with, for crest, a peacock's head issuant from a coronet.
> Three water-bougets [Roos].

The castle is part in Lincoln, part in Rotel', part in Nottingh.

[BOTTESFORD] Church com. Nottingham, a myle short of Belvoir Castle, as you come from Newark.

Carved upon the church doore old, as also with the peacock for a creast upon the pillars of the church :

> Roos.
> The same with a crest, viz. on a cap of maintenance a peacock in its pride.

North window, north yle, church:

> A standard, bearing ENGLAND, impaling the old coat of FRANCE.

In a low window beneath the north dore, church, three pictures not very large, one of Roos, two of the blood royall, one Crouch-back, I thinke.

> Rude sketch of a knight in chain mail, upon his surcoat the arms of Roos.
> Rude sketch of a knight, upon whose shield and surcoat appear the arms of ENGLAND.

Against the south wall, at the east end of the chancel, upon an altar-tombe, lyes a statue cutt in alablaster, in the fashion of the Black Prince, his creast under his head, a peacock.

Another right over against the former, and not unlike the fashion, for another Roos.

Upon the sides is divers small statues holding escocheons with single coates.

In the chancel, on the north side, upon an altar-tombe, lies the statue of a woman. Upon the side this coate is carved, old, and embosses on this forme [a heater shield] :

Roos.

To shew that anciently women did beare armes, and also of this forme.

Upon the same monument lies a small statue about a foot and halfe or two foot long cutt in blew marble. They say it was for him that built Belvoir Castle.

Rude sketch of a Knight Templar.

In this chancel are six faire monuments of the family of Mannors, Earles of Rutland, successively. The first lyes in the middle in a rownd cap, Hen. VIII. beard, his robe for the garter, and under it a surcoate with his armes painted upon it. Upon her surcoate, who was the heire of Roos, are her armes depicted also. 1500 and od.

In the middle of this village is a crosse, and at the foot of it, above the gresses, are four shields cutt, and these armes embossing, very old :

Roos.
Three catherine-wheels [ESPEC].a

NEWARKE Church, com. Nottingham.

North yle, church window, divers coates, especially the coates ot Leake, both with and without a border.

Argent, on a saltire engrailed sable five annulets or [LEEKE].

South side, chancel, a monument of Markham, and the armes old in the window :

Two bars wavy, on a chief or a demi-lion rampant gules [? for MARKHAM].

In the south window, the crosse yle, church, in very old glasse, towards the bottome, these following, and in this manner fairely depicted in six severall panes: the sheild of Deyncourt four times

a For an account of these monuments, &c., see Nichols's Leicestershire.

in every pane. The man supports one, the woman another, and two saints or angells two more. Neare the picture of the woman is an escocheon single, most probable 'twas the sheild of her family. For in that age impaleing of coates was not used. The men differ in sheilds below, but the four above in every pane were all alike.

Men's :

Argent, a fess dancetty between ten billets sable [DEYNCOURT].
The same, with the addition of a label of three points argent.
Azure, a fess dancetty between ten billets or, over all a bend gobony argent and gules.

Women's coates:

Gules, a maunche argent.
Lozengy argent and gules [FITZWILLIAM].
(Blank).
Azure, a fess dancetty between ten billets or.
Three similar shields.
Twenty-four more shields bearing the field azure and the charges or.
Kneeling effigy of a knight in chain mail, his hands raised, on his right shoulder an ailette or charged with a cross gules, in front of him a shield, bearing the coat of [DEYNCOURT].

Satterday August 23, to Stamford, com. Lincoln. Four parish churches in it.

In the hill before ye come into the towne, stands a lofty large crosse built by Edward III., in memory of Elianor his queene, whose corps rested there coming from the North. Upon the top of this crosse these three shields are often carved :

ENGLAND.
Three bends sinister, a bordure [PONTHIEU].
Quarterly, CASTILE and LEON.

Sunday, 24, to Huntingdon. In this march, before wee came to Stilton, wee mett with a body of horse lately raysed out of Suffolk and Essex, about 400, commanded by Colonel . . . . , Leiftenant-

Colonel Lehunt, Major . . . ., *Scotus*, and Captain Loe. The Major and about 100 were taken that night. *Gosnal, Minor, Wroth, Sym. et al' ceperunt.* They a little disputed Huntingdon, but wee entered, notwithstanding a large ditch encompassed it, lately scowred and cast up, and a breast worke and gate in the roade.

Theise rebells ran away to Cambridge; all of them back and breast, headpeice, brace of pistoll, officers more. Every troope consisted of 100.

Sunday, 25, rested at Huntingdon.

Four churches in Huntingdon.

Upon the east end of Alhallowes church, cutt upon a stone, 𝕿. 𝕹𝖔𝖜𝖊𝖑𝖑.

Sir William Vaughan's brigade consists of these regiments:

Queenes regiment, Prince Maurice, Sir William Vaughan's, Colonel Samuel Sandys.

Leiftenant-Colonel Slaughter is Major-Generall of the brigade.

Tuesday, August 26, to Uborne [Woburn] com. Bedford, and the King lay at the Earle of Bedford's howse there.

Wednesday, 27, to Wing. The King lay in the Earle of Carnarvon's howse, the army in the adjoyning closes.

Thursday. This morning one of our soldjers was hangd on the tree in Wing towne, for stealing the communion plate there.

This day we marchd by Bostoll [Borstall] Howse, com. Bucks, belonging to the Lady Denham. Sir William Campion is governour. A pallazado or rather a stockado without the graffe; a deepe graffe and wide, full of water; a palizado above the false bray, and another six or seven foot above that, neare the top of the curten.

Some of this fashioned palizadoes are upon the old walles at Monmouth.

The palizadoes at Woodstock stand upon the top of the curten as here, and the like at the foot of the false bray.

A sectional sketch is given of these fortifications.

At Worcester Prince Maurice has made without the ditch (that is dry on that side that goes to Droitwiche) a low breast work, and a

stockado without: the top of the breast work is not a foot about the
ground on the outside. Very necessary to safeguard a dry ditch and
wall.

The head quarters of our horse was at Burcester [Bicester].
His Majestie this Thursday, 28 of August, went to Oxford, his
guards to Islip, &c.

Friday rested.

Satterday, 30, to Shipton-upon-Stowre.

Sunday to Worcester, guards at Claynche [Claynes].

Munday, September 1°, rested.

Tuesday rested.

Wednesday, 3, to Bramiets [Bromyard], com. Hereford; there his
Majestie and the court lay ; the army lay in the feild.

Thursday the King with his own regiment went to Hereford;
the Scotts, hearing of his Majesties coming, had removed their seige
from Hereford on Tuesday before, being the second of September,
and marchd towards Gloucester.

Davie Lesley is their Leiftenant-Generall of the horse.

Craford was Major-Generall; he was slayne at a salley before the
towne; they weare gott neare the towne, and had made two breaches,
but were repulsed. Two mynes, and drayned the ditch: 3 or 4,000
and 1,500 horse of the Scotts.

The King's army rested this day. Wee quartered at Madley,
five myles beyond Hereford.

MADLEY Church, com. Hereford.

North window, church:

> Kneeling figure of a knight in complete armour of the xiii. century, with
> the hands upraised in the attitude of prayer, his sword suspended
> from a highly enriched belt, and his surcoat embroidered with Sable,
> three garbs argent [FELD or FIELD]; "under written 𝔚𝔞𝔩𝔱'𝔲𝔰 𝔢𝔱
> 𝔍𝔬𝔥'𝔢𝔰 𝔉𝔢𝔩𝔡𝔢 "—"sword between his legs."
>
> Outline of the effigy of a knight, upon which is written "broken, the same
> garbes."

Some of this family of Delafield built part of this faire churche,
and a howse is so called now.

In the next window, same side:

> The kneeling effigy of a knight in complete armour of the thirteenth century, the hands upraised in the attitude of prayer. The buckle of his sword-belt bears a small shield with this coat, Paly of four or and azure, on a fess gules three mullets argent. "The same coat upon him," *i. e.* his surcoat. "Under this, 'Pries p' Johan Rees et Alice . . . . et pur les almes de tous lur enfans et pur les almes de toutes cristiens.' "

A woman holding this coat in the next pane:

> A sketch of the arms is given, as borne by the knight.

Chancel, old:

> . . . . on a fess gules three mullets or, a label of five points azure, "twice."
> Gules, a chief compony or and azure, a bend argent.
> Or, five chevronels azure [DEANERY OF HEREFORD], "twice."

South window, church:

> Gules, a lion rampant or, a bordure engrailed [TALBOT].

This Thursday came newes that the Scotts horse were returned out of the North and come back neare Worcester.

The King knighted the Leift. Governour of Hereford, Sir Nicholas Throckmorton, and Sir William Layton the Leift.-Colonel of the King's lifeguards of foot.

Friday the King went to Lemster [Leominster], co. Hereford, and lay that night at Webley; his guards returned to their old quarters.

Satterday the King determined to goe to Aburgeny, but 'twas altered: the guards to Letton, His Majestie to Hereford.

Sunday to Ragland, guards to Treargaire, &c.

Thursday, Septemb. 11th. The King, attended with his guards, went to Aburgaveny; returned at night to Ragland. His buisines was to committ five cheife hinderers from releving Hereford.

ABERGAVENY Church, St. Maries.

East window, large and faire shield:

> Quarterly FRANCE and ENGLAND.

The same ; a label of three points argent, each charged with an ermine spot.

Per pale azure and gules, three lions rampant argent, [HERBERT] ; impaling, Quarterly FRANCE and ENGLAND, within a bordure argent.

HERBERT.

Argent, three cocks, or wyverns, legged or.

Argent, a lion rampant sable, crowned or.

Sable, a chevron between three [? spearheads] argent.

East window, north yle:

Quarterly FRANCE and ENGLAND, a label of three points argent. *Supporters*, two lions rampant or, each charged on the breast with a label of three points argent. *Crest*, upon a wreath vert, surmounting a helmet or, a lion passant gardant, charged with a label of three points argent, as before.

Quarterly FRANCE and ENGLAND ; beneath is written "The same, sans label."

Argent, a rose gules seeded of the field ; the shield surmounted by a helmet. On either side of this shield a portcullis.

North window, old : the borders are : Gules, three fleurs-de-lis or ; a maunch gules; and Valance his coate; and Azure, six lions rampant argent.

Gules, three fleurs-de-lis or.

At the bottome of the window lies a statue in wood; two cushions under his head, crosse-legd, a loose coate and belt. They call him the builder of the church.

Betweene the north yle and quire, upon two altar tombes, lyes two statues of women. Escocheons on the sides of this form [the ordinary shield of the latter part of the 14th century].

One was killed with a fall following a squirrel from the top of the castle wall. One of the family of Nevill. The other lyes with a peare betweene her hands and a shield very large upon her breast; they say she was choaked with a peare.[a] A Nevill; a hownd at her feet.

Rude sketch of a recumbent effigy, which, but for the pronoun "her" above, would pass for that of an ecclesiastic. The hands are folded on the breast, and upon the middle of the figure is a shield with this coat: three fleurs-de-lis.

[a] No doubt a heart; and the legend absurd.

In old glasse, south yle, chancel. First window:

Azure, three castles triple-towered or.
Checky azure and or, on a fess gules three fleurs-de-lis argent.

Second window:

ENGLAND, a label of three points, each charged with three fleurs-de-lis
or.
The kneeling figure of a knight, the visor apparently raised. From the
left shoulder is suspended a shield bearing, Sable, a cross argent.
Or, a maunche gules [HASTINGS].
Azure, six escocheons, 3, 2, and 1, sable, each charged with a lion
rampant argent.
HASTINGS.
Vair ermine and gules, two bars azure.

East window of this chappel, very faire:

The kneeling figure of a man, his coat embroidered with the arms of
Herbert. The figure of the female is not given, though alluded to
as "her picture;" "and under is written: 'Orate pro a'i'abus Will'i
Thomas militis et Alicie ux'is sue qui istam capellam et fenestram
vitrari fecerunt.'"

In the south window of the same chappel a statue crosse-legd.
This stands upright at his head:

A helmet of the thirteenth century, surmounted by a coronet, out of
which the crest, but which is undefinable, issues.

A greyhound at his feet.   Dyed because he killed his greyhound, say they.

Another betweene the pillars of this chappel and the quire.   Not
much unlike the former statue.   Upon an altar tombe.   A sword
and long dagger.   Not crosse-legged.   On his left arme a large
shield.   Under his head a wiverne:

Sketch of a helmet surmounted by the crest, a wyvern.

A Nevill, say they.   [The crest is that of Herbert.]

In the middle of this chappel a stately altar tombe; divers faire
statues round about the sides.

Upon the surface lyes two statues, a man and woman; the man on the left hand.

Under his head a helme, and forth of a wreath a maiden's head, a collar of S about his neck. At his head two angels support this shield [viz. a shield with the coat of Herbert].

Behind her head this:

Argent, a lion rampant sable, crowned or.

Bodyes in alablaster.

They call this forementioned monument Sir William Thomas, who was ancestor of the Herberts of Colbroke, Ragland, and Werndee.

1, Werndee; 2, Colbroke and Ragland.

Between the pillars of the quire and this chappel, another very faire altar tombe and two statues, not unlike the last mentioned. These shields are supported by angells round about the sides:

" Also at his head not impaled at all," viz. the coat of Herbert.

" This at her head," viz. Or, a chevron between three eagle's heads erased sable.

He is in long black haire. Under his head

A helmet surmounted by the crest, viz. on a wreath a bundle of " arrows " or.

This they call Sir Richard Herbert of Colbroke, in this parish.

Against the south wall of the same chappel, upon an altar tombe, arched and fairely painted, lyes a statue of a man in alablaster, a collar of S about his neck.[a]

These coates upon it:

HERBERT debruised by a bend sinister argent; impaling, Azure, semée of cross-crosslets, three boar's heads couped argent, a crescent for difference. [CRADOCK.]

Quarterly, HERBERT and CRADOCK.

[a] This is the monument of Sir Richard Herbert of Ewyas, ancestor of the Earls of Pembroke and Carnarvon.

A shield, the dexter side *blank;* impaling, Quarterly, 1, Argent, a chevron between six crosses moline, a bordure; 2, Argent, a saltire gules; 3 and 4 *blank.* Dexter, " man in armour supporter ;" sinister, " woman supporter." Crest, a " mermaid."

In the middle, under the arch,

A figure of the Virgin, standing ; on either side " angels," and at her feet " men and women praying to her;" above her head three crowns or, around which, " sitting," are the three persons of the Trinity, (represented as old men, crowned, and the Son holding his cross in his hand, who place on the Virgin's head the crowns, the " Father the upper crowne, Son on the right hand the middle, Holy Ghost[the] 3d."

On each side the Virgin Mary the pictures of three sons and a daughter, and their names written over their heads, those on the right hand Margaret Herbert, Mathew Herbert, William Herbert, George Herbert and his wife. On the left hand, John Herbert, Water Herbert, William Herbert, Jane Herbert.[a] Upon the verge this inscription, guilt fairely :

Hic jacet Richardus Herbert Armiger qui obiit xij die Septemb. a D'ni Mcccccx°. Et. a°. regni Regis Henrici Octavi 2° : cujus a'i'e p. d. a.

A faire monument in the same chappel for Judge Powel :

Azure, in chief three castles argent, in base a scaling ladder ; impaling, HERBERT.

Another altar tomb in the north chappel for Doctor Lewis, Admiral of the sea in Qu. Eliz. time.[b]

North window, crosse yle, these old :

Or, a maunch gules [HASTINGS].
MORTIMER.
Paly of six azure and or, on a fess gules three mullets argent.

Middle south window of the body of the church :

MORTIMER.

---

[a] These are the eight children of Sir Richard Herbert of Ewyas ; William was created Earl of Pembroke, 1551.
[b] David Lewis, Judge of the Admiralty.

GENESNELL impaling MORTIMER, called by Symonds, erroneously, " PEM-
BRIDGE and MORTIMER."

A very faire guilt roode left, and old organs.   At the east end of
the north yle church lyes a large statue for Jesse, and a branch did
spring from him, and on the boughs divers statues, but spoyld.

EWYAS HERALD [Harold] Church, com. Hereford.

Under an arch against the north wall, chancel, lyes a statue of a
woman, very old, holding betweene her hands either a peare or
heart [no doubt the latter].

Upon an altar tombe in the church yard, very faire, an inscription
and this coate.   For Thomas Cardiff, gentleman, buried 1638.

An " Indian bowe " in bend between two pheons.

Upon a high hill neare this church was a castle, but now ruined
and gone.

MANNINGTON [Monington] Church, com. Hereford.

In this church this coate severally, and some matches of either
family are painted on a wall:

Azure, a chevron between three " phesants " argent [or—TOMKYNS], impaling, Per bend imbattled argent and gules [BOYLE].

Tompkins married into this family, by whome as I conceive he
had this manour and pretty seate.[a]

Thursday, September 11.   His Majestie at Aburgaveny comitted
Sir Trevor Williams, but he was bayled.   Mr. Morgan of T.
[? Tredegar.] Mr. Herbert, of Colbroke.   Mr. Baker.   Mr. (blank),
cheife hinderers of the counties of Monmouth and Glamorgan to
releve Hereford.

During the time of the King's being at Ragland, when he first
came he sent Sir Marmaduke Langdale with his horse to Cardiffe,

---

[a] Not so.   His grandfather was of Monington, and married a coheiress of Baskerville.
C. 25, f. 26. Coll. Arms.

with Lord Astley and 100 foot out of Monmouth, (*blank*) foot out of Ragland, Chepstow, &c., to parley with the Glamorganshire peace army, who were agane reson. Both armyes mett eight myle off Cardiffe in Glamorganshire. The peace army seing Lord Astleyes resolution to fight, though not considerable in number, agreed to lay downe their armes and provide 1,000 men and armes within a moneth for the King, money, &c.

The next day or two after the enemy sent them ammunition and armes by sea, landed in Pembrokeshire. Then these rogues, hearing of the losse of Bristoll, joyned with the Pembrokeshire forces. Sir Marmaduke Langdale marched toward Brecknock.

Friday, September 12th. In the afternoone his Majestie, attended with his guards, left Ragland and marched some miles towards Hereford, but returned. The guards to Aburgaveny. Satterday the King rested at Ragland. Gerard's horse at this time the King was at Ragland were about Ludlowe : 2,000 of the enemyes horse about Lemster.

Sunday, 14. About noone his Majestie left Ragland, and marched to Monmouth; thence that night to Hereford.

Some matches of the Herberts in Monmouth church. Two churches in Monmouth.

Munday, 15 September. His Majestie in the morning, attended by his guards, marched some miles towards Bromyat [Bromyard] ; but by reason Gerard's horse had not orders soone enough to appear at the rendesvouz, &c., his Majestie returned to Hereford, accompanied with Prince Maurice and Generall Gerard, &c. His Majestie read a coppy of a letter from Montros, of his thorough victory in Scotland. Guards to Madley.

Tuesday Sir Marmaduke Langdale's horse came to quarter about Biford, &c.

Generall Gerard's horse at . . . . . .

Pointz his horse, above 2000, was come to Lemster.

This morning wee received orders to move, but remanded, so rested.

Tuesday, September 16. His Majestie dispatched letters of buisiness to Oxford, and sent them by Sir Henry Wrothe, whome he now knighted in the bishop's pallace in Hereford.

Wednesday, Sept. 17. The whole army mett at a rendesvouz upon Arthurstone Heath, neare Durston [Dorston] Castle, com. Hereford; and from thence his Majestie marched to Ham [Holm] Lacy, the seat of the Ld Viscount Scudamore.

This day, the nearest enemy (and whose buisines it was to attend the King's motion), vizt. Points and Rosseter's horse, were about Lemster, com. Hereford.

Guards to Rolston.

Thursday, 18th. The rendesvous was over Wye, at Stokedye in Herefordshire. Marched thence over the river Aroe [Arrow], betwixt Morden [Marden] and Wellin[g]ton, *eod. com.*

Intelligence this morning at the rendesvouz that the said enemy had marched all night, and were about betweene us and Worcester.

This night to Prestayne com. Radnor.

PRESTAYNE [Presteign] Church, com. Radnor.

West window, old:

MORTIMER.
Ermine, a lion rampant gules, crowned or, within a bordure sable bezanty, " CORNWALL."

North window chancel, old:

Sable, a maiden's head argent between five lozenges of the second, each charged with a mullet of the field.
CORNWALL.
Quarterly, MORTIMER and the Cross of St. George.

This in the north window chancel, very faire:

Sable, a maiden's head argent, her hair or, and a string of " pearle " round her head, between five plates, each charged with a mullet of the field.

East window:

Quarterly, 1 and 4, Argent, a cross moline sable ; 2 and 3, Azure, a fret or.
A shield prepared for six coats, two of which alone remain ; viz. 2, Two
  lions passant ; and 5, two bends sable, " HERLEY, miles."
Quarterly, 1 " gone " [but as 4?] and 4, a lion rampant, between six crosses;
  2 and 3, Azure, three fleurs-de-lis or ; impaling MORTIMER.
FRANCE and ENGLAND quarterly, a label of three points argent within the
  garter, " 𝔓 . . . 𝔄𝔯𝔱𝔥𝔲𝔯 under-written."
Azure, three boy's heads couped, crined or, the necks encircled by "snakes
  proper, VAUGHAN."
Gules, three fleurs-de-lis or.

Friday, Sept. 19th.   This day wee marched from Prestayne [Pres-
teign], and, except in the first three myle, wee saw never a house or
church, over the mountaynes.   They call it ten myle, but twenty
till wee come to Newtowne, com. Montgomery.   Satterday rested.

Sunday, 21 Sept.   Over the mountaynes, lesse barren then the
day before, by   , Sir Arthur Blanyes howse, to LlanVutlyn
[Llanfyllin], a borough towne in Montgomeryshire:

Munday 22.   Over such mountaynes to Chirke Castle, com.
Salop; there the King lay; . . . . Watts is governour.   The Guards
to Llangothlyn [Llangollen], a market towne com. Denbigh, three
myle from Chirke.   Newes this day that Colonel William Legg the
governour of Oxon was committed.   That Prince Rupert's commission was declared null.

That part of the out workes at Chester were betrayed to the
enemy by a Captain and Leiftenant, both apprehended.

The King sent to Watts to send to Lord Byron to Chester to hold
out twenty-four howres.

LLANGOTHLYN Church, com. Denbigh.

Towards the west end of the church, north side, is an altar tombe
and the statue of a bishop fairly cutt, old; they call him bishop
Cathlyn.

Tuesday his Majesty marched towards Chester attended with Mountague Earl of Lindsey, Earle of Corke, Earl of Lichfield, Lord Digbie, Lord Astley, Lord Gerard. His force with him were his owne regiment of Life Guards, consisting of these troopes: The King's, The Queenes, commanded by Sir Edward Brett, the Major of the regiment, Earle of Lichfeild's, Leiftenant-Colonel Gourden *Scotus* commanded it. (They were most Scotts officers.) Sir Henry Stradling's troope, which came from Carlisle with Sir Thomas Glemham: toto about 200. Lord General Charles Gerard was also then with the King with his gallant troope of Life Guard, 140 men.

Gerard's cornet—

Here is drawn a standard bearing a sphere, and the motto " At all that's round " below.

Colonel Herbert Price his horse.

Sir Marmaduke Langdale's brigade, Sir Thomas Blakeston's brigade, and Sir Wm. Vaughan's brigade, and Generall Gerard's horse marched before all night toward Holt Castle, com. [Denbigh:] a garrison of the King's, comanded by Sir Richard Lloyd, where wee have a passe of boates over the river. Their buisines was to fall upon those horse and foot that lay before Chester. The King went into Chester, and lay at Sir Fr. Gamul's howse; his guards watched in the street. The enemy who were gotten into the out workes, which secured the suburbs, had made a breach the day before, and had entered had it not bin most gallantly defended.

Wednesday, 24 September. Contrary to expectation, Pointz his horse were come betweene Nantwiche and Chester to releive those forces of their party who were afore Chester, and to fight the King, as appeares by his letters, intercepted by Sir Richard Lloyd, to this purpose, directed to Jones, who sometimes was student in Lincoln's Inn, and commanded the horse that beseiged Chester, thanking them for keeping their ground notwithstanding the King's approach, and tells them a neare relacion or accompt of the King's strength, of his tired over-marcht horse, of his number of dragoons, of his resolucion to engage them if possible, &c.

This morning Sir Marmaduke Langdale on Chester side of the river Dee, and not farr from Beeston Castle, charged Pointz his horse, beate them and toke some cornetts.   But they beate us agen for't.

About twelve of the clock, those horse which came with the King and 200 foot were drawne out of Chester.

Nine hundred prisoners of ours taken and carried to Nantwiche, whereof about twenty gentlemen of the King's owne troope.

Beeston Castle was beseiged at this time.

Thursday 25.   This night I saw a rainbow within a myle of Denbigh at five in the morning, and the moone shined bright; t'was just against the moone.   About nine and ten in the morning the King left Chester and went to Harding [Hawarden] Castle, governed by Sir William Neale, stayed three howres, and went that night to Denbigh Castle.   Sir Marmaduke Langdale's rendesvouz was early this morning within two myles of Holt Castle.

Denbigh Castle is governed by Mr. Salisbury, repaird by him and his kinred at their owne cost.   Had his commission from the King two years since.

Upon the top of the tower, this olde:

Mortimer.

Lower, over the same gate:

Mortimer.
Quarterly, Mortimer and Ulster.

In the church, within the out wall of the castle at Denbigh, called the Chappel of St. Tillilo [Hilary], round about the borders of the east window, this single feather in a black feild:

An ostrich feather argent, a scroll or.

These two, very large, same window:

Quarterly; Mortimer and Ulster, but the two first quarters "gone."
Or, a lion rampant "purple".
Badge of the fetterlock or.

South window :

A shield with the emblems of Christ's wounds.
A shield with the instruments of Christ's passion.
Sable, two battleaxes in saltire, handles argent, crowned or.

The parish church where they bury is a myle off.

Friday, 26 Sept. rested.

Satterday, 27, was a generall rendesvouz three myles from Denbigh.

Newes againe that Montrose had routed David Leshly about Kelso on the borders; that Prince Maurice was coming with 1000 horse to us, and was at Chirke.

All ours reanimated, and expected to follow Pointz to the North.

Sunday, 28. After sermon about noone came intelligence that the enemyes horse were over the river; a little afore we heard that they were gone toward Scarborough (so ill intelligence has the King); but they went butt into fresh quarters about Nantwich to refresh.

About one of the clock afternoone the King marched thorough Ruthyn, where there is a large castle and fortified, to Chirke Castle com. Denbigh. Watts knighted. Here Prince Maurice mett us with his troope and those of Prince Rupert's horse that came from Bristoll, Lucas his horse, &c.: toto 6 or 700.

Munday, 29. Leaving Oswestree (a garrison of the rebells) on the left hand, to Llandisilio and Llandrenio, com. Montgomery, where the army lay in the feild; some cheife in some howses.

Tuesday, from thence early at day breake, marched, leaving Shrewsbury three myle on the left hand; that night late and teadiously to Bridgnorth; the rere guard gott to Wenlock Magna, com. Salop. In this marche three or four alarmes by Shrewsbury horse, and five or six of them crosst the way and killd and took some.

Wednesday rested. 1° Octobr. Intelligence that the Devizes and Berkley Castle were both taken by Fairfax.

Thursday 2. The King marched to Lichfeild. Upon the rendesvouz going to Lichfeild the King knighted Sir   Horwood,[a] of com. Salop, no soldjer nor in armes.   This day Generall Gerard's regiment returned from the rendesvouz *quia* tired, to have refreshment under Bridgnorth garrison.   *Ego etiam.*   This day, by reason of the long and tedious marches, divers fell off, some, as six went into Bentall howse.   Prince Maurice this morning with his owne troope (partly comanded by Lord Mol[ineux], and partly by Sir Thomas Sandys) went toward Worcester.

Sir Thomas Glemham went to be Governour of Oxford.

After the battaile at Rowton Moore, com. Cestr. upon the rendesvouz neare Denbigh divers complaints came to the King and Generall about horses taken that were agen found; some tooke away their horses where they found them.   It was thus ordered by the King, according to the opinion of Lord Astley in this case.   One of Sir Marmaduke Langdale's soldjers was killed, his horse the enemy tooke, and anon one of Generall Gerard's soldjers tooke the horse away from the enemy; this horse was challenged at the rendesvouz, and 'twas adjudged to the first owner, Sir Marmaduke Langdale's man.   The reason was given, that, unlesse the enemy had had so much possession of the horse as to carry him to his quarters, it was nothing of validity to say that he was taken from the enemy.   So that, if the enemy had kept the horse twelve or twenty-four houres at his owne quarters, he had had a property in him, and he that then had taken the horse might have owned him by this old law of warr.

This is like a law of goods taken from shipps cast away.

Satterday 4th October.   The remainder of Sir Charles Lloyd's regiment came from the Devizes, about 60.

ENVILL, or ENFEILD, Church, com. Stafford.

These coates, and more, are very old in the windowes of this church:

---

[a] Not mentioned in the list of Knights, Coll. Arm., nor is his pedigree in the Visitation of Shropshire.

South window chancel:

Sable, a lion rampant argent.

East window, north yle, church:

Azure, a bend lozengy or.

North window, church:

MORTIMER.
Quarterly or and azure, four lions rampant counterchanged.

West window, north yle:

Per pale indented and azure or.
ENGLAND.

Against the north wall, in the chancel, upon an altar tombe, two statues, he in armour; this coate carved:

Quarterly, 1, Barry of six argent and azure, in chief three torteaux; "GREY."

The rest not given.

Now Mr. Henry Grey lives at the manor howse.

Garrisons com. Denbigh.

K.   Denbigh Castle.   Mr. Salisbury of that county is Governour; King made him Governour.

K.   Ruthyn Castle.   Captain Sword, made by Prince Rupert, is Deputy-Governour under Colonel Marke Trevor.   Sir Thomas Middleton did owe it.

K. Chirke Castle.   Captain Watts[a] Governor;   Lord Capell made him Governour.

K.   Holt Castle.   Sir Richard Lloyd is Governour;   King made him Governour.

Garrisons in Flintshire.

K.   Harding [Hawarden] Castle.   Sir William Neale is Governor; made by Prince Rupert.   The Earle of Derbyes howse, and lived there sometimes.

[a] Sir John Watts, knighted Sept. 23, 1645.   List of Knights, Coll. Arms.

K. Rudland [Rhuddlan] Castle, two myle from St. Asaph. Gilbert Byron, (brother to the Lord Byron,) is Governour, made by Lord Byron. The King's Castle.

K. Flint Castle. Colonel Mostyn is Governour. The King's owne castle.

Garrisons in Anglesey.

K. Beaumaris. Lord Bulkeley is Governour, Irish Baron. The King's castle.

Garrisons in Mountgomeryshire.

R. Mountgomery Castle. This castle was built by H. 3 to prevent the rising of the Welchmen. (Holinshed, 6 H. 3, p. 203 a.)

R. Red Castle. Hugh Price is Governour.

R. Welchpole. Sir Thomas Middleton is Governour; Mason is, in his absence. Tho. Farrer horse [house?]. Red Castle and Welchpole are within halfe a myle.

R. Abermarghnant, a garrison made about the time the King marched from Hereford to Chester; 'tis Lewis Vaughan's howse, four myle from Llan Vutlyn [Llanfyllin].

Garrisons in Merionethshire.

R. Harley [Harlech] Castle. William Owen is now Governour, and is constable during life, and now sheriffe.

Garrisons in Caernarvonshire.

K. Conway Castle. Archbishop of Yorke was Governour, and Sir John Owen.

K. Caernarvon Castle. John Bodwell is Governour. Onely these two.

ALVELEY Church, com. Salop, five myle from Bridgnorth.

In a south window, next the south dore of the church, three

times this escocheon, and underneath coat, helme, mantle, and creast:

> A shield surrounded by a "glory," two coats one above the other; 1, Barry nebuly of six or and sable [BLOUNT]; 2, Argent, a lion rampant gules within a bordure sable, bezanty [CORNWALL]; impaling, Quarterly per fess indented azure and argent, a lion passant in the first quarter [CROFT]; the whole surmounted by a helmet with, for crest, Out of a ducal coronet or, a demi-lion rampant gules, crowned or, between two human arms embowed, "armes gules, hands proper;" "mantle gules, dowbled argent."

In the chancel, an altar tombe for Grove, a mercer of London, (Grocer *added*):

> Ermine, on a chevron engrailed gules three escallops or, a crescent for difference, [GROVE] of London.

Now Mr. Grove lives here.

QUATFORD Church, com. Salop, a myle from Bridgnorth.

South window and north window of this church, this is old and small:

> MORTIMER.
> The same, the inescocheon charged with three [? nails sable, or a mistake for ermine].

An altar tombe against the north wall chancel; inscription in brasse circumscribed.

Quatt is the next parish, wher Sir Thomas Wolrich has an old seate.

Garrisons in com. Salop, 15 October, 1645.

K. Ludlow. Sir Michael Woodhowse Governour; *quond.* pag o' Marq. Hamilton.

K. Bridgnorth. Sir Lewis Kirke, Governour. Sir Thomas Woolrich was first Governour three years since; then Sir Lewis Kirke. 200 in the Castle.

Leift.-Governour Thomas Wyne, Sir Robert W. [Wynne's] son. Major Fr. Billingsley, jun., com. Salop.

K. High Arcall, the howse of Sir Richard Newport, now Lord Newport. Armorer is Governour.

R. Shrewsbury governed by a Committee.

R. Oswestree.

R. Wemm. Major Bryan is Governour.

R. Lindshall [Lilleshull] Abbey. Sir Richard Leveson owes it; Major Duckenfeild lost it.

R. Dawley Castle, seven myle from Bridgnorth, four myle from Wellington. Fouke is Governour; Duckenfeild was, and lost it.

R. Bromcroft Castle. Mr. Lutley owes it, the Lord Calvyn *Scotus* is Governour.

R. Benthall, Mr. B. howse, five myle from Bridgnorth. Thomas Brereton is Governour.

R. Stokesay, a howse of the Lord Craven's, four myle from Ludlow.

At this time the King rested, and had his court at Newarke; his army was thus disposed of—

The court, horseguards, and Sir Marmaduke Langdale's horse at Newarke, and Newarke horse, now about 300, there too.

Generall Gerard's horseguards at Belvoir, his regiment gone into Wales.

Earle of Northampton's regiment at Wirton, a garrison of ours commanded by Major Honywood.

Sir William Blakeston's, Prince Rupert's remainder, Lucas 50, &c. at Welbeck. Toto 120.

Queenes regiment at Shelford, taken by the enemy and all putt to the sword, refusing quarter when the King was at Newarke.

Munday, 13 October, Prince Rupert at Lichfield goeing to the King.

Captain Gattacre, of the county of Salop, killed in Bridgenorth by a quartermaster, the quartermaster killed too by him. One endeavoured to hang himselfe the next day here.

BRIDGENORTH Church.

East window, north yle, church:

> The kneeling figure of a knight in chain armour, over which he wears a surcoat marked "or," round the waist a belt "sable," from which the "sword" is suspended "on the right side." In front of him is a shield, Azure, a cross moline or.

North window, north yle, toward the west end:

> Two shields erased.
> Gules, fretty or.
> Azure, a chevron gules.
> . . ., on a chief gules three plates.
> Gules, a chevron or.

Against the north wall, same yle, upon an altar tombe, lyes the statue of a man in armour and a woman. Many escocheons painted on the side:

> Gules [Argent], on a chief or a hawk sable, "HOORD."
> The same impaling a crescent between three roses.

The Hoordes lived in this parish. Hoord's parke still.

Neare the former monument, and against the north wall, upon an altar tombe, lyes the statue of a woman fairely guilt in alablaster. This inscription is circumscribed and coate of armes:

> Here lyeth the body of Francis Fermer, daughter of Thomas Hoorde, Esq. and wife of Thomas Fermer, Esq. who dyed 10 day of July, 1570. On w. s. I. h. m.

> Quarterly; 1 and 4, Or, on a fess sable between three lion's heads erased [gules] three anchors erect [of the first, FARMER]; 2 and 3, A chevron between three escallops; impaling, 1, HOORD; 2, An inescocheon charged with three roundles or within a bordure.[a]

---

[a] For the coat of Palmer. See this, and six other coats not here given, in Vincent's Salop., Coll. Arm.

In the north window, neare the former monument, very small:

> Or, on a cross gules a hurt.
> Or, a fess gules.
> Or, three chevronels gules [CLARE].
> Quarterly or and gules [VERE].
> Gules, three fleurs-de-lis within a bordure or.
> Gules, a crescent subverted or, in base an escallop of the last.

In the same north window this picture of a saint:

> Rude sketch of a male figure, habited in a long robe marked " or." With
> his right hand he supports a staff having a cross pattée at the top, and
> on his left arm is a shield, bearing Argent, a cross pattée gules.

In the middle yle of the church a flat stone, and these fashioned and numberless shields are embossed upon it, and worne:

> A sketch of the stone is given, upon which is sculptured the shaft of a
> cross raised upon three steps, at the top a shield, and on either side six
> other shields, all blank.

This coate in the west window, church:

> Argent, on a bend cotised sable three cross-crosslets fitchy argent.

In the church within the Castle of Bridgenorth is nothing of observation.

Medeley. Upon this river of Seaverne they use here a little boate for one to sitt in; they call them corricles, laths within and leather without, from *corium*.

Friday, October 17, came intelligence to Bridgenorth the King had left Newarke, and gone towards Scotland to Montros the Sunday before.

That Sir Thomas Fairfax had taken Winchester from Ogle.

A provost martiall has power to hang two or three or all that he takes in actuall fault, but no power to make any cast dice; that is, as much or more than a generall can doe, without a councell of war, unles a proclamation be made a little before.

A parson may be tryed at a counsill of warr, and was so at Bridgenorth.

A Scott was tryed at a councel of warr there, and he putt on his hatt before them, and, being reprehended for it by the Governour, he told them he was equall to all except the Governour, and they committed him for it.

20 October. Severall Colonels whose regiments were in Bridgenorth.

Foot.

Sir Lewis Kirkes, Governour; Colonel John Corbett's; Colonel Billingsley's, the trained band,—this regiment watches in the towne; Sir Mich. Earnley's, one company of them; Sir Charles Lloyd's, came thither from the Devizes, 60.

Foot about in all, of all these, 260.

Horse.

Sir Francis Ottley the high sheriffe, Sir Edward Acton 10, Governour's troope 60;—Horse not 100.

Wednesday, October 22. Leift.-Colonel Slaughter marched out of Bridgnorth about two of the clock afternoone. Governour's troope commanded by Captain Singe 40, Sir Francis Otteleyes, &c. That night by eight to High Arcall. Thence marched thirty horse and twenty dragoons with us about twelve of the clock that night. By nine next day to Chirke.

Selden's Titles of Honor, p. 838, " Teste Rogero de Mortuomari de Chirk," in a patent Rot. Cart. 9 Edw. 2, n. 12.

CHIRKE Church, com. Denbigh.

South window, chancel:

Quarterly; 1 and 4, Per bend sinister ermine and erminois, a lion rampant or [LLOYD]; 2 and 3, Gules, a chevron sable between three armed heads argent; impaling, Argent, a chevron azure between three owls.

East window, north yle:

Same as last without the impalement.

This in the north window, same yle:

Gules, an armed head, "young face," the visor raised argent.

Under written thus:

Orate pro a'i'abus Will'i Edwards . . . . . arm . . . Lloyd, fratris ejus et omniu' parochia . . . . et pro a'i'abus om . . . . qui hanc capellam fieri fecerunt a° d'ni M . . . . decimo nono.

The Castle of Chirke; Sir Thomas Middleton owes it, and formerly lived there; as also Denbigh and Ruthyn, in the same county. Colonel Marke Trevor has the command of Ruthyn Castle. A leift. there under him. Prince Rupert putt him in. Captain Sword is Governor.

Coates of armes sett up by Sir Thomas Middleton in Chirke Castle: [a]

1, Gules, a lion rampant argent between three crescents or; 2, Quarterly argent and sable, four lions rampant counterchanged; 3, Azure, a lion passant argent; 4, Gules, three lions passant argent; 5, Argent, two bars azure, each charged with three martlets of the field; 6, Vert, a buck trippant argent, attired or; 7, Azure, on a bend argent three roses gules; 8, On a bend vert three wolf's heads erased argent, a mullet for difference; 9, Vert, a chevron ermine between three wolf's heads erased argent; 10, Gules, on a bend or three lions passant sable; 11, Argent, two choughs sable; 12, Gules, a lion rampant argent; 13, Or, a boar passant sable; 14, Barry of six argent and sable; 15, Barry of six argent and gules; 16, Gules, a label of three points or; impaling, 1, On a bend vert three wolf's heads erased argent, a mullet for difference; 2, Vert, a chevron ermine between three wolf's heads erased argent; 3, Gules, on a bend or three lions passant sable; 4, Argent, two choughs sable; 5, Sable, a chevron between three owls argent; 6, Gules, three snakes nowed, two with heads erect, the third in base, "proper." Motto: "In veritate triumpho."

SALISBURY—MIDDLETON.

[a] See Vincent's Wales, and Le Neve's Baronets, Coll. Arm. Sir Henry Salusbury married the daughter of Sir Thomas Middleton.

The 8th, 9th, 10th and 11th in the Baron are the same with the 1st, 2nd, 3rd and 4th in the Femme.

Officers in the warrs of Ireland.

Went out of England about March, anno dom. 1641.

Earle of Leicester was made Lord Leiftenant of Ireland and Generall, but he never went out of England.

A regiment of foot called the Earl of Leicester's regiment, commanded by Leiftenant-Colonell George Monke, *Angl.* A troope of horse also which was the generall's commanded by Captain Abraham Yardner, *Anglus*, Phisitian.

Regiments of foot raised in England.

Colonel Sir Simon Harcourt, *Angl.*, killed in Ireland, first regiment that went over.

Leiftenant Colonel G. Gibson;

Thomas Pagett, Major, brother to the Lord Pagett;

Colonel Sir Fulke Hunkes;

Leiftenant Colonel Tilyard, now Colonel in this warr in England 1645.

Major . . . . .

These were about Dublin and the Nase [Naas].

These two, with the Earl of Leicester's which was commanded by Warren, came over into England, first siege of Chester. After these, three were ruined at the battaile of Nantwiche.

Sir Michael Earnleyes regiment: Kirke, Leiftenant-Colonel, killed.

Lord Jones, Irish, was president of Connaght: had a regiment raysd in England. These two Earnleyes and Jones went into Connaght at first and there stayd.

Regiments of foot raysd in Ireland.

Colonel Sir Charles Coote, *Angl.*, estate there.

Colonel Sir Henry Tichborne, *Angl.*, estate there.

Lord Lambert, Irish } Regiments.
Lord Burlacy, Irish }

These four regiments were raysed about and in Dublyn, and the first beginning to suppresse the rebellion.

Some of these came over with Tilyard, 1,000 foot greencoates came with him, most of them lost at Yorke with Prince Rupert.

All officers and soldjers that went out of England had an oath given them to fight for the King and Parliament.

When the King called them to his assistance into England, he had an oath administered to them to. Most came to the King except those that left there to resist the rebells.

Divers companies of foot raysd by private gentlemen of that kingdome that never came into regiments.

Horse.

Lord Lisle's, eldest son to the Earl of Leicester, regiment now at London. Sir Richard Grenvill was Major. After the battaile of Rosse they both came over in[to] England.

1. Captain Sir William Vaughan. He brought over this regiment into England at Christmas 1643, landed in Nesson [Nesse] in Worral behind Chester.

Sir Thomas Lucas was Commissary Generall of the horse and was to have this regiment, but he stayd in Ireland.

Little before the battaile of Yorke, Sir William Vaughan, being Colonel, made Slaughter his Leiftenant-Colonel, who was Captaine Leiftenant to Sir Thomas Lucas in Ireland, and Major coming over; at the same time Radcliffe Duckenfield was made Major, and Beverley Usher his Leiftenant.

These three came over captaines: 1. Captain Croftes, killed at Longford in Shropshire, when they beat Mitton and 300 of Mitton's men killd, and one of theirs besides, and five taken. 2. Captain John Davalier, a Florentine, tooke his troope to Ludlowe, and is now Colonel. 3. Captain John Bomer, at first in Ireland a cornett to Captain Villiers. Toto, six troopes.

Now these are Captains, October, 1645. 1. Captain Bomer. 2. Armorer, now Governour of Arcall, Leiftenant to Croftes in Ireland. 3. James Vaughan, brother to Sir William. 4. Dixie, Leiftenant to Slaughter, first a corporall, Cornet to Sir Thomas Lucas and Leiftenant. 5. Brookes.

Divers single troopes in Ireland besides. Garrisoned in several places, and drawne out according to the severall designes.

An. Dni. 1644. Sir William Vaughan was Generall of Shropshire. In the winter he made these his garrisons to quarter his owne regiment:—

Shraydon Castle, commanded by Sir William his brother, a parson; lost it to the counties of Salop, Chester, &c. Cawes Castle, Davalier. High Arcall, Armorer. Linshall and Dawley, Major Duckenfeild.

October, 1645. When the King was at Newarke, he made Sir William Vaughan generall of the horse in the counties of Salop, Wigorn, Stafford, Hereford, South Wales, and North Wales.

Munday, October 26. Sir William Vaughan came to Chirke. We marched to Llanannis [Llanynys], Mr. Thelwall's howse, com. Denbigh.

In the chamber window—old:

> Gules, a spoonbill argent, legged sable.
> Argent, a bugle-horn sable, stringed.
> Gules, on a chevron between three boar's heads couped argent, as many trefoils sable, "THELWALL."

RUTHYN Church, com. Denbigh.

East window, chancel, old:—A shield (*blank*).

Under an arch, south wall of the belfray, betweene church and chancel, the statue.

> This statue is not described, and the portion of the inscription given is quite unintelligible.

Lowest north window, chancel, old:

> Argent, three bars azure, in chief three torteaux [GREY].

GREY, with a label of three points gules.

West window, church, old and faire:

Quarterly, 1 and 4, Gules, three water-bougets argent [Roos] ; 2 and 3, Argent, a fess between two barrulets gules.

Quarterly, 1 and 4, GREY; 2 and 3, Quarterly, 1 and 4, Gules, a maunch or [HASTINGS] ; 2 and 3, Barry, ... martlets [VALENCE].

Azure, a cinquefoil ermine.

South window, over the doore:

Quarterly, 1, Or, a lion rampant sable ; 2, Gules, a chevron or between three *(blank)* sable; 3 and 4 *(blank)*.

Monument of Parry:

Sable, three boar's heads couped argent.

Monument of Jones:

Argent, a chevron between three boar's heads couped sable.

LLANHAYDIR [Llanrhaiadr] Church, com. Denbigh.

East window, chancel:

Or, a lion rampant between three crescents argent. " LAUS DEO about in scrolls."

A male effigy in armour, and having a surcoat with these arms upon the breast and sleeves, viz., Gules, a lion rampant facing the sinister, " yᵉ lyon ramp. turned"; over head a scroll bearing this inscription " Jesu degne on us sinners have mercy."

"Thomas Salisbery."

Gules, a chevron sable between three " old women's heads" argent.

Sir Edwyn Lloyd lives in this parish.

" The effigies of Sir Thomas Salusbury, of Lleweny, Knight Banerent [Banneret,] son of Thomas Salusbury Esq.; he lived in the time of Edward 4, Ric. 3. He was dubed Knight Banerent by Henry 7. at Black Heath feild: obijt 1505."

A man in armour, the surcoat edged with " furr" and embroidered on " velvet," with a lion rampant between three crescents. Motto, " Sat est prostrasse leoni."

This picture is in the howse of the Lady Salusbury in the parish of Henllan.   This is a surcoate of velvet, over his armour; and so written on it as above.

Many monuments of the family of Salisbury are in the church of Whitchurch by Denbigh.

Friday, October 31, came intelligence to Denbigh to Sir William Vaughan that the enemy under the command of Mitton was advanced to Ruthyn, both horse and foot.

Satterday at noone wee had the alarm, for they were at Whitchurch, below the towne.   Their approach was handsomely disputed by our horse and foot above an howre in the hedges and lane.

Their number of foot, being 1500 at least, made ours retreat to the towne, which was not long disputed by reason of their forward advancing.   Our horse were putt to a disorderly retreat and flight, notwithstanding Sir William Vaughan drew many of them up upon a greene neare two myles off, but could not be made stand: a party of Arcall horse chargd the persuers, and were seconded by part of Prince Maurice's life-guard.

The foot were lett into the castle by the governour.   The horse gott to Llanrust that night, com. Denbigh, twelve miles distant. Next morning dispersed to quarters.   The governour of Denbigh wrote that the enemy was in his sight above double our number.

Tuesday, 4° Nov. returned a trumpet from Denbigh sent by Sir W. V. and told that their rendesvouz was at Northop, the day before, (see a copy of Mr. Salisburyes letter to the Governour of Denbigh p. 280) : and this morning being Tuesday came our foot to us out of the castle to Llanrust.   A regiment of Reformades against us in this buisines come from London under Mitton's (Brereton's) command.

Sir W. Vaughan's forces composed of those regiments and companies.

P. Maurice life guard in part.

Sir William V.'s owne regiment, with Arcall, Bridgnorth, and Chirke; Colonel Hurter [first written Rutter] that commanded the horse in Monmouth; Colonel Worden's; Shakerley, Leift.-Colonel; Colonel Sandys of Worcester—all 300.

Colonel Randal Egerton's, Major-Generall to Gerard; Colonel Whitley—both 200.

Colonel Gradyes regiment ; General Gerard's, and Colonel Davalier's—200.

Lord Byron's regiment 100.—Horse, toto 700.

Foot—P. Maurice firelocks in pt. 150; Ludlow Foot 90 ; Arcall Dragoons, 20; Chirke firelocks 20,—Foot, toto 280.

Sir Richard Wynn lives at Guydur [Gwydyr], a faire seate in the parish of Llanrust, yet in Carnarvonshire.

Vert, three eagles displayed in fess or, " WYNN."

This coate is twice, old, in his window, and contrary, one gardant, the other passant:

Quarterly gules and or, four lions passant guardant counterchanged.
Quarterly or and gules, four lions passant counterchanged.

Divers mottoes about this house, one is:

" Non mihi glis servus nec hospes hirudo."

Manan [Maynan], an old howse in the parish of [Eglwysfach], county of Carnarvon, neare Llanrust. This coate is often carved on the old wainescott, for Kyffin; and one Mr. Kyffin now lives there; they call him Cuffyn.

Argent, a chevron gules between three pheons argent, each pointing to the centre of the shield [KYFFIN].

This also is in a little paper pasted and painted upon the wainscott:

Quarterly, 1 and 4, Per fess argent and sable, a lion rampant counterchanged; 2 and 3, KYFFIN.

The roofe of the parlour adorned with the second coate, and W. K. 1576. [Here is sketched a buck's head.]

The roof of the chamber over the parlour was the old roofe of the chappel of Conway abbey. In another chamber thus painted:

A coat similar to the last, excepting that the first and fourth coats are parted per bend sinister.

And in some places party per fesse. In another party per bend sinister ermine and erminois.

This family of Cuffyn came out of Flintshire; the ruine of the A. [Abbeys] was the raysing of them. One of the family fled for killing a man formerly, at last returned and changed his name to Vaughan, for he was little of stature, for so Vaughan signifies.

The Abbey of Conway stands neare this howse called Manan; 'twas antiently built at Aberconway, but one of the princes there (as is reported) likt his seate and gave him leave to build in any part of Carnarvonshire els. The abbot likt none better then this seate, but 'twas out of Carnarvonsh. over the river in Denbighsh. So this abbey was made part of Carnarvonsh. This is the countrey story. Now the family of Wynn lives in this abbey; theire coate is:

Gules, three boar's heads erased, palewise, argent.

This coate is painted also in the abbey howse:

Gules, a " man's head erased " argent, " or proper."

St. GEORGE Parish, com. Denbigh.

Against the north wall hangs coate armour, mantle, helme, and creast of one of the family of Holland:

Azure, a lion rampant guardant between six fleurs-de-lis or [HOLLAND]. 700*l.* per annum *inter* two sisters.

Colonel Price lives in this parish at Kinmill: he married the heire of David Holland the son of Peirs H.

ST. ASAPH Cathedral, com. Flint.

East window of the quire:

Quarterly, MORTIMER and ULSTER.
Gules, three cushions or [REDMAN].

Bishop Robert Redman [consecrated 1471]. The same coate is carved upon the organ loft; there was formerly the picture of a soldjer and these [*sc.* cushions].

This quire is pretty handsome, but poore in respect of others.

Upon the flore neare the north wall at the east end of the quire lyes the statue of a bishop cutt in stone; an arch over his head a foot above the ground, with miter and crosier.

The body of the cathedral is rude and slovenly clay flore, only a scurvy stone walke in the middle. No other monuments in the church.

Another church here called St. ASAPH Church.

South window:

Quarterly FRANCE and ENGLAND.

The bishop has a howse here,—a good parsonage howse in England.

Wednesday rested, 5°.

Thursday, 6°, to St. George parish, the rest quartered thereabouts.

Friday, 7° Nov. was a generall rendesvouz on Denbigh greene. This night the head-quarter was at Llanraydor, Sir Evan Lloyd's howse.

Satterday marched to Llansanfraid. Some over the water in Merionethshire.

Sunday, to Llanvutlyn, written Llanvilling in the mapp; a towne where the King lay about two months before as he marched from Hereford to Chester. All, both horse and foot, lay there.

Munday, Nov. 10, to Newtowne. In this march a leiftenant of horse and a trooper fell out, and had a single combate in private about a horse. Both fought a horseback; the lieftenant shott him in the thigh, and the trooper him in the sholder, disarmed the leiftenant, and tooke away his horse and pistolls.

Here the van of quartermasters tooke Captaine Vyner and seven of his men prisoners; the rest of his troope were at the seige of Chester then.

Tuesday to Knighton, a pretty towne, com. Radnor. Here Mr. Crowder the sheriffe of the shire lives.

KNIGHTON Church, com. Radnor.

South window:

Quarterly, FRANCE and ENGLAND.

Painted on the wall:

Quarterly, 1 and 4, On a fess between three lions passant, three crosses potent; 2 and 3, Sable, a chevron argent between three spearheads "bloody," "PRICE."

This Crowder married Mr. Herbert Price' sister of Brecknock.

WIGMORE Church, com. Hereford, two myle from Brampton Bryan.

(Selden's Titles of Honor, p. 840, "Rogero de Mortuomari de Wigmore," Teste to a patent Rot. Cart. 9 E. 2.)

East window, south yle church, very old and large:

MORTIMER. "The inescocheon A, and a label of nine poynts sable, very small."
MORTIMER, without the label on the inescocheon.
The same, the inescocheon "all argent, yͤ portrait of a lyon onely."

Same yle a flat stone and the portrait of a man in armour, the inscription circumscribed, but imperfect. This shield:

Three "greyhounds" courant.

In the north window of the south chappel of the church, small:

MORTIMER, the inescocheon argent; dimidiated with, Argent, three fusils in fess gules.
BOHUN, dimidiated with, Argent, a fess between four barrulets gules.
BOHUN.
MORTIMER.
"All the Mortimer's coate here is b. three barrulets o."

Sir Gilly Merrick lived here in the castle. Sir Robert Harley was borne here in this castle; his father lived in it before Sir Gilly. Harley ruined it at the beginning of the Parliament. At the rendesvouz neare Brampton Bryan (both castle and church are demolisht), a Dr. of Physick kept the castle.

Wednesday, Nov. 12. This party dispersed. Prince M. guards to Bewdley, Bridgenorth horse thither; the rest with Sir William V. to Lemster, com. Hereford.

The inhabitants of Brecknockshire had pulld downe the castle of Brecknock, and walls of the towne. Colonel Herbert Price they petitioned out to the King afore.

Monmouth taken by the countrey people.

The people of the Forest of Deane had made turnpikes in the avenues and passes into the countrey, and sufferd none to enter without their leave. The Parliament soldjers cap in hand for a night's quarter.

The countrey people of Merionethshire at times also beseige and block up the King's castle of Aberusty [Aberystwith].

Thursday, Lord Gerard's troope of Reformades, &c. came into Herefordshire, and quartered a myle from Lemster.

Prince Rupert and Prince Maurice now at Worcester.

When Sir W. V. marched out of Denbighshire, the enemy lay in this manner; three troopes of horse and three troopes of dragoons at Bretton, Welch side, two myle from Chester. Colonel Jones lay at Darleston with a regiment of 400 horse, and another of 400 firelocks called Jones his regiments. They have a bridge over the Dee at Egleston. More lye at Wrexham.

Staffordshire horse gone.

They drew out of these garrisons to fight us, vizt. Wem, Oswistree, Red Castle, Montgomery, Nottingham, Derby, Stafford; Vine's troope of 50; besides Mitton brought 500 horse and foot.

Satterday, about two in the morning, came intelligence that Mitton was advancing toward Lemster. Sir William Vaughan drew out and marched that night; quartered at Sutton and Morton, &c. com. Hereford.

Sir Henry Linghen has a faire howse in Sutton, an able parish.

Morton Church, com. Hereford.

Against the east wall, a small and neate monument for Mr. Dauncer, lately erected; his son now lives here. 'Tis a church lease, not 200*l*. p. a.

> Gules, on a chevron between three cinquefoils argent three ogresses; impalement blank.

Sunday, the firelocks and Gerard's troope went to Worcester with Sir William Vaughan; the rest of the horse removed to Maunsell, &c.

The countrey people told us the Scotts at the seige of Hereford eate the piggs which they cutt out of a sowes belly.

In Derb: the Scotts dranke, " Swill the King's health."

This day we removed to Mansfield Parva, &c.

Thursday removed to Delwyn.

Delwyn [Dilwyn] Church, com. Hereford.

East window of the chancel, these five, very large and old, each about a foot broad:

> England.
> The same with a label of five points azure, each charged with three fleurs-de-lis or.
> Or, five chevronels azure [Deanery of Hereford].
> Gules, three fleurs-de-lis or [? meant for the See of Hereford].
> Per pale azure and gules, a fess between two chevrons ermine.

The borders of the window adorned with [castles] or in gules [*i. e.* the border being gules] and B. [fleurs-de-lis] or.

South window, chancel, old:

> Gules, a lion rampant within a bordure engrailed or [Talbot].

North window, chancel:

> Argent, five bends sinister gules.
> Gules, a fess argent, in chief three annulets argent; " imperfect."

In the lower north window of the chancel these two coates and this picture are fairely aud largely painted, and putt in since the old glasse was made:

> Gules, a chief "imperfect."
>
> Azure, a bend argent, cotised or, between six martlets of the same, impaling, Gules, on a chief argent three martlets sable.
>
> The kneeling figure of a knight clad in armour of the thirteenth century marked " or," the hands joined in the attitude of prayer. He has a sword-belt, also marked " or," and his surcoat is embroidered with the arms described as on the dexter side of the last-named shield.

Under an arch in the middle of the north wall of the chancel lyes this statue, cutt in stone:

> The recumbent effigy of a Knight Templar, his right hand grasps the hilt of his sword, and on his left arm is a shield bearing a lion rampant within a bordure engrailed, " lyon and border carved and embosse out."

In the chancel, upon a flat stone of this fashion, this is thus carved, very old, shield simply carved:

> A flat stone, broad at the head and narrowing towards the feet, having two antique crosses within circles sculptured at the head and foot, and in the centre a shield of arms, viz. Barry, a bend between six martlets, on the bend an inescocheon charged, apparently, with two labels, the one of four, the other of three points.

East window, south yle, church:

> Quarterly, FRANCE and ENGLAND, a label of three points argent, each point charged with a canton, " colour gone " [LIONEL DUKE OF CLARENCE]. MORTIMER.

First south window, south yle:

> Azure, three boar's heads couped, armed argent, between seven cross-crosslets fitchy gules; " tusks argent" [CRADOCK].

Second window.

> Argent, on a cross azure five escallops or.

The north window of the chappel, in the north yle of the church, is fairely adorned with the pictures of the twelve Apostles, these two shields at bottome:

> Azure, a lion rampant argent, charged on the breast with a demi-cross botony, the dexter side removed, or, within a bordure engrailed of the last.
>
> The same, but charged with a mullet argent, pierced or, in place of the cross botony.

At the church gate stands a howse and square with pillars and two doores, which they call a Palme-howse; it formerly stood in the churchyard.

> Sketches of a stool, with "leather or cloth" top, exactly similar to the modern camp-stool, showing it when open and when closed. "Brasse."

A water wheele six foot in diameter, six spokes, and about four inches thick.

> A sketch of the water-wheel, with the "trough to convey ye water."

This will turne spitts, two chernes, and beate in a morter.

Munday night, November 22; Tuesday morning, 23. Colonel Gradyes and Generall Gerard's regiments, lying at Pembridge, at three of the clock in the morning were beate up, one or two killd, most lost their horses and armes.

Stokesay, Montgomery, and Martin of New Radnor did it.

Tuesday, those horse under Sir William Vaughan's command, marched to Lemster.

LEMSTER [LEOMINSTER] Church, com. Hereford.

Within it is a double church; the north side is very ancient, the other part was built later. The Fryars had also a church neare this.

In the north yle window of the old church, called St. Anthonyes Church, very old:

> Quarterly, Per fess indented argent and azure, in the first quarter a lion passant guardant or [CROFT].
> The same.

An old altar-tombe with alablaster on the topp, in black lynes the two pictures, and in a large forme the effigies of our Saviour on the crosse.

> Thome Phillips, ob. 1530, & Isabela ux. ejus.

In the middle yle of the church, neare a lower north pillar, upon an altar-tombe lyes this fashiond statue of a woman fairely carved:

> The figure of a female habited in a long robe with hanging sleeves doubled ermine, the collar folded down, having the neck bare. Round her neck "a cheyne buckled," the waist encircled by a "great belt and buckle," and the hands joined upon the breast. The hair, which is confined across the forehead by a fillet, is extended on either side of the head, forming two enormous plaits.

For the Lady Jane Clifford who built the west window, and gave three commons to the poore of this parish.[a]

A flat stone in the chancel, the pictures of a man and woman scratcht in black lynes. This coate between them, he in armor:

> Hic jacent corpora Radulfi Hakesluit et Eliz. ux'is sue, qui obierunt 1 Maii A.D. M° ccccc.xvii. q. a. p. d. a.[b]

> Quarterly, 1, three battleaxes in fess [HAKLUYT]; 2, three towers; 3, three "imperfect;" 4, three birds "sable."

The inscription circumscribed. Eaton, in this parish, was an ancient seate of this family.

Upon the same in other characters:

> Hic jacet corpus Milonis Hackluit gen. qui ob. 21 Junii 1621.

---

[a] Matilda Mowbray, niece of Sir Walter Clifford. See Gough's Camden, vol. ii. p. 458.

[b] The date given in Camden is May 1, 1507; in C. 25, f. 4, Coll. Arm. May 10, 1527. The well-known compiler of the Voyages, &c. was of this family.

Another.

> Catharine, wife of John Barneby, Esq. daughter to Sir Tho. Cornwall
> knight, ob. 30 Sep. 1633.

> A lion passant between three escallops [for Barneby; but ? if correct],
> impaling CORNWALL.

On the south side of the south yle, in the chancel, are three arches within the wall, each lower than other; in the seat a little above it the hole for holy water. [He gives a sketch of them].

These three were for confession. [They are merely *sedilia*].

This escocheon is upon an old flat stone in the south yle of the church. The inscription is circumscribed, very old, in this letter, set very close W.

> A fess between three leopard's heads erased [? an error for eagles—BRADFORD].[a]

The priory adjoynes to the church, habitable in part; the Queenes right, Mr. Coningsby the lease.

Lemster is famous for fine wool, which makes the finest black and scarlet cloth.

A parcell of ground called the Ore, which runs to Kingsland, is the finest; 'tis sold for 40*s*. the stone, 12^{1b}. to the stone, and commonly twelve fleices to the stone.

Sunday, October 26, 1645. At Newarke, Prince Rupert, Generall Gerard, and Sir Richard Willys came into the presence, when the King had almost dyned. Prince Rupert came in discontentedly, with his hands at his side, and approached very neare the King, whereat his Majestie presently commanded all to be taken away, and rising from the table walked to a corner of the roome. They three presented themselves before his Majestie, and first Willys spake after this manner.[b]

*   *   *   *   *   *   *   *   *

King. Say no more; this is a time unseasonable for you to command here.

---

[a] This and the monuments of Hakluyt and Barnaby are given in C. 25, f. 4, Coll. Arm.

[b] This part of the manuscript was purposely torn away, as will be seen by the Diary i the following page.

G. All that Sir Richard Willys desires is very reasonable, for, if gentlemen must be putt out upon every occasion and aspersion, it will discourage all from serving your Majestie.

K. What doth this concerne you ? you for your part have received as much honour as any man, and I did not think you would have come to me in this manner.

*   *   *   *   *   *   *   *   *

G. I am sure, and can prove, that Digby was the cause that I was owted from my comand in Wales.

K. Whosoever says it . . . . but a child . . . .

[The dialogue was then continued, as shown by the initial letters, by Rupert, the King, Gerard, and Willys.]

[*K.*] Why then do you not obey me, but come to expostulate with me?

. . . . . Majestie is ill informed . . . . . .

[*K.*] I am but a child, Digby . . . . . What can . . . . Rebell say more?

K. O nephewe, 'tis of great concernment, and requires consideration.

Here the Prince said something concerning Bristoll. Whereat the King sighed and said, O nephewe, and stopt. Then he would say no more.

P. Lord Digby is the man that has caused all these distractions amongst us.

King. They are all rogues and rascalls that sayes soe, and in effecte traytors that seeke to dishonor my best subjects.

Here Gerard bowed himselfe and went out. The Prince shewed no reverence, but went out prowdly with his hands at his side.

All the trayne followed them, and the King left in private with Sir Richard Willys.

Then Sir Richard Willys told the King that a corporall and tenn boyes were able to doe as much service as all his commissioners in Newarke.

Such stuff was printed as I have torne out, for, being many times since in Sir Richard Willys' company, 'tis all a feynd * * lye, for he said not one word to the King all that while, and Lord Gerard said most, and that was concerning Lord Digby.

This Sir Richard told me October 28, 1659. The coming to Newarke, as afore said, and at a councel of warr proposing what was to be done, Sir Richard propounded that his Majestie would putt all his garrison soldjers in a body and march after Fairfax, then about Taunton. Newarke river was fordable, and in it 4,000 good foot.

[He here notes.] This following belongs to p. 119, [meaning the part relating to the scene at Newark.]

There was then Newarke, Ashby, Tutbury, Lichfield, Belvoir, Weston, Bridgnorth, Denbigh, and other garrisons. Slight them all and all inland garrisons, keep your ports, as Exeter and Bristoll, &c. and you will have canon and a very considerable army to fight Fairfax. Besides, Goring's army in the West was then good too.

The King likt it well; Ashburnham embraced Sir Richard for the proposition, and so did Lord Digby like it. But they delayd, and the cowardly commissioners that lingered for compounding, they put queries. Where shall wee have winter quarters? Digby and Ashburn-ham were jealous Sir Richard should get too much with the King's favour. 3,000*l.* was raysed by the Ingrams and the Northern gent. to give the King in his necessity, and that they might have a governor that would make good compositions for them, and this gott Sir Richard out of that government, and there did go away with him and his officers 800 soldjers, and, had it not been for Sir Richard himselfe, when his men heard that he was turned out of the government, they had quitted all the guards and all left the King's service: for at the first noyse of it many of them toare their colors in the market place; which was not done by his instigation, or insinuation, but out of love to him, and shewing their discontent.

MAY IT PLEASE YOUR MOST EXCELLENT MAJESTIE,

Whereas in all humility wee came to present ourselves this day unto your Majestie to make our severall grevances knowne, wee find wee have drawne upon us some misconstruction by the manner of it, by reason your Majestie thought it appeared as a mutiny; wee shall therefore with all humblenes and cleernesse present unto your Majestie that wee the persons subscribed, who from the beginning of this unhappy warr have given such testimonyes to your Majestie and the world of our fidelity and zeale to your Majesties person and cause, doe thinke ourselves as unhappy, to lye under that censure, and, as wee know in our conscience ourselves innocent and free from it, wee doe in all humility therefore, least we should hazard ourselves upon a second misinterpretation, present these reasons of our humblest desires unto your sacred Majestie rather in writing then personally, which are these :

That many of us, trusted in high commands in your Majesties service, have not onely our commissions taken away without any reason or cause expressed, whereby our honours are blemished to the world, our fortunes ruined, and wee rendered incapable of trust or command from any foraigne prince. But many others, as wee have cause to feare, designed to suffer in the same manner. Our intentions in our addressing ourselves to your Majestie were, and our submissive desires now are, that your Majestie wilbe gratiously pleased that such of us as now labour under the opinion of unworthinesse and incapacity to serve your Majestie may at a councel of warr receive knowledge of the causes of your Majesties displeasure, and have the justice and liberty of our defence against what can be objected against us, and in particular concerning this government. And, if upon the severest examination our integrity and loyalty to your Majestie shall appeare, that then your Majestie wilbe gratiously pleased to grant us either reparation in honour against the calumny of our enemyes, or liberty to passe into other parts, which are the humblest desires of

Your Majesties most obedient loyall subjects and servants,

RUPERT, MAURICE, CHARLES GERARD, ME. TUCHET, RICH. WILLYS, CHA. COMPTON, EDW. VILLERS, CHA. WHELER, SIMON FANSHAW, THO. DANIEL, PHIL. HONYWOOD, WILL. WILLYS, JOHN FISHER, WILL. ROLLESTON, WM. BELENDEN, SOMERSET FOX, HEN. OSBORNE, JO. SCHRYMSHERE, RICH. HATTON, SEBAST. BUNCKLEY, JO. JAMES, ROBT. DALISON.[a]

CHARLES R.

Trusty and welbeloved, wee greet you well. By our former letters wee expresst our care to prevent the inconvenience that might arise to the country and our service if our nephew Prince Rupert and Prince Maurice, with their trayne and followers, should make any long abode at Worcester, or other our

---

[a] This Petition is printed in Evelyn's Memoirs, but without the signatures.

quarters, which by your letters to Sir Edward Walker wee perceive was not without cause. As your care therein, and of our service, is very acceptable unto us, so wee desire your continuance thereof. Our nephewes stay in those our quarters hath already been longer then wee expected. And because wee perceive it is like to be enlarged in regard to passes which have been sent them from London are such as they thought not fitt to accept of, Our will and command is, that you declare unto them that our pleasure is, that they deliver to you a lyst of all their owne servants which they intend to take with them, whome wee will you to accommodate, as well as you may, with quarters and other necessaryes for them during their residency with you, which wee presume will not be long. And that for all others who adhere to them, as well those who have passes from us as those who have not, Our command is, that you signify our pleasure unto them that they leave our quarters by the first of December next, for that wee may not beare the inconvenience of the eating out of our quarters by those who have so abandoned our service. Herein you are to be very carefull to give us a speedy accompt of your proceedings, for which this shalbe your warrant.

Given at our Court at Oxford, this 23 of November, 1645.
By his Majesties command,

ED. WALKER.

Superscribed thus :—

To our trusty and welbeloved Colonel Samuel Sandys, Governour of our citty and garrison of Worcester.

Munday, Nov. 31, to Tenbury. At Lemster was a strong guard; every night they watcht by regiments, every third night turne.

TENBURY Church, com. Wigorn.

East window, chancel, old:

Argent, on a bend azure three cinquefoils or [COKESEY].
MORTIMER.
Checky or and azure [WARREN].

This picture is in the north window, chancel, praying to our Saviour:

The kneeling figure of a man, habited in a long coat with open hanging sleeves, the head bare. At his girdle a dagger hilted or. Underneath is written "Johannes Hull."

Against the north wall of the chancel, under an arch, lyes a small statue about two foot long, well cutt:

> Recumbent figure of a Knight Templar, the hands joined in prayer over the breast, rudely sketched.[a]

West window, church, the glasse very old:

> A shield within a quatrefoil; Gules, a chevron between three mullets argent.

East window, north yle, is painted with the root of Jesse.

The Scotts broke this font in pieces, and of the next parishes also.

At the bottome of a window, south side of the church, lyes a statue of rude bignes, about seven foot long; his sheild whereon his armes are carved is two foot and halfe long.

> Recumbent figure of a Knight Templar, his feet resting upon some animal. The right hand grasps the hilt of the sword, the left the scabbard below; on the left arm a shield is suspended charged with the coat last described. "Buckle of the spurr leather [in the] middle."

Sir Gilbert Cornwal told me this was for Sturmy, a great man in this partes.

In the south yle, church, an altar-tombe and two statues cutt, lying thereon, he in the moderne armour.

> Thomas Acton, of Sutton, Esq. ob. 2 Jan. 1546, and Mary his wife, daughter of Sir Thomas Lacon, of Willy, Knight, ob. 1564; two sons, Lancelot and Gabriel, who died young; and Joice their onely daughter and heire, who married Sir Thomas Lucy, of Charlcott, Knight.
>
> A fess within a bordure engrailed ermine [ACTON]; impaling, Quarterly per fess indented, in first quarter a girfalcon [LACON]. *Crest,* an arm embowed, holding in the hand a sword, "on the sword-point a bore head."

Base and treble:—

> Strep. Come, my Daphne, come away,
>   Wee doe wast the cristall day.
> Da.   'Tis Strephon calls; what would my love?
> S.   Come follow to the mirtle grove,
>   Where Venus shall prepare
>   Rich chaplets for your haire.

[a] See the notice of this effigy in Nash's Worcestershire, and also of a similarly diminutive effigy at Mapowder Church in Hutchins's Dorsetshire.

D.   Were I shutt up within a tree,
          I'de rend my barke to follow thee.
S.   My shepheardesse, make hast,
          The minutes fly too fast.
D.   In those cooler shades will I,
          Bind as Cupid, kisse thine eye.
S.   On thy bosome there I'll stray,
          In such warme snow who would not loose his way.
Chor. Weele laugh and leave this world behind,
          And gods themselves that see shall envy thee and me,
       But never find such joyes
          Whiles they embrace a deity.
       Tell me not I my love mispend,
          'Tis time lost to reprove me ;
       Enjoy thou thine, I have my end,
          So Cloris onely love me.
       Tell me not other flocks are full,
          Myne poore ; let them despise me
       That more abound in milke and wooll,
          So Cloris onely prise me.
       Tire others' easier eares with these
          Unapperteyning storyes,
       He never feeles the world's desease
          That cares not for her glories.
       Nor pitty thou that wiser art
          Whose thoughts lye wide of mine,
       Let me alone with mine owne heart,
          And ile ne're envy thine.
       Nor blame whoever blames my witt,
          That seekes no higher prise,
       Then in unenvyed shades to sett
          And sing of Cloris' eyes :

Depart thou fatall feaver from me, now depart, thinke not my hart
To thy dull flames shall be a sacrifice.
A maid dread Cupid hath then on the altar laid, by thee betrayed,
A rich oblation to restore thine eyes :
But yet my bare acknowledgment can testifie thou hadst no craft
To bend thy bow against a foe that aymes to catch the shaft.
Nor did feare thee at my bosome all thy arts at once did move,
She that receives a thousand sheaves, she can no more but love.

No more, phisitians, let me tire your braynes no more, pray give it ore,
I have a cure that phisick never read.
Although ye skillfull doctors, all the world doth know, in learning flow,
You may as well make practise on the dead ;
But if my Gerard do but view me with the bewty of his lookes,
I make no doubt to live without phisitians and their books.
Tis he that with his balmy kisses can restore my latest breath,
What blisse is this to have a kisse can raise a maid from death.

To you that tell me of another world I bowe, and will allowe
Your sacred precepts if you grant me this,
That he whome I accept of best that deity may goe with me ;
Without his presence there can be no blisse.
Go teach your tenets of eternity to those that aged be,
Do not persuade a loveful maid there's any heaven but he ;
But yet methinkes an icy slumber doth possesse my fiery braine,
Pray bid him dye if you see I doe never wake againe.

For the Belly ake or the Grease molten in a horse.

Brimstone beaten to powder, black sope to make it into a paste, and give him the quantity of a hen egg. Stirr him and keepe him warme. Or onely a spoonfull of diapente in strong ale.

Gald Back.

Wheaten flower and soot mixed with the white of an egg, made into a soft past. Or strong ale boyld with wheaten bread. Make a poltis; lay it on with red flocks.

Mr. Humfrey Walker of Llanvane, com. Salop, neare Radnor-shire, pretty seate.

Passeganger. In a court of guard the benches which the soldjers lye on they call swet bankes.

Roundhead. Carrett beard. Essex calves.

To take away Cornes.

Take a good peice of the leane of veale and bynd the same to the corne over night, and by the next morning it will be so supple as you may pull it off.

Bard. Kye at Oswestree.

Mr. Jones of Caus, com. Flint, now prisoner in Chester Castle.

Wednesday, December 2, 1645.   To the Rock, com. Wigorn.

Friday, to Kinver, betweene Kiderminster and Bridgnorth.

Satterday, 5, to Bridgnorth.   Here Lt.-Colonel Sloughter's troope and Colonel Dixies stayed; and Colonel Gradyes.   Major Generall and Whitleyes to Hereford.

Beeston Castle surrendered after it had endured a tedious seige·

Sir William Vaughan with his troope to Ludlowe, but his men not admitted.

Captain Bowmer and Captain Vaughan to Arcall, which was shutt up by three or four petty garrisons.

Lord Byron sent word that Lathom Howse was lost, com. Lancaster, the seate of the Earle of Derby.

Thursday, December 18.   Sir William Vaughan drew out the horse he had with him afore, and some of Dudley and Ludlowe, 6 or 700 foot commanded by Lieutenant-Colonel Smyth, horse 5 or 600; marched from Bridgnorth, and had a rendesvouz towards S.

Friday morning came intelligence to B. that Hereford was lost. About a fortnight before this Sir Nicholas Throckmorton, the Lieutenant-Governour of Hereford, told Sir Thomas Lunsford that he lost Monmouth basely.   Sir Thomas told him he lyed; to fight they prepared, but stopt by the guards.   Twas referd to six gentlemen, but could not end it; they were both confined.

The Governour and Sir Henry Linghen escaped to Ludlow.

To make severall locks for the port, or doore, or drawing, to be putt on at uncertaine times.   .

Beeston Castle held out, and had but one dayes provision left; the captaine and his company marched out with all their baggage, arms, match lighted, bullett in mouth, &c.   Their ammunition was so spent that the enemy gave the soldjer many shootes of powder to make the conditions good. *Ita* Lord Brereton told me. This castle was built by Ranulph Earle of Chester, after his returne from the Holy Warr, 4. H. 3. 1220. (Holinshed p. 202 b.)

23 of December. Lord Astleigh came to Worcester, being generall of these four countyes; Sir Charles Lucas with him, Lord Generall of the horse.

Munday, December 29. Colonel Bagott with his party shutt the Lord Loughborough and his party out of the Close of Lichfield.

Tuesday, Lord Loughborough, &c., went to Tedbury.

Jan. 12. To Ashby from Lichfield.

TUDBURY.

Munday, January 14. Those horse which were the remnant of Generall Gerard's army, viz., his owne life guard, commanded by his brother Sir Gilbert Gerard, 100. Major-Generall Egerton's, Colonel Whitleyes, Leiutenant-Colonel Bambrigg, Major Paramore, with Colonel Molesworth's, the remnant of Prince Maurice's regiment of horse,—Toto 300, were beate up by the forces of the garrisons of Stafford, Derby, Pamsley Howse, Alton Castle, Caswall, and Barton. Above 100 horse and 20 troopers lost, no officers.

Friday, January 18. Leiftenant Moore, who was Leiftenant to Gerard's troope, went into the enemy to Derby, with twenty-four of those Reformades, saucie fellowes most.

Satterday, the enemy fell into Tudbury agen, and did no hurt; one of them killd.

Satterday, Captain Wright, sent by the Lord Loughborough from Ashby, surprised Ashly Howse, within four myle of Coventry; tooke the Governour, Hunt, the coblar of Coventry, and his brother, and the rest, about ten; all their horse were gone out; fired the howse; 'twas Mr. Chamberlanes howse, his son did it. Four or five dayes after, another party was sent from Ashby, and tooke 3 or 4 canoniers, a captain, and others, within four myle of Belvoir Castle.

January . Lord Loughborough sent 300 foot, with four

colours, under the command of Colonel Roper, and above 100 horse under the command of Colonel Stamford, towards the releife of Chester, and the expectation of meeting Irish forces.

Thursday, Jan. 29, came some gentlemen and about thirty troopers to Ashby from Newarke, and came thorough the enemyes quarters that beseige that place.

Satterday night, ult. January, about 12 of the clock, came a party of horse and dragoons into the towne of Ashby, plundered the mercers', sadlers', and suttlers' shopps, and the inns of the horses, especially those that came from Newarke and Tudbury with Colonel Egerton.

No gentleman taken, and few or none other, though divers lay there in the towne; none killd. Were gone before two of the clock, six muskets sallied on them.

Tuesday, 3rd February, came intelligence to Ashby that Belvoir Castle was surrendered, and that the governour for his owne security had articled with the enemy, and sent four hostages to Lichfeild; he and his men were convoyed to Lichfeild.

Dartmouth taken by storme.

Wednesday, Feb. 11. Those foot and horse returned home to Ashby, and the party togeather were above 2000, tooke Riccardin [Wrockwardine] church.

W. Shute, in his Heroicke Acts of his Excellencie of Prince Maurice of Nassau. The taking Breda by a turfe boat, p. 117. The taking of the Fort of Zutphen, 1590, by boares and soldjers clad in women's clothes, p. 124. The Duke of Parma's Cornett. The Image of Christ, &c. p. 131.

Mr. Joscelin in his Saxon Dictionary. MS. in Bibl. Cottoniana. Nowel in his Dictionary of the same tongue. Selden, p. 114.

Alfricus his Saxon Grammar, ibidem.

King John's sending to the King of Morocco to change his Christianity for Muhumetanisme. Idem, p. 104.

Rot. Parl. 18 H. 6. That every of your leiges may omitt the kissing of you in doing their homage. Idem, p. 32.

Cole Orton Church, com. Leicester.

In the north yle of the church against the wall is a lofty monument with these coates and inscription, besides many quarterings of the Beaumonts:

> Azure, a lion rampant within an orle of fleurs-de-lis or [Beaumont].
> The same; impaling, Sable, three dovecotes argent [Sapcote.]
> Argent, a chevron engrailed gules between three shovelers proper [Lovis].

Here lyeth the bodies of Sir Henry Beaumont, Kt. and lady Elizabeth his wife, which Sir Henry was son to Nicholas Beaumont, Esq., and Elizabeth was daughter and heire of Lovis, Esq. by whome he had one onely son Sir Thomas Beaumont, Kt. who married the daughter and heire of Henry Sapcotts, Esq. which Sir Henry [died] 31 of March, 1607, the Lady Elizabeth 26 of March, 1608.

Divers matches of this family in the east window of this yle lately sett up. The manor howse is lately burnt, being a garrison of the Parliament's. Belonging to the Lord Beaumont.

Grancester [Granchester] Church, com. Cantebr.

North window chancel:

> Vert, a fess indented counter-indented ermine; impaling, Gules, a chevron azure between three birds or.
> The same; impaling, Gules, on a fess sable a mullet between two annulets argent.

South window chancel:

> Quarterly gules and or, in first quarter a mullet argent [Vere].
> Vere; impaling, Vert, a fess indented counter-indented ermine.

South window of the church:

> Gules, a bend or, in chief a martlet of the last.
> The same; impaling, Argent, on a bend engrailed sable three torteaux.

This [viz. the first] coate divers times in all the south windowes, and the picture of a man kneeling, and **John Audele.**

Within the wall under the uppermost south window, under an arch, is an altar tombe, and upon the marble was the pictures of a man and woman inlayed in brasse, but gone, with the inscription and shield, probably his whose coate that bend and martlet is.

Against the south wall of the chancel is a neate little monument with an inscription for Dr. Byng,[a] and these shields:

> Quarterly sable and argent, in first quarter a lion rampant of the second, "BYNG"; impaling, Quarterly 1 and 4, Sable, three lion's heads erased argent [RANDAL]; 2 and 3, Sable, a chevron or between three wolf's heads erased argent.
>
> Quarterly, "RANDAL"; and Sable, a chevron or between three wolf's heads erased argent.

[The following is the letter of Mr. Salesbury to the Governor of Denbigh referred to in p. 258.]

FOR SIR WILLIAM VAUGHAN.

Sir, I wish you be as free from danger as I hope wee are secure and in good condition here.   Of your foot being received under the castle wall, I received them in, though I conceived I had no need of them for defence of this place; yet, having I doubt not provision enough, their valour and good service meriting my compassion, I freely enterteynd them.   I judge the enemy had a force that came the other way over the greene equall in number or thereaboutes to what you fought with.   Mitton, and the foot, I am informed, quarter in the towne, and most of the horse in the country about.   God blesse us all !

Your friend and servant,   WILLIAM SALESBURY.

Denbigh Castle,   What way you will resolve to looke
1º Nov. 1645   I leave to your own discretion.
ii at night.

Ex. cum originali per R. S.

---

[a] Thomas Byng, Master of Clare Hall, Cambridge, and Regius Professor of Civil Law.

INDEX.

INDEX OF SUBJECTS.

WESTMINSTER: PRINTED BY J. B. NICHOLS AND SONS, 25, PARLIAMENT STREET.